The Great Water

The Great Water

A DOCUMENTARY HISTORY OF MICHIGAN

Edited by Matthew R. Thick

MICHIGAN STATE UNIVERSITY PRESS | *East Lansing*

♾ The paper used in this publication meets the minimum requirements
of ANSI/NISO z39.48-1992 (R 1997) (Permanence of Paper).

Michigan State University Press
East Lansing, Michigan 48823-5245

Printed and bound in the United States of America.

27 26 25 24 23 22 21 20 19 18   1 2 3 4 5 6 7 8 9 10

LIBRARY OF CONGRESS CATALOGING-IN-PUBLICATION DATA IS AVAILABLE
Names: Thick, Matthew R., editor.
Title: The great water : a documentary history of Michigan / edited by Matthew R. Thick.
Description: East Lansing : Michigan State University Press, 2018.
| Includes bibliographical references.
Identifiers: LCCN 2017011161| ISBN 9781611862676 (pbk. : alk. paper)
| ISBN 9781609175504 (pdf) | ISBN 9781628953183 (epub) | ISBN 9781628963182 (kindle)
Subjects: LCSH: Michigan—History—Sources.
Classification: LCC F566 .G795 2018 | DDC 977.4—dc23
LC record available at https://lccn.loc.gov/2017011161

Book design by Charlie Sharp, Sharp Des!gns, East Lansing, MI
Cover design by Erin Kirk New
Cover image of Mackinac Bridge is from iStock.com/ 954images.

Michigan State University Press is a member of the Green Press Initiative and is committed to developing
and encouraging ecologically responsible publishing practices. For more information about the Green
Press Initiative and the use of recycled paper in book publishing, please visit *www.greenpressinitiative.org*.

Visit Michigan State University Press at *www.msupress.org*

For my dad, Lewis Thick

CONTENTS

CHAPTER 8. The White Pine Era: The Lumber Industry

CHAPTER 9. Wealth from Underground: The Mining Industry

CHAPTER 10. Social Change: Women's Rights and Progressivism

CHAPTER 11. A New Industry: The Horseless Carriage

CHAPTER 12. Hard Times: The Depression and the New Deal

CHAPTER 13. Organizing Labor: Unionization of Michigan Workers

CHAPTER 14. Arsenal of Democracy: World War II

CHAPTER 15. Fight for Equality: Civil Rights

CHAPTER 16. The Buckle of the Rust Belt: Economic Decline

CHAPTER 17. Preserving the State: Environment and Health

CHAPTER 18. Challenges Old and New: Michigan's Infrastructure

PREFACE

Michigan has a very long history. Its first hunters arrived ten thousand years ago, its first farmers arrived about six thousand years after that, and three hundred years ago people from various places of the globe began to call Michigan their home. Most arrived by their own volition, some at the volition of others. Collectively, it is their words, what they left behind for future generations to discover, that make up Michigan's history.

What follows is a Michigan history documentary reader. These documents cover important aspects of Michigan's history from its original inhabitants to the present. This reader is designed to provoke a discussion about Michigan's past. While most pieces included here are windows into the lives of the people who lived during the events under study, several chapters include items that offer opposing views or different ideas about the same subject. Further, this reader includes the words of figures great and small, adding depth to historical discussion.

Because Michigan's history is incredibly expansive, some topics and figures will not be represented; nevertheless, the pieces included touch on the important themes in Michigan history. Readers can obtain an understanding of the development of political structures for numerous groups, such as the power dynamics of the Anishinaabeg and other Great Lakes American Indian groups, French and British political assertion in the region, and, of course, the development of Michigan statehood within the United States. In addition, the documents demonstrate Michigan's social organization and cultural growth. For example, religion was a driver for migration into Michigan. Several Native American groups migrated to the region following prophetic visions, and Quakers came to Michigan to undermine southern slavery, work they believed was a holy crusade. Not only does this reader show how the mix of vastly different societies and cultures became a driver for change, it also highlights the importance of Michigan's geologic makeup, its geographic location, and the varied ideas and positions of those who made Michigan their home.

The book is roughly arranged in chronological order, but some chapters deal with events whose documents are better situated thematically. Chapters include items that may cover a few decades or a century. In addition, the documents have been edited for clarity. Some of the original spellings or grammatical errors have been left intact, so long as the point can be understood. Some words are spelled inconsistently by different authors, and these have been left as the author wrote them. For example, readers might see "Ojibwa" in one document and "Ojibway" in another, though these refer to the same group. Further, to maintain the integrity of the documents and historical inquiry, offensive language has been left intact.

Some chapters contain more editorial notes than others, of course, since some references require added contextual explanation. It was a goal, however, to keep editorial comments to a minimum to allow readers the opportunity to create their own questions and ideas about the documents. Accordingly, this collection would work well in a Michigan history classroom or could be read concurrently with a history of the state (see the recommended readings at the end of this collection).

Michigan's location within the Great Lakes has made it the crossroad of worlds. Its vast resources of water, food, land, trees, metals, and minerals attracted various groups, thus becoming a center of cross-cultural and cross-social interaction. Reading the stories and letters and personal accounts of those who have called Michigan "home" gives special insight and depth into those interactions, therefore providing a better understanding of the region, North America, and the world.

ACKNOWLEDGMENTS

Any academic endeavor is best accomplished with help. I owe thanks to numerous people who assisted me along the way: the staffs of the Bentley Historical Library in Ann Arbor, the Burton Historical Collection at the Detroit Public Library, and the Ada Historical Society; Mark Fedder, Tom Gerhardt, and Ray Fortier of the Manistee Historical Museum; Jeremy Dimick and Heather Moore at the Perry Archives, Sloan Museum in Flint; Paul Gifford and Matthew Wolverton at the Frances Willson Thompson Library of the University of Michigan–Flint; Gregory Miller of the Scharchburg Archives at Kettering University; Rosemary Michelin and Beth Gruber from the Marquette Regional History Center; Vincent Duffy and Jack Lessenberry of Michigan Radio; Osama Siblani of *Arab American News*; and my research assistant, Mary Wooley.

CHAPTER 1

Native Michigan: The Anishinaabeg

Michigan's documentary journey begins with the Anishinaabeg (uh-NISH-in-AH-beg), which is sometimes translated as the "chosen people" or the "real people." The Anishinaabeg, a name by which the Ojibwa (Chippewa or Ojibway), Odawa (Ottawa or Adawe), Potawatomi, and a few other groups refer to themselves, were not the first human inhabitants of what would become Michigan. However, they inhabited the region for centuries before Europeans came. In fact, the word "Michigan" derives from *Kitchi Gami*, meaning "Great Water" in Anishinaabe-mowin, the language of the Anishinaabeg. The Anishinaabeg were typically categorized as "prehistorical," suggesting they are a people without a history, which is entirely untrue. As the following documents will show, the Anishinaabeg have a clear history that contributed to a high level of political, social, and cultural development.

To the Anishinaabeg, stories have a spirit. They are alive, and the storyteller has a great responsibility to honor the story and tell it as it was told to her or him. Stories accomplish multiple tasks: they are histories, they preserve tradition, they entertain, they offer explanations about the world, and they provide practical advice.

The Migration of the Anishinaabe

Traditional/Edward Benton-Banai

Many centuries ago, the Anishinaabeg inhabited northeastern North America. From there, they migrated westward, eventually settling in the Great Lakes region. According to the traditional story, while the Anishinaabeg lived on the shores of the "Great Salt Water," seven prophets came to inform them of an impending journey. They must embark on this journey, said the prophets, in order to escape destruction from the "Light-skinned Race." There would be seven stops along the way, the first on a turtle-shaped island near the current city of Montreal; the last, Madeline Island in Lake Superior. It is important to note generations passed between each stop—some versions of this story suggest the migration took centuries to complete. The following excerpt comes from the Ojibwa version of this tradition, beginning with the third stop of this migration, near present-day Detroit.

[The] third stopping place was very likely the shores of the Detroit River that connects Lake St. Clair and Lake Huron in the North to Lake Erie in the South. It is said that again the Sacred Megis appeared to the people out of the water. . . .

In this period, three groups began to emerge in the Ojibway nation. Each group took upon themselves certain tasks necessary for the survival of the people. There came to be a very strong spiritual sense that bound these groups together.

The group called the Ish-ko-day'-wa-tomi (fire people) were charged with the safekeeping of the Sacred Fire. As the people moved on the migration, this group guarded the coals of the Sacred Fire as it was carried along. These people were later called the O-day'-wa-tomi, and, still later, the Potawatomi.

The group called the O-daw-wahg' (trader people) were responsible for providing food goods and supplies to all the nation. They took charge of the major hunting and trading expeditions. These people were later called the Ottawa.

The people that retained the name Ojibway were the faith keepers of the nation. They were entrusted with the keeping of the sacred scrolls and Waterdrum of the Midewiwin [the Anishinaabeg religion]. These people were later mistakenly referred to as the Chippewa.

All the Anishinabe people became known as the nation of the Three Fires to recognize how these groups provided for all their needs. . . .

The people picked up the Waterdrum and continued their westward journey. They were attacked along the way by the nations later called the Sauks and the Foxes. The people pushed on until they came to a large body of fresh water. Here, the Sacred Fire rested for a long time. . . . It is possible that this camping place of the migration was on the eastern shore of Lake Michigan. At this point many people drifted off by groups to look for a place to cross the great water. They knew that their journey must take them to the West, but some of the people traveled South in an attempt to go around the water. Many felt that the direction of the migration had become lost and that the people had missed their fourth stopping place. Time passed so that there were many births and deaths among the people. Giti-gan-nug' (gardens) were raised and o-day-na-wing' (villages) were established. As related in the Second Fire, people began to wander away from the teachings of the Midewiwin Lodge. Many became preoccupied with satisfying the things needed for physical survival but neglected the spiritual side of life. Many lost the direction in their lives that comes from Spirit Ceremony and Sweat Lodge. Only a few of the people, mostly elders, were able to keep the Sacred Fire alive. But the prophecies said that "a boy would be born to show the Anishinabe back to the sacred ways." It was prophesied that he would show the way to "the stepping stones to the future of the Anishinabe people." That boy did come among the people. He had a dream of stones that led across the water. The Mide people paid attention to this dream and led the people back to the river that cut the land like a knife. They followed the river to the North. The river turned into a lake, and at a place where the river was formed again, they rested awhile on an island. This island is known today as Walpole Island. They continued following the river further and came to the northern sea of freshwater that they had heard about when they first came to this region. They followed its eastern shore until, at last, they discovered a series of islands that led across the water. By moving the people by canoe, a way was found to the West over these "stepping stones." And so, the prophecy of the Third Fire came true for the people. They found "the path to their chosen ground, a land in the West to which they must move their families." Here they would find "the food that grows on water."

On the largest island in this chain, the Sacred Megis appeared to the Anishinabe. Here the people gathered. This is the island known today as Manitoulin Island. Slowly, the Anishinabe gathered until Manitoulin Island became known as the capital of the Ojibway nation. Here, the Midewiwin Way grew in following and the Clan System flourished. Truly, the boy with the dream did lead the people back to the sacred ways. Manitoulin Island became the fourth major stopping place of the migration. It is said that the voice of the Waterdrum could be heard even several days journey from Manitoulin Island.

For some time the main body of the migration stayed on this island, but it was not until the people settled at Baw-wa-ting' that the Waterdrum was given a home in which to rest and sing. Here again, the people found the Megis Shell. There was a small island here where powerful ceremonies were held. People now call this place Sault Ste. Marie. The fishing was excellent in the fast water. Skilled fishermen could run the rapids with a canoe while standing backwards in the bow. They would be carrying an ah-sub-bi' (net) on the end of a long pole. By the time they got to the quiet water of the river, their canoe would be full of beautiful Mi-ti-goo-ka-maig' (whitefish). There was so much food in the village that this place came to support many families. Baw-wa-ting' became the fifth stopping place of the migration. Many years later, in the time of the Fifth Fire, Baw-wa-ting' would become a big trading center between the Anishinabe and the Light-Skinned Race. . . .

From *The Mishomis Book: The Voice of the Ojibway* by Edward Benton-Banai (Hayward, WI: Indian Country Communications, 1988), 98–101. Reprinted with permission from Indian Country Communications.

When Nenibozhoo Killed a Bear

Traditional/Howard Webkamigad

There are hundreds, perhaps thousands, of tales involving the figure Nenibozhoo, sometimes spelled Nanabojo. Nenibozhoo is a trickster spirit according to Anishinaabeg tradition.

Nenibozhoo was out hunting and he killed a bear. After he had skinned it and cleaned it, he began to cook the bear. When he was about to begin eating, he was disturbed by the squeaking of trees rubbing against each other, it annoyed him. Again, as he was about to take a bite of the bear meat, the trees made the irritating sound. So Nenibozhoo climbed up the tree to go and untangle them where they were rubbing against each other. As he was attempting to untangle the trees, he got his hand stuck between the trees. At that moment he heard some wolves running nearby. Nenibozhoo shouted to them,

"Don't come here." He said to them, "Keep on running in that direction."

Then the wolves thought, "Let's go to where Nenibozhoo is at, he may have something there for us to eat."

So they went there, and sure enough they saw the bear, which was already nicely cooked, and they proceeded to eat up all of the bear meat.

So when the wolves left, that is when Nenibozhoo slid down from the tree. He was very angry at the tree for trapping his hand, for this was a tree he was trying to help. Nenibozhoo broke off a small shrub and he began whipping the birch tree that had trapped his hand, and he left welts on the bark of the tree. That is why the birch tree now has markings on its bark.

So after he had slid down from the birch tree and after he had finished punishing the birch tree, he began to look for some bear meat to eat. But it was all gone, having been eaten up by the wolves, all that was left was a pile of bones. That is when he saw the bear's head.

"I will eat that. I will crawl in there," he supposedly thought.

He pondered over his predicament, as he did not know how he would get inside the bear's head to eat it. So, then he changed himself into a small snake, and he was now able to crawl inside of the head. He ate all he could, and he had eaten too much for he could not crawl back out of the head. So the bear's head was now stuck on his head as he returned to his normal shape.

He began to walk, and he was unable to see, so he bumped into a tree. He asked the tree, "Who are you?"

"I am the basswood."

Then Nenibozhoo knew he was heading too far inland. So he must have turned around and began walking again and eventually, he bumps into another tree.

"Who are you?" he asks this tree.

"I am called the pine," replied the tree. Then Nenibozhoo knew he was going toward the big lake.

Eventually, he could tell he was going downhill and that is when he bumped into another tree. He asked this tree, "Who are you?"

"I am called the cedar."

"Oh!" said Nenibozhoo. He was pleased. "I will soon be arriving at the water's edge."

He soon feels the grasses under his feet and then he steps into the water and he continues to wade into the water. He is getting further out into the lake, it is much too deep for him to keep wading, so he now begins to swim. That is when he is spotted by several hunters who happened to be going by in a canoe.

"Look at that, it's a bear," they said. "Let's go and kill it," they said further.

So they approached what they thought was a bear, and they caught up to him, and that is when one of them clobbered the bear's head with a paddle, and he hit it so hard that it split the bear's head, which Nenibozhoo had been wearing.

So then Nenibozhoo got out of the water and he was last seen running into the woods and he was gone.

That is it.

From *Ottawa Stories from the Springs*, translated and edited by Howard Webkamigad
(East Lansing: Michigan State University Press, 2015), 27–31.

History of the Ottawa

Andrew J. Blackbird

In my first recollection of the country of Arbor Croche, which is sixty years ago [ca. 1825], there was nothing but small shrubbery here and there in small patches, such as wild cherry trees, but the most of it was grassy plain; and such an abundance of wild strawberries, raspberries and blackberries that they fairly perfumed the air of the whole coast with fragrant scent of ripe fruit. The wild pigeons and every variety of feathered songsters filled all the groves, warbling their songs joyfully and feasting upon these wild fruits of nature; and in these waters the fishes were so plentiful that as you lift up the anchor-stone of your net in the morning, your net would be so loaded with delicious whitefish as to fairly float with all its weight of the sinkers. As you look towards the course of your net, you see the fins of the fishes sticking out of the water in every way. Then I never knew my people to want for anything to eat or to wear, as we always had plenty of wild meat and plenty of fish, corn, vegetables, and wild fruits. I thought (and yet I may be mistaken) that my people were very happy in those days, at least I was as happy myself as a lark, or as the brown thrush that sat daily on the uppermost branches of the stubby growth of a basswood tree which stood near by upon the hill where we often played under its shade, lodging our little arrows among the thick branches of the tree and then shooting them down again for sport.

Early in the morning as the sun peeped from the east, as I would yet be lying close to my mother's bosom, this brown thrush would begin his warbling songs perched upon the uppermost branches of the basswood tree that stood close to our lodge. I would then say to myself, as I listened to him, "here comes again my little orator," and I used to try to understand what he had to say; and sometimes thought I understood some of its utterances as follows: "Good morning, good morning! arise, arise! shoot, shoot! come along, come along!" etc., every word repeated twice. Even then, and so young as I was, I used to think that little bird had a language which God or the Great Spirit had given him, and every bird of the forest understood what he had to say, and that he was appointed to preach to other birds, to tell them to be happy, to be thankful for the blessings they enjoy among the summer green branches of the forests, and the plenty of wild fruits to eat. The larger boys used to amuse themselves by playing a ball called Paw-kaw-doway [lacrosse], foot-racing, wrestling, bow-arrow shooting, and trying to beat one another shooting the greatest number of chipmunks and squirrels in a day, etc.

I never heard any boy or any grown person utter any bad language, even if they were out of patience with anything. Swearing or profanity was never heard among the Ottawa and Chippewa tribes of Indians, and not even found in their language. Scarcely any drunkenness, only once in a great while the old folks used to have a kind of short spree; particularly when there was any special occasion of a great feast going on. But all the young folks did not drink intoxicating liquors as a beverage in those days. And we always rested in perfect safety at night in our dwellings, and the doorways of our lodges had no fastenings to them, but simply a frail mat or a blanket was hung over our doorways which might be easily pushed or thrown one side without any noise if theft or any other mischief was intended. But we were not afraid for any such thing to happen us, because we knew that every child of the forest was observing and living under the precepts which their forefathers taught them, and the children were taught almost daily by their parents from infancy unto manhood and womanhood, or until they were separated from their families.

These precepts or moral commandments by which the Ottawa and Chippewa nations of Indians were governed in their primitive state, were almost the same as the Ten Commandments which the God Almighty himself delivered to Moses on Mount Sinai on tables of stone. Very few of these divine precepts are not found among the precepts of the Ottawa and Chippewa Indians, except with regard to the Sabbath day to keep it holy; almost every other commandment can be found, only there are more, as there were about twenty of these "uncivilized" precepts. They also believed, in their primitive state, that the eye of this Great Being is the sun by day, and by night the moon and stars, and, therefore, that God or the Great Spirit sees all things everywhere, night and day, and it would be impossible to hide our actions, either good or bad, from the eye of this Great Being. Even the very threshold or crevice of your wigwam will be a witness against you, if you should commit any criminal action when no human eye could observe your criminal doings, but surely your criminal actions will be revealed in some future time to your disgrace and shame. These were continual inculcations to the children by their parents, and in every feast and council, by the "Instructors of the Precepts" to the people or to the audience of the council. For these reasons the Ottawas and Chippewas in their primitive state were strictly honest and upright in their dealings with their fellow-beings. Their word of promise was as good as a promissory note, even better, as these notes sometimes are neglected and not performed according to their promises; but the Indian promise was very sure and punctual, although, as they had no timepieces, they measured their time by the sun. If an Indian promised to execute a certain obligation at such time, at so many days, and at such height of the sun, when that time comes he would be there punctually to fulfill this obligation. This was formerly the character of the Ottawa and Chippewa Indians of Michigan. But now, our living is altogether different, as we are continually suffering under great anxiety and perplexity, and continually being robbed and cheated in various ways.

Our houses have been forcibly entered for thieving purposes and murder; people have been knocked down and robbed; great safes have been blown open with powder in our little town and their contents carried away, and even children of the Caucasian race are heard cursing and blaspheming the name of their Great Creator, upon whose pleasure we depended for our existence. . . .

Again, most every historian, or annalist so-called, who writes about the Island of Mackinac and the Straits and vicinity, tells us that the definition or the meaning of the word "Michilimackinac" in the Ottawa and Chippewa language, is "large turtle," derived from the word Mi-she-mi-kinock in the Chippewa language. That is, "Mi-she" as one of the adnominals or adjectives in the Ottawa and Chippewa languages, which would signify tremendous in size; and "Mikinock" is the name of mud turtle—meaning, therefore, "monstrous large turtle," as the historians would have it. But we consider this to be a clear error. Where-ever those annalists, or those who write about the Island of Mackinac, obtain their information as to the definition of the word Michilimackinac, I don't know, when our tradition is so direct and so clear with regard to the historical definition of that word, and is far from being derived from the word "Michimikinock," as the historians have told us. Our tradition says that when the Island was first discovered by the Ottawas, which was some time before America was known as an existing country by the white man, there was a small independent tribe, a remnant race of Indians who occupied this island, who became confederated with the Ottawa when the Ottawas were living at Manitoulin, formerly called Ottawa Island, which is situated north of Lake Huron. The Ottawas thought a good deal of this unfortunate race of people, as they were kind of interesting sort of people; but, unfortunately, they had most powerful enemies, who every now and then would come among them to make war with them. Their enemies were of the Iroquois of New York. Therefore, once in the dead of the winter while the Ottawas were having a great jubilee and war dances at their island, now Manitoulin, on account of the great conquest over the We-ne-be-goes of Wisconsin, of which I will speak more fully in subsequent chapters, during which time the Senecas of New York, of the Iroquois family of Indians, came upon the remnant race and fought them, and almost entirely annihilated them. But two escaped to tell the story, who effected their escape by flight and by hiding in one of the natural caves at the island, and therefore that was the end of this race. And according to our understanding and traditions the tribal name of those disastrous people was "Mi-shi-ne-macki-naw-go," which is still existing to this day as a monument of their former existence; for the Ottawas and Chippewas named this little island "Mi-shi-ne-mackinong" for memorial sake of those their former confederates, which word is the locative case of the Indian noun

"Michinemackinawgo." Therefore, we contend, this is properly where the name Michilimackinac is originated.

From *History of the Ottawa and Chippewa Indians of Michigan: A Grammar of their Language, and a Personal and Family History of the Author* by Andrew J. Blackbird
(Ypsilanti, MI: Ypsilantian Job Printing House, 1887), 9–13, 19–22.

An Ojibwa Battle with the Iroquois

Traditional/Charles Kawbawgam

This event took place sometime between 1655 and 1670 at Iroquois Point, near Sault Ste. Marie. The date varies according to different sources. However, the specific date is of little importance.

A great war party of Iroquois came up from the lower lakes. As they paddled along the shore of the Georgian bay, the Ojibwas in that neighborhood pushed on ahead of them and gave warning of their approach. The Ojibwas traveled day and night to the Ault, gathering numbers as they went, till they reached Lake Superior and felt able to fight. They then camped secretly at Point aux Pins, while the Iroquois passed them the next day and camped on the other side of the water at Iroquois Point. As they went along, not knowing that they were watched, the Iroquois began to sing their war songs, and when they landed they had a war dance.

The Ojibwa chief called for two strong medicine men to go scouting. The scouts were unarmed for they were to go in spirit form. Presently the Ojibwas waiting on the beach, heard a beaver in the water and heard the whistle of an otter. These were the two medicine men. They swam across the bay going ashore between Whiskey [probably Waiska] Bay and Iroquois Point, and resumed their own forms. They went through the woods towards the other point and as soon as it was dark, crept up and counted the Iroquois. Then they went back to their landing place, recrossed the bay in animal form, and returned to camp, arriving about dawn. They knew from a spirit that the Iroquois would continue their dance all day and night for four days. And the Ojibwa chief understood that by that time they would be all tired out.

Most Iroquois war parties carry along one woman. The squaw with this party dreamed every night that the Iroquois were all going to be killed by the Ojibwas. She told the Iroquois chief but he thought nothing of it.

In the morning that the medicine men came back to Point aux Pins, the Ojibwas moved across to Whiskey Bay to wait till it was time to attack.

On the fourth day they sent two more scouts to find out when the Iroquois were going to sleep. About the same time, the whole band of Ojibwas began to move through the woods toward the enemy camp. Meantime the scouts were working back and forth and reported at last that all the Iroquois seemed to be asleep.

The Ojibwas gradually drew up and surrounded them till the scouts had only a little way to go to take their reports to the chief. Near dawn he ordered the men to attack. The Iroquois, tired out after their long war dance, were taken entirely by surprise. They were slaughtered in heaps. Only two were spared. The Ojibwas took these two, cut off their ears, noses, fingers and toes, gave them supplies enough to get home and sent back this message: That that party of Iroquois wasn't big enough to give the Ojibwas a little fun and that if any more felt like coming, they could count on getting the same welcome. The Ojibwas cut off the heads of the slain and set them up, one after another, along the beach in a line that stretched about half a mile.

From *Ojibwa Myths and Halfbreed Tales, 1893–1895*, collected by Homer Kidder, 1918, housed in the American Philosophical Society, Philadelphia.

CHAPTER 2

Pays d'en Haut: Arrival of the French

Though there had been a French presence in North America since Jacques Cartier's voyages in the early sixteenth century, French officials in Europe took little interest in the New World until nearly 130 years later. At this time, the Anishinaabeg and the Iroquois were in the midst of a devastating war (see "An Ojibwa Battle with the Iroquois" in chapter 1), one that displaced and upset numerous groups of Huron, France's first Indian allies (it is important to note that the Huron are not Anishinaabeg). By the late seventeenth century, French priests and explorers reached what would become Michigan. The French dubbed the Great Lakes region *Pays d'en Haut*, or "Upper Country."

During this period, the Anishinaabeg permitted the French to live among them, and the "gifts" the French handed out to the Indians were actually tribute. One Anishinaabeg group that displayed incredible power and influence were the Ottawa at Michilimackinac. The French relied heavily on Indian support because without their Anishinaabeg allies, they could have been easily pushed off the continent by their enemies, the Iroquois and the English. Still, Catholic priests, such as Fathers René Menard and Jacques Marquette, were important to French expansion and exploration of the Great Lakes, and the fur trade became important to both France and the original peoples.

Letter on Ministering to the Huron

Father René Menard

In this letter, Menard relates his experiences proselytizing to Huron near present-day L'Anse in the Upper Peninsula. These particular Huron were refugees, dispersed by wars with the Iroquois.

June 2, 1661

I have seen nothing in this Christendom that has not edified me. Nevertheless, evil tongues have not failed to find cause of scandal in it, as did of old the gentiles in St. Paul's infirmities, considering that there was more to be lost than gained in God's service. After all, God's kindness, which has guided me, has shown me that it was not without design that Paradise was to be peopled with these poor folk who, although they seem to be of the lowest degree, are men as well as the Europeans and the other nations of the earth. One of my first visits at the spot where we were to winter was to a hovel, the most miserable cabin of all, erected under a large decayed tree, which served as a shelter for it on one side, and upheld some branches of cedar and Hemlock which kept off the wind on the other. I entered almost on all fours, and under that tree I found a treasure. It was a woman, abandoned by her Husband and her daughter, who had left her two little children, and they were dying; one was about 2, and the other 3 years old. I began to speak of the faith to this poor afflicted creature, and she heard me with pleasure which she expressed in these words: "My brother," she said to me, "I know well enough that my people do not approve thy discourses; but, for my part, I relish them very much, and what thou sayest is full of consolation." At the same time, she drew out from underneath the tree a piece of dried fish, of which she deprived herself to pay me for my visit. But I prized much more highly the Opportunity that God gave me for assuring myself of the salvation of the 2 little Innocents, by administering baptism to them. I returned some days afterward to see that good creature, and I found her fully resolved to serve God; and, in fact, she began from that day to come and pray to God night and morning—so constantly, that she never failed to do so, no matter what affairs she had on hand or how pressed she Was to obtain her wretched livelihood. The younger of those little Innocents did not long delay in surrendering to Heaven the first-fruits of this Mission, whose devotions he practiced during the short time that he survived his baptism. For, noticing that his Mother prayed to God before eating, he at once, of his own accord, acquired the habit of lifting his hand to his forehead to make the sign of the cross, before drinking and eating. This he continued to do until the end—a somewhat extraordinary thing in a Child who was not yet 2 years old.

The second person whom God gave us was a poor old man, sick unto death, at 3 Rivers. When his people came down, and I could no longer approach him on account of their jugglers, who surrounded him at all hours, that good man, upon whom God had his designs, was not yet ripe for Heaven. The affliction that befell him during the voyage greatly humiliated him; for a squall struck him on Lake Superior, and, to save his life, he lost all that he had gone to get at 3 Rivers. As old age and poverty are held in great contempt among the savages, he was obliged to take refuge with Our Nahakwatkse, his sister, the good widow of whom I have already spoken. On one occasion, he tried to jeer at our Mysteries in my presence, but, as our cause is an excellent one, I took him up on a point whereon he gave me a fairly good chance. He was unable to reply, and, yielding to grace and to the Holy Ghost, he came to see me on the following day and asked me to make him pray; and ever since then he has borne himself openly before his countrymen as a disciple of Jesus Christ, so that I have baptized him Jean Amikous.

The third who seems predestined for Paradise is a Young man about 30 years of age, who for a long time has excited the admiration of our savages by resisting, with a constancy unknown among them, all the temptations of the spirit of impurity, which are probably as frequent here as in any other place in the world. This chosen soul had sometimes approached me on the road, and expressed to me a great desire to become a Christian. But I heard that he was not married, and I persuaded myself that he was worse than those who were settled. I found here, however, that in fact he was not so; and, what is more, that, although he was sought after because he was clever and belonged to a great family, he nevertheless rejected the advances of all the girls or women who loved him, and that they could never draw any licentious or indecent word from him—so much so that none amused themselves by importuning him in that direction. He was one of the first who came to visit me as soon as I had withdrawn into my little hermitage. I asked him, after several excellent conversations, how it happened that he was not married, and whether he intended to remain always in that state. "No, my Brother," he said; "what I am resolved to do is not to live in the fashion of my people, or to [bind] myself with any woman who has a coarse mind, such as I find very common here in that sex. I will never marry unless I find a chaste woman, who is not abandoned like those of this country. I am not in a hurry; and, if I do not find one, I am quite satisfied to remain as I am with my brother during the remainder of my life. Moreover, when thou findest that I am doing any other thing than what I tell thee, thou mayst exclude me from prayer." These bold words afterward seemed to me to have been inspired by Jesus, who had taken possession of that great heart and had preserved it until the hour of its salvation. This winter, a feast of fornication was held by order of the medicine-men of the country, to restore the health of a man sick beyond hope of recovery. The good neophyte, whom I named Louis in baptism, was begged and earnestly urged to be present, to complete the number of the guests; but he refused. When his relatives urged and scolded him to induce him to go, he got up and went out by one door of the cabin; and after remaining for some time at a certain place praying to God, he reentered by another door, giving cause for laughter to those who were present. As he is alone in this kind of life he is obliged to endure a thousand insults on all sides. To this, thank God, he is already inured. His only answer to all that they may say is a slight smile; and he never flinches or relaxes on a single point when his duty as a Christian is in question.

The 4th chosen Soul who has been found is the elder sister of our Louis, a widow burdened with 5 Children—a very quiet woman, who is occupied all day long with the affairs of her little household. She brought me the oldest of her Children, a girl 10 years old, and begged me to instruct her, in order that, as she said, God might have pity on her and restore her health, which she had lost some months ago. She was suffering from a chronic catarrh, which hindered her in speaking, and choked her voice. I made her pray, and then had her bled. The bleeding produced its effect, and she recovered her voice. This induced the Mother to come with all her family and ask that they also might pray to God. I baptized them after a thorough Instruction and trial of their piety. The good creature loves us very much, and her great charity contributes toward our subsistence. I named the Mother Plathéhahsmie.

The 5th person whom I found worthy of Holy baptism is another widow. She has had no children by her husband, to whom she was given in her youth by her parents. The Iroquois took him from her, 6 years ago. This woman, who came to me of her own accord to ask to be instructed, has during all the time of her widowhood lived with great reserve, remaining ever at the Side of her Mother, who is of an exceedingly taciturn nature, and who strongly disapproves of the visits of the Young men. It seems as if God chose her in the place of some Christian women of 3 Rivers, who had taken refuge in her cabin. For she began to serve God so fervently that the others left her: and she heeded my words and the impulses of grace more than anything that deranged persons could say in their ill humor.

Finally, the 6th is an old man, about 80 years of age, who is blind and unable to come and pray to God in our house. This good man also listens to me with pleasure, as soon as I speak to him of Paradise. He has applied himself to learning the prayers, and he repeats them day and night, in the hope of finding everlasting life at the moment of death, which cannot be far off in his case.

(These are all) who have hitherto seemed to me to be ripe for Heaven, and whom

I have found sufficiently well prepared for receiving baptism; for in some others who come to pray I have not found such manifest proofs of their faith and piety. What I can say generally with reference to our neophytes is that in each one of them we observe, in particular, a certain spirit of charity and gratitude toward us. Thus, when they have anything out of the ordinary, either meat or fish, they do not fail to share it with us; and they do not wait, like those down below [he might be speaking of Michilimackinac], for any acknowledgment on our part: for here we have neither bread, nor peas, nor corn, nor prunes to give them as down below. As to our petty wares, knives or beads, not only are they abundantly provided with these, but, as I have only a few, and as it is impossible to obtain any more, all the ways by which I might gratify them are closed to me. I left 3 Rivers with 60 or 80 small beads; if I should give them away, I would reach the end of them within a month. . . . I have also wished for Tobacco; everything can be done with that Money. After all, the desire for those things that would seem to me to be necessary has been very moderate. God shows me by experience that I can serve him without that and many other things. . . .

There has been no winter here, to speak of. Our great bay of Ste. Thérèse, on whose shore we have wintered, has been frozen over only since the middle of February. I have said Holy Mass every day from All Saints' Day to March, without any fear that the elements would freeze or that I would need any fire at the altar. I brought with me only a pint of Spanish wine, which is very little, considering the great distance, for a person who has no other consolation in the world but that august sacrifice. Alas! I know not when that wine will fail me; and I know not whether any one will ever bring me some. Vines are not to be seen here anymore than other comforts which are fairly common down below. God has preserved my altar-bread inside a small box, which was quite ruined by the Water that entered it, and it may last me till the autumn of the year 1662. It is a long time until then, and matters will assume another shape, to determine me either to remain here or to leave this place, as I may deem best for God's greater glory. I must push on to the last post, the Bay of St. Esprit, 100 leagues from here [Chequamegon Bay]. There the savages have their rendezvous in the early spring, and there we must decide either to leave the country entirely, or to settle permanently in some place where we may hope to grow wheat. I pray the Father of Light to direct the purposes of these poor people toward his own greater glory.

Here is a summary of what has occurred from the 1st of March to the 1st of June. The savages are living on moose-meat, which came very opportunely. The supply of fish failed, and those who wished to keep lent suffered greatly; those who did not keep it, did not suffer. The Savages invite us every day to their feasts. We decamped from our winter quarters on Easter Saturday, to proceed to a very pleasant river where there was good hunting, and where the savages found what was needed for their subsistence. Game and fish failed us; so we left the savages, and 6 of us Frenchmen embarking in three canoes, we continued our navigation. At the end of two days, we arrived at that formidable portage which is a short league in length, midway between the trembling lands [bogs] wherein one sinks of necessity, sometimes more, sometimes less.

On the 1st of May, we performed our devotions in the Cabins of some Algonquins, who stole a part of our provisions during the night. We left them, and found this great lake all bordered with ice. At a distance of 2 leagues from that place, we arrived among other Algonquins where, fearing lest the same thing might happen to us as among the former ones, we passed on, and after 5 days we finally reached the main body. There I learned that the bodies of [blank in MS.] and 2 others, who had been drowned in the autumn, had been found, so bad was the weather for several days that Canoes and men were lost. The winter and white frosts continued until the middle of May. On Ascension Day, I saw a Huron who had started 11 days before from the Tobacco nation. He told me that people were dying of hunger in his country; that, toward the end of May, the Iroquois had fallen upon 14 persons, and killed 4 men upon the spot; that the Natwesix (Nadouesis or Nadouesieux) had appeared some time afterward and killed 5 Hurons, while the latter had killed 8 Nadwesiou; that dysentery had carried off 40 Poutewat and 60 others; that his people had left the country and traveled a distance of 5 days' journey hitherward; that he had come by land in eight days, by a difficult road. . . .

Private letters will tell you the remainder. I commend myself with all my heart to all our Fathers and Brethren, to whom I would Write si liceret per chartem et atramentum. But I have not even a Penknife.

Of Yourself, Reverend Father,
The very humble And obedient
servant in Jesus Christ,
René Menard

Father Menard to Jerome Lelamant, June 2, 1661, in *The Jesuit Relations and Allied Documents: Travels and Explorations of the Jesuit Missionaries in New France, 1610—1791*, vol. 46 (Cleveland: Burrows Brothers Company, 1899), 127–45.

Travels among the Menominee and Mascouten

Father Jacques Marquette

The feast of The Immaculate Conception of the Blessed Virgin—whom I have always invoked since I have been in this country of the Outaouacs [Ottawa], to obtain from God the grace of being able to visit the Nations who dwell along the Missisipi River—was precisely the day on which Monsieur Jollyet arrived with orders from Monsieur the Count de Frontenac, Our Governor, and Monsieur Talon, Our Intendant, to accomplish this discovery with me. I was all the more delighted at this good news, since I saw that my plans were about to be accomplished; and since I found myself in the blessed necessity of exposing my life for the salvation of all these peoples, and especially of the Ilinois, who had very urgently entreated me, when I was at the point of St. Esprit, to carry the word of God to their country.

We were not long in preparing all our equipment, although we were about to begin a voyage, the duration of which we could not foresee. Indian corn, with some smoked meat, constituted all our provisions; with these we embarked—Monsieur Jollyet and myself, with 5 men—in 2 bark canoes, fully resolved to do and suffer everything for so glorious an undertaking.

Accordingly, on the 17th day of May, 1673, we started from the Mission of St. Ignace at Michilimakinac, where I then was. The joy that we felt at being selected for this expedition animated our courage, and rendered the labor of paddling from morning to night agreeable to us. And because we were going to seek unknown countries, we took every precaution in our power, so that, if our undertaking were hazardous, it should not be foolhardy. To that end, we obtained all the Information that we could from the savages who had frequented those regions; and we even traced out from their reports a map of the whole of that new country; on it we indicated the rivers which we were to navigate, the names of the peoples and of the places through which we were to pass, the course of the great river, and the direction we were to follow when we reached it.

Above all, I placed our voyage under the protection of the Blessed Virgin Immaculate, promising her that, if she granted us the favor of discovering the great river, I would give it the Name of the Conception, and that I would also make the first mission that I should establish among those new peoples, bear the same name. This I have actually done, among the Ilinois.

With all these precautions, we joyfully plied our paddles on a portion of Lake Huron [present-day Lake Michigan], on That of the Ilinois and on the Bay des Puants [Green Bay].

The first Nation that we came to was that of the folle avoine [literally translated, "people of the wild rice," Menominee]. I entered their river, to go and visit these peoples to whom we have preached the Gospel for several years,—in consequence of which, there are several good Christians among them. The wild oat, whose name they bear because it is found in their country, is a sort of grass, which grows naturally in the small rivers with muddy bottoms, and in swampy places. It greatly resembles the wild oats that grow amid our wheat. The ears grow upon hollow stems, jointed at intervals; they emerge from the water about the month of June, and continue growing until they rise about two feet above it. The grain is not larger than that of our oats, but it is twice as long, and the meal therefrom is much more abundant. The savages gather and prepare it for food as follows. In The month of September, which is the suitable time for the harvest, they go in canoes through these fields of wild oats; they shake its ears into the canoe, on both sides, as they pass through. The grain falls out easily, if it be ripe, and they obtain their supply in a short time. But, in order to clean it from the straw, and to remove it from a husk in which it is enclosed, they dry it in the smoke, upon a wooden grating, under which they maintain a slow fire for some days. When the oats are thoroughly dry, they put them in a skin made into a bag, thrust it into a hole dug in the ground for this purpose, and tread it with their feet—so long and so vigorously that the grain separates from the straw, and is very easily winnowed. After this, they pound it to reduce it to flour,—or even, without pounding it, they boil it in water, and season it with fat. Cooked in this fashion, the wild oats have almost as delicate a taste as rice has when no better seasoning is added.

I told these peoples of the folle avoine of my design to go and discover those remote nations, in order to teach them the Mysteries of Our Holy Religion. They were greatly surprised to hear it, and did their best to dissuade me. They represented to me that I would meet Nations who never show mercy to strangers, but break their heads without any cause; and that war was kindled between various peoples who dwelt upon our route, which exposed us to the further manifest danger of being killed by the bands of warriors who are ever in the field. They also said that the great river was very dangerous, when one does not know the difficult places; that it was full of horrible monsters, which devoured men and canoes together; that there was even a demon, who was heard from a great distance, who barred the way, and swallowed up all who ventured to approach him; finally that the heat was so excessive in those countries that it would inevitably cause our death.

I thanked them for the good advice that they gave me, but told them that I could not follow it, because the salvation of souls was at stake, for which I would be delighted to give my life; that I scoffed at the alleged demon; that we would easily defend ourselves against those marine monsters; and, moreover, that we would be on our guard to avoid the other dangers with which they threatened us. After making them pray to God, and giving them some instruction, I separated from them. Embarking then in our canoes, we arrived shortly afterward at the bottom of the Bay des Puants, where our Fathers labor successfully for the conversion of these peoples, over two thousand of whom they have baptized while they have been there.

This bay bears a name which has a meaning not so offensive in the language of the savages; For they call it la baye sallé ["salt bay"] rather than Bay des Puans,—although with them this is almost the same and this is also the name which they give to the sea. This led us to make very careful researches to ascertain whether there were not some salt-water springs in this quarter, as there are among the Hiroquois [Iroquois], but we found none. We conclude, therefore, that this name has been given to it on account of the quantity of mire and mud which is seen there, whence noisome vapors constantly arise, causing the loudest and most continual thunder that I have ever heard.

We left [Bay des Puans] to enter the river that discharges into it; it is very beautiful at its mouth, and flows gently; it is full of bustards, ducks, teal, and other birds, attracted thither by the wild oats, of which they are very fond. But, after ascending the river a short distance, it becomes very difficult of passage, on account of both the currents and the sharp rocks, which cut the canoes and the feet of those who are obliged to drag them, especially when the waters are low. Nevertheless, we successfully passed those rapids; and on approaching Machkoutens, the fire Nation, I had the curiosity to drink the mineral waters of the river that is not far from that village. I also took time to look for a medicinal plant which a savage, who knows its secret, showed to Father Alloues with many ceremonies. Its root is employed to counteract snake-bites, God having been pleased to give this antidote against a poison which is very common in these countries. It is very pungent, and tastes like powder when crushed with the teeth; it must be masticated and placed upon the bite inflicted by the snake. The reptile has so great a horror of it that it even flees from a person who has rubbed himself with it. The plant bears several stalks, a foot high, with rather long leaves; and a white flower, which greatly resembles the wallflower. I put some in my canoe, in order to examine it at leisure while we continued to advance toward Maskoutens, where we arrived on the 7th of June.

From *The Jesuit Relations and Allied Documents: Travels and Explorations of the Jesuit Missionaries in New France, 1610—1791*, vol. 59 (Cleveland: Burrows Brothers Company, 1899), 89–101.

Plan for Detroit

Antoine de la Mothe Cadillac

October 18, 1700

Sir, It is my duty to give you an exact account of all that I have done regarding the establishment of Detroit since it was referred to you at the time when I was in France, and concerning which you were good enough to converse with me. . . .

It is greatly to be feared that the execution of this scheme has been delayed too long, from the news we have that the English have fortified themselves on a river which discharges itself into Lake Ontario, and that they will extend their posts toward Lake Erie.

If our Colony were not full of envy, disunion, cabal and intrigue, no opposition would have been offered to taking possession of a post [that is] so advantageous that, if it were separated from all those we [now] have, we should be compelled in a short time to abandon all; for it is that alone which will make the Colony and its commerce entirely safe, and cause the certain ruin of the English colonies. For that reason it is very important that it should not pass into other hands, which would be inevitable if we deferred taking it any longer.

The objections which have been raised also at the wrong time, in the belief that this post might cause us to be forever at war with the Iroquois, are now removed by the peace which has been concluded with them. That tribe was not in a position to keep up the war any longer, and will not be able to begin it again very soon; therefore there could not be a more suitable time for establishing Detroit, which will be fortified more quickly than the Iroquois can make up the loss of their numbers.

It is an incontestable fact, that the strength of the savages lies in the remoteness of the French, and that ours increases against them with our proximity. For it is certain that, with a little Indian corn, these people have no difficulty in traversing two hundred leagues to come and take some one's life by stealth; and when we want to get to their lands, we are obliged to provide ourselves with stores of all kinds and to make great preparations, which involves the King in extraordinary expenses, and always with very little effect since it is like beating drums to catch hares.

But, on the contrary, when we are the neighbors of that tribe and are within easy reach of them, they will be kept in awe and will find themselves forced to maintain peace since they will be unable to do otherwise unless they wish to ruin themselves irretrievably.

It would be in vain to establish this post if they would not comply with my memorandum; for if only a garrison pure and simple were kept up there, it would be liable to the revolutions which usually take place in the frontier posts, and it would make no impression on the minds of the Iroquois and of our allies, and much less still on those of the English. In order to succeed thoroughly, it would be well (in my opinion) to adopt the following measures.

1. To go and station ourselves there with a hundred men, one half of whom should be soldiers and the other Canadians. In order to carry out this expedition with all necessary despatch, and to undeceive the Englishmen at once as to having any claim there and to take from them all hope of establishing any relations with our allies, this strength is sufficient for the first year. For this number is absolutely necessary to me for fortifying [the place] and for taking the proper steps for the subsistence of those who wish to settle there subsequently.

2. The year after, the fort being secure from insult, it is well to allow twenty or thirty families to settle there, and to bring their cattle and other necessary things which they will willingly do at their own cost and expense; and this may be continued as it is permitted in all the other settlements of the Colony.

3. It is no less necessary that the King should send two hundred picked men who should, as far as may be, be of different trades and also rather young.

4. It is not advisable that I, any more than the other officers, soldiers and inhabitants, should do any trade with the savages, in order to take away from the people of the other established posts their cause for complaint, as to which they are very active. . . .

5. We must establish at this post missionaries of different communities such as Jesuits and other Fathers, and ecclesiastics of the foreign missions; they are laborers in the vineyard, and should be received without distinction to labor at the vine of the Lord, with orders in particular to teach the young savages the French language, [that] being the only means to civilize and humanize them, and to instil into their hearts and their minds the law of religion and of the monarch. We take wild beasts at their birth, birds in their nests, to tame them and set them free. But in order to succeed better in that, it would be necessary for the King to favor these same missionaries with his bounty and his alms, in proportion as they instruct the children of the Savages at their houses, on the evidence which the Commandant and other officers give of it.

6. The third or fourth year we shall be able to set Ursulines there, or other nuns, to whom His Majesty could grant the same favors.

7. It would be important that there should be a hospital for sick or infirm Savages, for there is nothing more urgent for gaining their friendship than the care taken of them in their illnesses. . . .

8. It would be absolutely necessary also to allow the soldiers and Canadians to

marry the savage maidens when they have been instructed in religion and know the French language which they will learn all the more eagerly (provided we labor carefully to that end) because they always prefer a Frenchman for a husband to any savage. . . .

9. Marriages of this kind will strengthen the friendship of these tribes. . . .

We shall find, in the execution of this scheme, not only the glory of His Majesty but also that of God magnificently extended; for by this means his worship and his religion will be established in the midst of the tribes, and the deplorable sacrifices which they offer to Baal entirely abolished. . . .

As I am taking my son with me to Detroit, I beg the Minister to be so good as to grant him an ensigncy or an order for the first vacancy. . . . The Colony sends two persons for the matters which concern it, and to manage the sale of the beaver skins; instructions have been given them, and there is reason to hope that they will conform to them, and that they will do their duty better than the first [men sent].

Permit me to assure you that I am, with deep respect
Your very humble and very obedient servant
Lamothe Cadillac

Cadillac to Unknown, October 18, 1700, in *Michigan Pioneer and Historical Collections* (hereafter abbreviated *MPHC*), vol. 33 (Lansing: Robert Smith Printing Company, 1904), 96–101.

Furs at Detroit

For most Frenchmen, interest in North America centered on the fur trade. By the mid-seventeenth century, French officials encouraged settlement and the development of farms in hopes to mirror the growth of the British North American colonies. However, most emigrants, perhaps looking for adventure and better pay than farming could offer, engaged in the fur trade once they arrived.

November 13, 1702

Returns that were derived from trade and from hunting at Fort Ponchartrain at Detroit, which were received at Quebec this present year of 1702

Be It Known

By the first convoy, which arrived at Montreal in the month of June

Beaver pelts which were delivered to the Office of the Farm on August 3, 1702:

- Greasy, semi-greasy, & green [used by Native trappers for some time]: 570 lbs. 2 oz., @ 3.25 livre per lb. = 1,852.9 livre
- Muscovy [unused]: 127 lbs. 7 oz., at 3 livre per lb. = 382.31 l.
- Dry, from winter: 1,683 lbs. 10 oz., @ 2 livre per lb. = 3,367.25 l.
- Furs and hides which were sold at auction, October 10 and 11, 1702:
- 365 tanned elk: 318 lbs., @ 7.13 livre per lb. = 2,265.75 l.
- 1,199 deer: 964 lbs., @ 2.21 livre per lb. = 2,132.86 l.
- 598 bears: 534 lbs., @ 3.75 livre per lb. = 2,002.5 l.
- 3,967 raccoons: 3,717 lbs., @ 0.41 livre per lb. = 1,533.26 l.
- 495 otters: 404 lbs., @ 3.75 livre per lb. = 1,517.43 l.
- tanned moose: 51 lbs., @ 10.69 livre per lb. = 545.06 l.
- bobcats: 88 lbs., @ 0.98 livre per lb. = 85.8 l.
- 29 timber wolves: 25 lbs., @ 3.15 livre per lb. = 80.33 l.
- 54 bear cubs: 45 lbs., @ 1.28 livre per lb. = 57.23 l.
- 12 foxes, 12 fishers, and 6 panthers: 30 lbs., @ 1.39 livre per lb. = 41.63 l.

By the second and last convoy, which arrived in the month of October

Beaver pelts which were delivered to the Office of the Farm on November 2, 1702:

- Greasy, semi-greasy, and green: 680 lbs., 2 oz., @ 3.25 livre per lb. = 2,213.65 l.
- Muscovy: 6 lbs. 14 oz., @ 3 livre per lb. = 20.63 l.
- Dry, from winter: 1,328 lbs. 14 oz., @ 2 livre per lb. = 2,657.75 l.

Furs and hides which were sold at auction, October 28, 1702:

- tanned elk: 341 lbs., @ 6.38 livre per lb. = 2,173.88 l.
- deer: 889 lbs., @ 1.8 livre per lb. = 1,600.2 l.
- otters: 317 lbs., @ 4.13 livre per lb. = 1,307.1 l.
- bears: 336 lbs., @ 3 livre per lb. = 1,008 l.
- raccoons: 1,654 lbs., @ 0.56 livre per lb. = 930.38 l.
- bobcats: 64 lbs., @ 1.99 livre per lb. = 127.2 l.
- bear cubs: 84 lbs., @ 1.13 livre per lb. = 94.5 l.
- foxes: 21 lbs., @ 2.29 livre per lb. = 48.
- fishers: 2 lbs., @ 3.34 livre per lb. = 6.68 l.

"Compte de la depense faite pour Établissement et Commerce du Fort Ponchartrain du Detroit, et des retours en sont provenir pendant la premiere aneé de cet Etablissement," November 13, 1702, National Archives of Quebec, Series C11 A, vol. 20.

CHAPTER 3

Indian Country: The British in Michigan

After the French defeat in the French and Indian War, Great Britain took control over what would become Michigan. Many Michigan native groups looked forward to the transition since the British promised to expand trade and tributes. However, the British failed to follow up on their promises, and many British leaders, particularly the new governor of North America, Lord Jeffery Amherst, maintained a hostile attitude toward Indians. Grievances against the British mounted until the Indians could take no more. In 1763, Great Lakes Natives launched a coordinated attack on the British that compelled British officials to take a more conciliatory approach. Although Michigan was and had been Indian country when the British assumed control, Pontiac's War made it official, at least in the point of view of the British.

Pontiac's War

Robert Navarre

Navarre was a notary living in Detroit during Pontiac's siege.

This adventure was soon noised about among the people of the whole village who came to hear the message of the Master of Life [Kitchi Manito, often reduced in translation by nonnatives to "Great Spirit"], and then went to carry it to the neighboring villages. The members of these villages came to see the pretended traveler [Neolin, the Delaware prophet who preached that whites were responsible for the evils within Indian society], and the news was spread from village to village and finally reached Pontiac. He believed all this, as we believe an article of faith, and instilled it into the minds of all those in his council. They listened to him as to an oracle, and told him that he had only to speak and they were all ready to do what he demanded of them.

Pontiac, delighted at the success of his harangue, told the Hurons and the Pottawattamies to return to their villages, and that in four days he would go to the Fort [Detroit] with his young men for the peace-pipe dance, and that while the dancers were engaged some other young men would roam around in the Fort to spy out all that was being done, the number of men the English had in the garrison, the number of traders, and the houses they occupied. All of this happened as he had said.

The first Sunday, or rather Sunday, the first day of May, about three o'clock in the afternoon, as the French were coming out of vespers, Pontiac came with forty men that he had chosen and presented himself at the entrance gate. But the Commandant, who had got wind of something in the conduct of the Indians, had ordered the sentinels not to let any come in. This surprised Pontiac. Seeing that they refused admission to him and his whole band who expected to enter as usual, they sent for Mr. LaButte, their interpreter, to say in their behalf to the Commandant that they had come to amuse him and dance the peace-pipe dance. At the request of Mr. LaButte they received permission. They took up their position to the number of thirty before the house in which Mr. Campbell lived, the second in command, and began to dance and beat a post, and relate their warlike exploits. And from time to time they leaped about the commander-in-chief and the accompanying officers who were watching the Indians perform, saying to them in defiance that they had beaten the English at various times and would do so again.

After they had finished talking they demanded bread, tobacco, and beer, which were given to them. They remained long enough so that the ten others who had the word could note all that was going on in the Fort. And nobody, the English or French, mistrusted them, since it is frequently their custom to roam around anywhere unhindered. After these ten had made the round of the Fort and closely examined everything, they came back to join the dancers, and all, as if nothing had happened, went away to their village which was located a little distance above the Fort on the other side of the river in the direction of east northeast, where, according to the orders of Pontiac, the Ottawa chief, all the Indians had encamped the previous Friday.

After their return to the village all the spies reported point by point to their chiefs what they had seen: the movements of the English, and the approximate number of the garrison. Following this report Pontiac sent his messengers to the Hurons and the Pottawattamies to inform them by means of wampum belts of what had happened at the fort. Mackatepelecite, the second chief of the Ottawas, and another Indian highly regarded among them, were dispatched to Takay, the chief of the bad Huron band, who received them with enthusiasm and promised that he and his village were ready to obey the first demand of their great chief.

Pontiac, wholly occupied with his project and nourishing in his heart a poison which was to be fateful for the English, and perhaps for the French, sent runners the following day, Monday, the 2nd day of May, to each of the Huron and Pottawattamy villages to discover the real feeling of each of these two nations, for he feared to be crossed in his plans. These emissaries had orders to notify these nations for him that Thursday, the 5th of May, at mid-day, a grand council would be held in the Pottawattamy village which was situated between two and three miles below the Fort toward the southwest, and that the three nations should meet there and that no woman should be allowed to attend for fear of betraying their plans.

When the appointed day had come all the Ottawas with Pontiac at their head, and the bad band of Hurons in charge of Takay, repaired to the Pottawattamy village where the expected council was to be held. Care had been taken to send the women out of the village so that they might not hear anything of that should be decided. Pontiac ordered sentinels to be placed around the village in order not to be disturbed in their council. When all these precautions had been taken each Indian seated himself in the circle according to rank, and Pontiac at the head, as great chief of all, began to speak. He said:

"It is important for us, my brothers, that we exterminate from our lands this nation which seeks only to destroy us. You see as well as I that we can no longer supply our needs, as we have done, from our brothers, the French. The English sell us goods twice as dear as the French do, and their goods do not last. Scarcely have we bought a blanket or something else to cover ourselves with before we must think of getting another; and when we wish to set out for our winter camps they do not want to give us any credit as our brothers, the French, do.

"When I go to see the English commander and say to him that some of our comrades are dead, instead of bewailing their death, as our French brothers do, he laughs at me and at you. If I ask anything for our sick, he refuses with the reply that he has no use for us. From all this you can well see that they are seeking our ruin. Therefore, my brothers, we must all swear their destruction and wait no longer. Nothing prevents us; they are few in numbers, and we can accomplish it. All the nations who are our brothers attack them,—why should we not attack? Are we not men like them?

Have I not shown you the wampum belts which I received from our Great Father, the Frenchman? He tells us to strike them,—why do we not listen to his words? What do we fear? It is time. Do we fear that our brothers, the French, who are here among us will prevent us? They do not know our plans, and they could not hinder anyway, if they would. You all know as well as I that when the English came upon our lands to drive out our Father, [the last French commandant of Detroit, François Marie-Picoté, sieur de] Belestre, they took away all the Frenchmen's guns and that they now have no arms to protect themselves with. Therefore, it is time for us to strike. If there are any French who side with them, let us strike them as well as the English. Remember what the Master of Life told our brother, the Wolf, to do. That concerns us all as well as others. I have sent wampum belts and messengers to our brothers, the Ottawas of Michillimackinack, and to those of the Thames River to join us. They will not be slow in coming, but while we wait let us strike anyway. There is no more time to lose. When the English are defeated we shall then see what there is left to do, and we shall stop up the ways hither so that they may never come upon our lands."

From *Journal of Pontiac's Conspiracy* by Robert Navarre, translated by R. Clyde Ford
(Detroit: Clarence M. Burton and Speaker Hines Printing Company, 1912), 32–40.

The Fall of Fort Michilimackinac

George Etherington

June 12, 1763

Sir: Notwithstanding what I wrote you [Henry Gladwin, commander of Fort Detroit] in my last, that all the savages were arrived, & that everything seemed in perfect tranquility; yet on the second instant the Chippewas who live in a plain near this fort, assembled to play ball, as they had done almost every day since their arrival; They play'd from morning till noon, then throwing their ball close to the gate, and observing Lieut. Leslie and me a few paces out of it, they came behind us, seized, and carried us into the woods. In the meantime the rest rushed into the fort, where they found their squaws, whom they had previously planted there, with their hatchets hid under their blankets, which they took and in an instant killed Lieut. Gamet and fifteen rank and file, and a trader named Tracy; they wounded two and took the rest of the garrison prisoners, five of which they have since killed.

They made prisoners of all the English traders, and robb'd them of everything they had; but offered no violence to any of the persons and properties of the Frenchmen.

When this massacre was over Mssrs. Langlad [Charles Langlade] and Farti, the interpreter came down to the place where Lieut. Leslie and me were prisoners, and on their giving themselves as security to return us when demanded, they obtained leave for us to go to the fort under a guard of savages, which gave time by the assistance of the above mentioned gentlemen to send for the Oatewas, who came down on the first notice and were very much displeased at what the Chippewas had done.

Since the arrival of the Oatewas they have done everything in their power to serve us, and with what prisoners the Chippewas have given them and what they have bought, I have now with me Lieut. Leslie and eleven privates, & the other four of the garrison who are yet living remain in the hands of the Chippewas.

The Chippewas, who are superior in numbers to the Outawas, have declared in council to them that if they do not remove us out of the fort, that they will cut off all communication to this post; by which means all the convoys of merchants from Montreal, Labay, St. Joseph & the upper posts would perish; but if the news of your posts being attack'd (which they say was the reason they took up the hatchet here) be false, and you can send up a strong reinforcement with provisions, etc., accompany'd by some of your savages, I believe the post might be re-established again. Since this affair happened, two canoes arrived from Montreal which put it in my power to make a present to the Outawa nation, who very well deserve anything that can be done for them.

I have been very much obliged to Messrs. Langlad and Farti, the interpreter, as likewise the Jesuit for the many good offices they have done us on this occasion; the priest seems inclinable to go down to your post for a day or two, which I am very glad of, as he is a very good man and has a great deal to say with the savages hereabout, who will believe everything he tells them on his return, which I hope will be soon.

The Outawas say they will take Lieut. Leslie, me, and the eleven men which I mentioned before was in their hands, up to their village & there keep us till they hear what is done at your post, they having sent this canoe for that purpose. I refer you to the priest for the particulars of this melancholy affair, and am,

Dear Sir, Yours very sincerely,
Geo. Etherington

George Etherington to Henry Gladwin, June 12, 1763, from *The Gladwin Manuscripts*, edited by Charles Moore (Lansing: Robert Smith Printing Company, 1897), 631–32.

Alexander Henry

The morning was sultry. A Chipeway came to tell me that his nation was going to play at *bag'gat'iway* with the Sacs or Saakies, another Indian nation, for a high wager. He invited me to witness the sport, adding that the commandant was to be there, and would bet on the side of the Chipeways. In consequence of this information, I went to the commandant, and expostulated with him a little, representing that the Indians might possibly have some sinister end in view; but the commandant only smiled at my suspicions.

Baggatiway, called, by the Canadians, *le jeu de la crosse*, is played with a bat and ball. The bat is about four feet in length, curved, and terminating in a sort of racket. Two posts are planted in the ground, at a considerable distance from each other, as a mile, or more. Each party has its post, and the game consists in throwing the ball up to the post of the adversary. The ball, at the beginning, is placed in the middle of the course, and each party endeavors as well to throw the ball out of the direction of its own post, as into that of the adversary's.

I did not go myself to see the match which was now to be played without the fort, because, there being a canoe prepared to depart, on the following day, for Montreal, I employed myself in writing letters to my friend; and even when a fellow-trader, Mr. Tracy, happened to call upon me, saying that another canoe had just arrived from Detroit, and proposing that I should go with him to the beach, to inquire the news, it so happened that I still remained, to finish my letters; promising to follow Mr. Tracy, in the course of a few minutes. Mr. Tracey had not gone more than twenty paces from my door, when I heard an Indian war-cry, and a noise of general confusion.

Going instantly to my window, I saw a crowd of Indians, within the fort, furiously cutting down and scalping every Englishman they found. In particular, I witnessed the fate of Lieutenant Jemette.

I had, in the room in which I was, a fowling-piece, loaded with swan-shot. This I immediately seized, and held it for a few minutes, waiting to hear the drum beat to arms. In this dreadful interval, I saw several of my countrymen fall, and more than one struggling between the knees of an Indian, who, holding him in this manner, scalped him, while yet living.

At length, disappointed in the hope of seeing the resistance made to the enemy, and sensible, of course, that no effort, of my own unassisted arm, could avail against four hundred Indians, I thought only of seeking shelter. Amid the slaughter which was raging, I observed many of the Canadian inhabitants of the fort, calmly looking on, neither opposing the Indians, nor suffering injury; and, from this circumstance, I conceived a hope of finding security in their houses.

Between the yard-door of my own house, and that of M. Langlade, my next neighbor, there was only a low fence, over which I easily climbed. At my entrance, I found the whole family at the windows, gazing at the scene of blood before them. I addressed myself immediately to M. Langalde, begging that he would put me into some place of safety, until the heat of the affair should be over; an act of charity by which he might perhaps preserve me from the general massacre; but while I uttered my petition, M. Langlade, who had looked for a moment at me, turned again to the window, shrugging his shoulders, and intimating, that he could do nothing for me: "*Que voudriez-vous que j'en ferais?*" [What can I do about it?]

This was a moment of despair; but, the next, a Pani [probably "Pawnee"] woman, a slave of M. Langalde's, beckoned to me to follow her. She brought me to a door, which she opened, desiring me to enter, and telling me that it led to the garret, where I must go and conceal myself. I joyfully obeyed her directions; and she, having followed me up to the garret-door, locked it after me, and with great presence of mind took away the key.

This shelter obtained, if shelter I could hope to find it, I was naturally anxious to know what might still be passing without. Through an aperture, which afforded me a view of the area of the fort, I beheld, in shapes the foulest and most terrible, the ferocious triumphs of the barbarian conquerors. The dead were scalped and mangled; the dying were writhing and shrieking, under the unsatiated knife and tomahawk; and, from the bodies of some, ripped open, their butchers were drinking the blood, scooped up in the hollow of joined hands, and quaffed amid shouts of rage and victory. I was shaken, not only with horror, but with fear. The sufferings which I witnessed, I seemed on the point of experiencing. No long time elapsed, before every one being destroyed, who could be found, there was a general cry of "All is finished!" At the same instant, I heard some of the Indians enter the house in which I was.

The garret was separated from the room below, only by a layer of single boards, at once the flooring of the one and the ceiling of the other. I could therefore hear every thing that passed; and, the Indians no sooner came in, than they inquired, whether or not any Englishman were in the house? M. Langlade replied, that "He could not say—he did not know if any"—answers in which he did not exceed the truth, for the Pani woman had not only hidden me by stealth, but kept my secret, and her own. M. Langlade was therefore, as I presume, as far from a wish to destroy me, as he was careless about saving me, when he added to these answers, that "They might examine for themselves, and would soon be satisfied, as to the object of their questions." Saying this, he brought them to the garret door.

From *Travels and Adventures in Canada and the Indian Territories, Between the Years 1760 and 1776: in two parts* by Alexander Henry (New York: I. Riley, 1809), 77–81.

Proclamation of 1763

King George III

October 7, 1763

And whereas it is just and reasonable, and essential to our Interest, and the Security of our Colonies, that the several Nations or Tribes of Indians with whom We are connected, and who live under our Protection, should not be molested or disturbed in the Possession of such Parts of Our Dominions and Territories as, not having been ceded to or purchased by Us, are reserved to them, or any of them, as their Hunting Grounds, We do therefore, with the Advice of our Privy Council, declare it to be our Royal Will and Pleasure, that no Governor or Commander in Chief in any of our Colonies of Quebec, East Florida, or West Florida, do presume, upon any Pretence whatever, to grant Warrants of Survey, or pass any Patents for Lands beyond the Bounds of their respective Governments, as described in their Commissions; as also that no Governor or Commander in Chief in any of our other Colonies or Plantations in America do presume for the present, and until our further Pleasure be known, to grant Warrants of Survey, or pass Patents for any Lands beyond the Heads or Sources of any of the Rivers which fall into the Atlantic Ocean from the West and North West, or upon any Lands whatever, which, not having been ceded to or purchased by Us as aforesaid, are reserved to the said Indians, or any of them. . . .

And We do hereby strictly forbid, on Pain of our Displeasure, all our loving Subjects from making any Purchases or Settlements whatever, or taking Possession of any of the Lands above reserved, without our especial leave and Licence for that Purpose first obtained.

And, We do further strictly enjoin and require all Persons whatever who have either wilfully or inadvertently seated themselves upon any Lands within the Countries above described, or upon any other Lands which, not having been ceded to or purchased by Us, are still reserved to the said Indians as aforesaid, forthwith to remove themselves from such Settlements. And whereas great Frauds and Abuses have been committed in purchasing Lands of the Indians, to the great Prejudice of our Interests, and to the great Dissatisfaction of the said Indians; In order, therefore, to prevent such Irregularities for the future, and to the end that the Indians may be convinced of our Justice and determined Resolution to remove all reasonable Cause of Discontent, We do, with the Advice of our Privy Council strictly enjoin and require, that no private Person do presume to make any purchase from the said Indians of any Lands reserved to the said Indians, within those parts of our Colonies where, We have thought proper to allow Settlement; but that, if at any Time any of the Said Indians should be inclined to dispose of the said Lands, the same shall be Purchased only for Us, in our Name, at some public Meeting or Assembly of the said Indians, to be held for that Purpose by the Governor or Commander in Chief of our Colony respectively within which they shall lie; and in case they shall lie within the limits of any Proprietary Government, they shall be purchased only for the Use and in the name of such Proprietaries, conformable to such Directions and Instructions as We or they shall think proper to give for that Purpose; And we do, by the Advice of our Privy Council, declare and enjoin, that the Trade with the said Indians shall be free and open to all our Subjects whatever, provided that every Person who may incline to Trade with the said Indians do take out a Licence for carrying on such Trade from the Governor or Commander in Chief of any of our Colonies respectively where such Person shall reside, and also give Security to observe such Regulations as We shall at any Time think fit, by ourselves or by our Commissaries to be appointed for this Purpose, to direct and appoint for the Benefit of the said Trade:

And we do hereby authorize, enjoin, and require the Governors and Commanders in Chief of all our Colonies respectively, as well those under Our immediate Government as those under the Government and Direction of Proprietaries, to grant such Licences without Fee or Reward, taking especial Care to insert therein a Condition, that such Licence shall be void, and the Security forfeited in case the Person to whom the same is granted shall refuse or neglect to observe such Regulations as We shall think proper to prescribe as aforesaid.

And we do further expressly enjoin and require all Officers whatever, as well Military as those Employed in the Management and Direction of Indian Affairs, within the Territories reserved as aforesaid for the use of the said Indians, to seize and apprehend all Persons whatever, who standing charged with Treason, Misprisions of Treason, Murders, or other Felonies or Misdemeanors, shall fly from Justice and take Refuge in the said Territory, and to send them under a proper guard to the Colony where the Crime was committed of which they stand accused, in order to take their Trial for the same.

Given at our Court at St. James's the 7th Day of October 1763, in the Third Year of our Reign.

"Royal Proclamation No. 1," from PrimaryDocuments.ca, https://primarydocuments.ca/documents/ RoyalProc11763Oct7.

Detroit Liquor Declaration

Merchants of Detroit

The introduction of alcohol from Europe was devastating for many Native peoples. In Great Lakes Native groups, visions and dreams are incredibly important, and one method to produce these visions was fasting for long periods. Knowing this helps us to understand why Great Lakes Natives were attracted to strong drinks—it was far easier to drink alcohol to obtain a vision than it was to starve oneself. In other words, alcohol, for many Natives, developed religious significance. European traders often took advantage of this, but it also led to competition among themselves. Knowing that alcohol severely impaired judgment, though realizing if they failed to use it in trade, someone else would, a group of British merchants in Detroit looked for a solution to this problem.

June 13, 1775

Whereas the Subscribers find the selling of Rum or other Spirituous Liquors among the Indians at their Settlements, Detrimental to trade and Dangerous to the Subjects, Do hereby Oblige ourselves to the following Regulations:

In order the Better to regulate the sale of Rum to the Savages, and Confine it entirely to the Fort, We hereby agree to establish a General Rum store in this Fort, for which purpose we promise to Deliver into said Store an equal proportion of Rum and Kegs necessary for that purpose, which Store shall be regulated by a Committee herein after named & appointed for that Intent.

None of us the Concerned in This agreement Shall under any pretence whatsoever Sell, Vend, or Barter with any Indian or Indians, Male or Female any Rum or other Spirituous Liquors for any Commodity whatsoever, which shall be Brought for sale by said Indians; but every [illegible word] Skins, Furs, Trinkets, Sugar, grease or Tallow, in short every thing the Savages may bring to market to Dispose of for Rum, the same shall be bought at the general Store only it being our true Intent & meaning that no Indian or Squaw shall receive Directly or indirectly either by Present or otherwise in any of our houses Give them one small glass of Rum at any time during the Continuance of our Said general Store & that no Skins or furs whatsoever shall be exchanged with Indians on any Pretence.

That we will not Vend or sell any Spirituous Liquors whatsoever to any Person or persons intending to Retail or otherwise dispose of the same to savages of any Nation

Whatsoever neither will we on our own people's account send or Carry any Rum or Spirituous Liquor among any tribe or nations of Indians with an intent to Vend the same to said Indians.

We further Oblige ourselves not to Vend or Dispose of Rum or Spirituous Liquor to any person or persons Residing or Sojourning among the Savages or to any person commenced in traffick with them in any way whatsoever unless the person who purchase those Liquors Shall bind him or themselves under Oath properly taken before the Commanding Officer or some other Magistrate not to dispose of Vend or sell by Retail or otherwise the said Liquor to Savages or any Person intending to Sell the Same to Savages.

"Liquor Declaration," Detroit, Michigan Papers, 1775–1888, Bentley Historical Library. University of Michigan, Ann Arbor.

CHAPTER 4

Under the Stars and Stripes:
The Michigan Territory

The United States acquired what would become Michigan following the Revolutionary War in 1783. After several incarnations and moving borders, the Michigan Territory was organized in 1805, and residents and officials soon faced several challenges. For one, a fire that year destroyed much of the capital, Detroit, and newly appointed territorial officials, despite understanding the urgency and importance of rebuilding, disagreed, argued, and undermined each other's efforts to such an extent that it took years to launch any major reconstruction projects. Meanwhile, a vast majority of the land in Michigan remained legally and physically with Indians. In 1805, Americans claimed legal title to a small strip of land, six miles wide, from the River Raisin to Lake St. Clair, Mackinac Island, and parts of the mainland at the Straits of Mackinac. Thus, Washington officials tasked William Hull, Michigan's first territorial governor, with acquiring legal title of more lands from the original inhabitants.

The War of 1812 was another challenge, and Michigan was a major front during this conflict. At first, things did not go well for Michigan, and the documents in this chapter regarding this war involve the fall of Detroit and explanations why this happened.

Population growth was also a problem for Michigan early on. Not only did veterans of the War of 1812 spread rumors of the horrible conditions of the territory, some officials reinforced these perceptions in their reports. Some have claimed that these rumors and official reports stifled migration to Michigan. Because of this, the

Territory's early residents and officials advertised the better aspects of Michigan in hopes to encourage settlement.

Perhaps the final challenge to the Michigan Territory was the boundary dispute with Ohio, better known as the Toledo War. At the time, it was believed the mouth of the Maumee River, present-day Toledo, Ohio, would become the economic center of the West. Michigan and Ohio each claimed the region. The dispute became so heated that Michigan's territorial governor, Stevens T. Mason, ordered the militia to march south and physically occupy Toledo. Although Michigan had rightful claim to the area based on language set forth in the Northwest Ordinance of 1787, many officials in Washington, DC, including President Andrew Jackson, favored Ohio.

Treaty of Detroit, 1807

*The Ottowa, Chippewa, Wyandot, and Potawatomi Nations
and William Hull on Behalf of the United States*

November 17, 1807

Articles of a treaty made at Detroit, this seventeenth day of November, in the year of our Lord, one thousand eight hundred and seven, by William Hull, governor of the territory of Michigan, and superintendent of Indian affairs, and sole commissioner of the United States, to conclude and sign a treaty or treaties, with the several nations of Indians, north west of the river Ohio, on the one part, and the sachems, chiefs, and warriors of the Ottoway, Chippeway, Wyandotte, and Pottawatamie nations of Indians, on the other part. To confirm and perpetuate the friendship, which happily subsists between the United States and the nations aforesaid, to manifest the sincerity of that friendship, and to settle arrangements mutually beneficial to the parties; after a full explanation and perfect understanding, the following articles are agreed to, which, when ratified by the President, by and with the advice and consent of the Senate of the United States, shall be binding on them, and the respective nations of Indians.

ARTICLE 1

The sachems, chiefs, and warriors of the nations aforesaid, in consideration of money and goods, to be paid to the said nations, by the government of the United States as hereafter stipulated; do hereby agree to cede and forever quit claim, and do in behalf of their nations hereby cede, relinquish, and forever quit claim, unto the said United States, all right, title, and interest, which the said nations now have, or claim, or ever had, or claimed, in, or unto, the lands comprehended within the following described lines and boundaries: Beginning at the mouth of the Miami [Maumee] river of the lakes, and running thence up the middle thereof, to the mouth of the great Au Glaize river [a tributary of the Maumee], thence running due north, until it intersects a parallel of latitude, to be drawn from the outlet of lake Huron, which forms the river Sinclair [St. Clair River]; thence running north east the course, that may be found, will lead in a direct line, to White Rock, in lake Huron, thence due east, until it intersects the boundary line between the United States and Upper Canada, in said lake, thence southwardly, following the said boundary line, down said lake, through river Sinclair, lake St. Clair, and the river Detroit, into lake Erie, to a point due east of the aforesaid Miami river, thence west to the place of beginning.

ARTICLE 2

It is hereby stipulated and agreed on the part of the United States, as a consideration for the lands, ceded by the nations aforesaid, in the preceding article, that there shall be paid to the said nations, at Detroit, ten thousand dollars, in money, goods, implements of husbandry, or domestic animals, (at the option of the said nations, seasonably signified, through the superintendent of Indian affairs, residing with the said nations, to the department of war,) as soon as practicable, after the ratification of the treaty, by the President, with the advice and consent of the Senate of the United States; of this sum, three thousand three hundred and thirty three dollars thirty three cents and four mills, shall be paid to the Ottoway nation, three thousand three hundred and thirty three dollars thirty three cents and four mills, to the Chippeway nation, one thousand six hundred sixty six dollars sixty six cents and six mills, to the Wyandotte nation, one thousand six hundred sixty six dollars sixty six cents and six mills, to the Pottawatamie nation, and likewise an annuity forever, of two thousand four hundred dollars, to be paid at Detroit, in manner as aforesaid: the first payment to be made on the first day of September next, and to be paid to the different nations, in the following proportions: eight hundred dollars to the Ottoways, eight hundred dollars to the Chippeways, four hundred dollars to the Wyandottes, and four hundred dollars to such of the Pottawatamies, as now reside on the river Huron of lake Erie, the river Raisin, and in the vicinity of the said rivers.

ARTICLE 3

It is further stipulated and agreed, if at any time hereafter, the said nations should be of the opinion, that it would be more for their interest, that the annuity aforesaid should be paid by instalments, the United States will agree to a reasonable commutation for the annuity, and pay it accordingly.

ARTICLE 4

The United States, to manifest their liberality, and disposition to encourage the said Indians, in agriculture, further stipulate, to furnish the said Indians with two blacksmiths, one to reside with the Chippeways, at Saguina [Saginaw], and the other to reside with the Ottaways, at the Miami, during the term of ten years; said blacksmiths are to do such work for the said nations as shall be most useful to them.

ARTICLE 5

It is further agreed and stipulated, that the said Indian nations shall enjoy the privilege of hunting and fishing on the lands ceded as aforesaid, as long as they remain the property of the United States.

ARTICLE 6

It is distinctly to be understood, for the accommodation of the said Indians, that the following tracts of land within the cession aforesaid, shall be, and hereby are reserved to the said Indian nations, one tract of land six miles square, on the Miami of lake Erie, above Roche dè Boeuf, to include the village, where Tondaganie, (or the Dog) now lives. Also, three miles square on the said river, (above the twelve miles square ceded to the United States by the treaty of Greenville) including what is called Presque Isle; also four miles square on the Miami bay, including the villages where Meshkemau and Waugau now live; also, three miles square on the river Raisin, at a place called Macon, and where the river Macon falls into the river Raizin, which place is about fourteen miles from the mouth of said river Raizin; also, two sections of one mile square each, on the river Rouge, at Seginsiwin's village; also two sections of one mile square each, at Tonquish's village, near the river Rouge; also three miles square on lake St. Clair, above the river Huron, to include Machonce's village; also, six sections, each section containing one mile square, within the cession aforesaid, in such situations as the said Indians shall elect, subject, however, to the approbation of the President of the United States, as to the places of location. It is further understood and agreed, that whenever the reservations cannot conveniently be laid out in squares, they shall be laid out in paralelograms, or other figures, as found most practicable and convenient, so as to contain the area specified in miles, and in all cases they are to be located in such manner, and in such situations, as not to interfere with any improvements of the French or other white people, or any former cessions.

ARTICLE 7

The said nations of Indians acknowledge themselves to be under the protection of the United States, and no other power, and will prove by their conduct that that are worthy of so great a blessing.

In testimony whereof, the said William Hull, and the sachems and war chiefs representing the said nations, have hereunto set their hands and seals.

Done at Detroit, in the territory of Michigan, the day and year first above written.

From *Indian Affairs: Laws and Treaties*, vol. 2, *Treaties*, compiled and edited by Charles J. Kappler (Washington, DC: Government Printing Office, 1904), electronic version available through Oklahoma State University Library, http://digital.library.okstate.edu.

The War of 1812

General Isaac Brock to General William Hull

Head Quarters, Sandwich, August 15, 1812

Sir—The force at my disposal authorizes me to require of you [General William Hull] the immediate surrender of Fort Detroit. It is far from my inclination to join in a war of extermination, but you must be aware, that the numerous body of Indians who have attached themselves to my troops, will be beyond my control the moment the contest commences, you will find me disposed to enter into such conditions as will satisfy the most scrupulous sense of honor. Leut.-colonel M. Donnell and Major Gligg are fully authorized to conclude any arrangement that may lead to prevent the unnecessary effusion of blood.

I have the honor to be
Sir, your most obedient servant
Isaac Brock, Major-General

Isaac Brock to William Hull, August 15, 1812, folder "1812, Aug, 1–15," box 2, William Hull Papers, Burton Historical Collection, Detroit Public Library.

General Hull to General Brock

Headquarters, Detroit, August 15, 1812

Sir—I have received your letter of this date. I have no other reply to make than to inform you that I am prepared to meet any power which may be at your disposal and any consequences which may result from any exertion of it you may think proper to make.

Hull to Brock, August 15, 1812, folder "1812, Aug, 1–15," Box 2, William Hull Papers,
Burton Historical Collection, Detroit Public Library.

General Hull to Secretary of War William Eustis

August 26, 1812

Sir,

Enclosed are the articles of capitulation by which the Fort of Detroit has been surrendered to Major General Brock, commanding his Britannic Majesty's forces in Upper Canada, and by which the troops have become prisoners of war. My situation at present forbids me from detailing the particular causes which have led to this unfortunate event—I will however general observe that after the surrender of Michilimackinac, almost every tribe, and nation of Indians excepting a part of the Miamis, and Delawares, north from beyond lake Superior, West from beyond the Mississippi, South from the Ohio, and Wabash and east from every part of Upper Canada, and from all the Intermediate Country, joined in open hostility, under the British standard, against the army I commanded; contrary to the most solemn assurances of a large portion of them to remain neutral; even the Ottawa Chiefs from Arbe crotch who formed the delegation to Washington the last summer in whose friendship I know you had great confidence, are among the hostile tribes, and several of them distinguished leaders—Among the vast number of chiefs who led the hostile bands, Tecumsee, Marpot, Logan, Walkinthewater, Split Log &c are considered the principals—This numerous assemblage of savages, under the entire influence and direction of the British Commander, enabled him totally to obstruct the only communication, which I had with my country—This communication had been opened from the settlements in the State of Ohio, two hundred miles through a wilderness, by the fatigues of the army, which I marched to the frontier on the River Detroit—The body of the Lake being commanded by the British armed ships, and, the shores &, river by gun boats, the army was totally deprived of all communication by water. On this extensive road it depended for transportation of provisions, military stores medicine, clothing, and every other supply on pack horses—all its operations were successful until its arrival at Detroit, and in a few days, it passed into the enemy's country, and all opposition seemed to fall before it—One month it remained in possession of this Country, and was fed from its resources—In different directions, detachments penetrated, sixty miles in the settled part of the province, and the inhabitants seemed satisfied with the change in the situation, which appeared to be taking place—The Militia from Amherstburg were daily deserting, and the whole country then under the control of the army, was asking for protection. The Indians generally in the first instance appeared to be neutralized, and determined to take no part in the contest. The Fort of Amherstburg [also known as Fort Malden] was eighteen miles below my encampment. Not a single cannon or mortar was on wheels suitable to carry before that place. I consulted my officers, whether it was expedient to make an attempt on it with the bayonet alone without cannon to make a break in the first instance—The council I called was of the Opinion it was not—The greatest industry was exerted in making preparation, and it was not until the 7th of August that 2 24-pounders, and three Howitzers were prepared. It was then my intention to have proceeded on the enterprise. While the operations of the were delayed by these preparations, the clouds of adversity had been for some time, and seemed still thickly to be gathering around me—The surrender of Michilimackinac opened the Northern hive of Indians, and they were swarming down in every direction. Reinforcements from Niagara had arrived at Amherstburg under the command of Colonel Proctor—The desertion of the Militia ceased—Besides the reinforcements that came by water, I received information of a very considerable force under the command of Chambers on the River Le Trench with four field pieces, and collecting the Militia on his route, evidently destined for Amherstburg; and in addition to this combination, and increase of force, contrary to all my expectations, the Wyandots, Chippewas, Ottawas, Pottawatmies, Munsees, Delewares &c with whom I had the most friendly intercourse, at once passed over to Amherstburg, and accepted the tomahawk and scalping Knife—There being now a vast number of Indians at the British post, they were sent to the River Huron, Brownstown, and Maguardo to intercept my communication. To open this communication, I detached Major Vanhorne of the Ohio volunteers with two hundred men to proceed as far as the River Raisin, under an expectation he would meet Captain Brush with one hundred and fifty men, Volunteers from the State of Ohio, and a quantity of provisions for the army—An ambuscade was formed at Brownstown, & Major Vanhornes detachment, defeated and returned to camp, without affecting the object of the expedition. . . .

Under this sudden and unexpected change of things, and having received an express [informing me] that there was no prospect of any cooperation from that quarter, and the two sent officers of the Artillery having stated to me an opinion that it would be extremely difficult, if not impossible to pass the turkey river and River aux Cannard, with the 24 pounders, and that they could not be transported by water as the Queen Sharloote which carried 18 24-pounders, lay in the River Detroit above the mouth of the River Auxcannard, and as it appeared indispensably necessary to open the communication to the River Raisin, and the Miami, I found myself compelled to suspend the operation against Amherstburg, and concentrate the main force of the army at Detroit. Fully intending, at that time after the communication was opened to recross the river, and pursue the object at Amherstburg, and strongly desirous of continuing protection to a very large number of the inhabitants of upper Canada, who had voluntarily accepted it under my proclamation, I established a fortress on the banks of the River a little below Detroit, calculating for a garrison of Three hundred men. On the evening of the 7th, and morning of the 8th inst the army, expecting the garrison of 250 Infantry, and a corps of Artillerists, all under the command of Major Denny of the Ohio Volunteers, recrossed the river, and encamped at Detroit. In pursuance of the object of opening the communication, on which I considered the existence of the army depending, a detachment of six hundred men under the command of Lt Colonel Miller was immediately ordered. . . . Nothing however but honor was acquired by the victory; and it is a painful consideration, that the blood of seventy five gallant men could only open the communication, as far as the points of their bayonets extended. The necessary care of the sick and wounded, and a very severe storm of rain rendered their return to camp indispensably necessary for their own comfort. Captain Brush with his small detachment, and the provisions being still at the River Raisin, and in a situation to be destroyed by the savages, on the 13th inst in the evening I permitted Colonels McArthur & Cass to select from their Regts four hundred of their most effective men, and proceed, an upper route through the woods which I had sent an express to Captain Brush to take, and had directed the Militia of the river Raisin to accompany him as a reinforcement. The force of the enemy continually increasing, and the necessity of opening the communication, & acting on the defensive, becoming more apparent, I had previous to detaching Colonels McArthur & Cass on the 11th instant evacuated, and destroyed the Post on the opposite bank. On the 13th in the evening Genl Brock arrived at Amherstburg about the hour Colonels McArthur & Cass marched, of which at that time I had received no information. On the 15th I received a summons from him to surrender Fort Detroit. . . . At this time I had received no information from Colonels McArthur & Cass. An express was immediately sent strongly escorted with orders for them to return. On the 15th as soon as Genl Brock received my letter, his Batteries opened on the Town, and Fort, and continued until evening—In the evening all the British Ships of war came nearly as far up the river as Sandwich, three miles below Detroit at day light on the 16th (at which time I had received no information from Colonels McArthur &Cass, my expresses, sent the evening before, and in the night, having prevented from passing by numerous bodies of Indians) the cannonade recommenced, and in a short time I received information, that the British army and Indians were landing below the Spring wells, under the cover of their ships of war. At this time the whole effective force at my disposal at Detroit did not exceed Eight hundred men. Being new troops, and unaccustomed to a camp life, having performed a laborious march; having been engaged in a number of battles & skirmishes in which many had fallen, and more had received wounds; in addition to which a large number being sick, and unprovided with medicine, and the comforts necessary for their situation; are the general causes by which the strength of the army was thus reduced. The Fort at this time was filled with women, and children, and the old and decrepit people of the town & Country; they were unsafe in the town, as it was entirely open, and exposed to the enemy's Batteries—back of the Fort, above or below it, there was no safety for them on account of the Indians. In the first instance, the enemy's fire was principally directed against our batteries; towards the close it was directed against the Fort alone, and almost every shot, and shell had their effect.

It now became necessary, either to fight the enemy in the field; collect the whole force in the Fort; or propose terms of Capitulation. I could not have carried into the field more than six hundred men, and left any adequate force in the Fort. There were landed at that time of the Enemy a regular force of much more than that number, and twice the number of Indians. Considering this great inequality of force, I did not think it expedient to adopt the first measure. The second must have been attended with a great sacrifice of blood, and no possible advantage, because the contest could not have been sustained more than a day for the want of powder, and but a very few days for the want of provisions; In addition to this, Colonels McArthur & Cass would have been in a most hazardous situation. I feared nothing but the last alternative. I have dared to adopt it—I well know the high responsibility of the measure, and I take the whole of it on myself. It was dictated by a sense of duty, and a full conviction of its expediency—The bands of savages which had then joined the British force were numerous beyond any former example. Their numbers have since increased, and the history of the Barbarians of the North of Europe does not furnish examples of more greedy violence than these savages exhibited. A large portion of the brave and gallant officers and men, I commanded, would cheerfully have contested until the last cartridge had been expended, and the bayonets had been worn to the sockets. I could not consent to the useless sacrifice of such brave men, when I knew it was impossible for me to sustain my situation. It was impossible in the nature of things that an army could have been furnished with the necessary supplies of provision, military stores, clothing and comforts for the sick on pack horses, through a wilderness of two hundred miles, filled with hostile savages—It was impossible, Sir, that this little army, worn down by fatigue, by sickness, by wounds, and [illegible word] could have supported itself not only against the collected force of the northern nations of Indians; but against the United strength of Upper Canada, whose population consists of more than twenty times the number contained in the Territory of Michigan, aided by the principal part of the regular forced of the province, and the wealth and influence of the North West and other trading establishments among the Indians which have in their employment, and under the entire control more than two thousand white men. Before I close this dispatch it is a duty I owe my respectable associates in command, Colonels McArthur, Findlay, Cass, and Lieut Colonel Miller, to express my obligation to them for the prompt and judicious manner they have performed their respective duties. If aught has taken place during the campaign, which is honorable to the army, these officers are entitled to a large share of it—If the last act should be disapproved, no part of the censure belongs to them. . . . I have only to solicit as early an investigation of my conduct, as my situation, and the state of things will admit; and to add the further request, that the Government will not be unmindful of my associates in captivity, and of the families of those brave men who have fallen in the contest.

Very respectfully
W Hull

William Hull to William Eustis, August 26, 1812, *MPHC*, vol. 40, 460–71.

Colonel Lewis Cass to Secretary Eustis

Washington, September 10, 1812

Sir,

Having been ordered on to this place by Col McArthur, for the purpose of communicating to the Government such particulars respecting the expedition lately commanded by Brig. Gen. Hull and its disastrous result, as might enable them correctly to appreciate the conduct of the officers and men and to develop the causes, which produced so foul a stain upon the national character, I have the honor to submit to your consideration the following statement. When the forces landed with an ardent zeal and stimulated with the hope of conquest, no enemy appeared within the view of us, and had an immediate and vigorous attack been made upon Malden, it would doubt-less have fallen an easy victory. I know Gen. Hull afterwards declared, he regretted this attack had not been made and he had every reason to believe success would have crowned his efforts. The reason given for delaying our operations, was to mount our heavy cannon and to afford to the Canadian Militia time and opportunity to quit an obnoxious service. In the course of two weeks, the number of their militia, who were embodied, had decreased by desertion from six hundred to one hundred men, and in the course of three weeks, the cannon were mounted, the ammunition fixed and every preparation made for an immediate investment of the Fort. At a counsel, at which were present all the field officers, and which was held two days before our preparations were completed, it was unanimously agreed to make an immediate attempt to accomplish the object of the expedition. If by waiting two days we could have the service of our heavy artillery, it was agreed to wait, if not it was determined to go without it and attempt the place by storm. This opinion appeared to correspond with the views of the General and the day was appointed for commencing our march. He declared to me, that he considered himself pledged to lead the army to Malden. The ammunition was placed in the wagons, the Cannon were embarked on board the floating batteries, and every requisite article was prepared. The spirit and zeal, the ardor and anima-tion displayed by the officers and men on learning the near accomplishment of their wishes was a sure and sacred pledge, that in the hour of trial, they would not be found wanting in their duty to their Country and themselves. But a change of measures, in opposition to the wishes and opinions of all the Officers was adopted by the General. The plan of attacking Malden was abandoned, and instead of acting offensively, we broke up our Camp, evacuated Canada and recrossed the river in the night, without even the shadow of an enemy to injure us. We left to the tender mercy of the enemy the miserable Canadians, who had joined us, and the *protection* we afforded them was but a passport to vengeance. This fatal and unaccountable step dispirited the troops and destroyed the little confidence, which a series of timid, irresolute and indecisive measures had left in the Commanding officer. . . .

On the 13th the British took a position opposite to Detroit and began to throw up works. During that and the two following days, they pursued their object without interruption and established a battery for two eighteen pounders, and an eight inch howitzer. About sunset on the evening of the 14th, a detachment of 350 men from the Regiments commanded by Colo McArthur and myself was ordered to march to the River Raisin, to escort the provisions, which had some time remained there protected by a party under the command of Capt. Brush. On Saturday the 15th about 1 o'clock, a flag of truce arrived from Sandwich, bearing a summons from Gov. Brock, for the surrender of the Town and Fort of Detroit, stating he could no longer restrain the fury of the savages. To this an immediate and spirited refusal was returned. About 4 o'clock their batteries began to play upon the Town. The fire was returned and continued without interruption and with little effect till dark. Their shells were thrown till eleven o'clock. At day light the firing on both sides recommenced. About the same time the enemy began to land troops, at the spring wells three miles below Detroit, protected by two of their armed vessels. Between 6 and 7 o'clock they had effected their landing and immediately took up their line of march. They moved in a close column of platoons, twelve in front, upon the bank of the River.

The fourth Regiment was stationed in the Fort, the Ohio volunteers and a part of the Michigan Militia behind some pickets in a situation, in which the whole flank of the enemy would have been exposed. The residue of the Michigan Militia were in the upper part of the Town to resist the incursions of the Savages. Two twenty four pounders loaded with grape shot were posted upon a commanding eminence ready to sweep the advancing column. In this situation, the superiority of our position was apparent and our troops in the eager expectation of victory, awaited the approach of the enemy. Not a sigh of discontent broke upon the ear, not a look of cowardice met the eye. Every man expected a proud day for his Country, and each was anxious, that his individual exertion should contribute to the general result. When the head of their column arrived within about five hundred yards of our line, orders were received from Gen. Hull for the whole to retreat to the Fort, and for the twenty-four pounders not to open upon the enemy. One universal burst of indignation was apparent upon the receipt of this order. Those, whose conviction was the deliberate result of a dispassionate examination of passing events, saw the folly and impropriety of crowding 1100 men into a little work, which 300 could fully man, and into which the shot and shells of the enemy were continually falling. The Fort was in this manner filled, the men were directed to stack their arms, and scarcely was an opportunity afforded of moving. Shortly after a white flag was hung out upon the walls. A British officer rode up to enquire the cause. A communication passed between the Commanding Generals, which ended in the capitulation submitted to you. In entering into this capitulation, the General took counsel from his own feelings only. Not an officer was consulted. Not one anticipated a surrender, till he saw the white flag displayed. Even the women were indignant at so shameful a degradation of the American character. And all felt as they should have felt, but he who held in his hands the reins of authority. . . .

If we had been defeated we had nothing to do but to retreat to the Fort, and make the best defense which circumstances and our situation rendered practicable. But basely to surrender without firing a gun, tamely to submit without raising a bayonet, disgracefully to pass in review before an enemy as inferior in the quality as in the number of his forces were circumstances, which excited feelings of indignations more easily felt than described. To see the whole of our men flushed with the hope of victory, eagerly awaiting the approaching contest, to see them afterwards dispirited, hopeless and desponding at least 500 shedding tears because they were not allowed to meet their Country's foe, and to fight their Country's battles, excited sensations, which no American has ever before had cause to feel, and which I trust in God will never again be felt, while one man remains to defend the standard of the Union. I am expressly authorized to state that Col. McArthur, Col. Findlay, and Lt. Col. Miller view this transaction in the light, in which I do. They know and feel, that no circumstance in our situation, none in that of the enemy can excuse a capitulation so dishonorable and unjustifiable. This too is the universal sentiment among the troops. And I shall be surprised to learn, that there is one man, who thinks it was necessary to sheath his sword, or to lay down his musket.

I was informed by Gen. Hull the morning after the capitulation, that the British forces consisted of 1800 regular, and that he surrendered to prevent the effusion of human blood. That he magnified their regular force nearly fivefold there can be no doubt. Whether the philanthropical reason assigned by him is a sufficient justification for surrendering a fortified Town, an Army and a Territory is for the Government to determine. Confident I am, had the courage and conduct of the General been equal to the spirit and zeal of the troops, the event would have been as brilliant & successful as it now is disastrous and dishonorable.

Very respectfully
Lewis Cass

Lewis Cass to William Eustis, September 10, 1812, *MPHC*, vol. 40, 477–85.

A Description of the Landscape of the Michigan Territory

Edward Tiffin

Even after the threats of the British and Indians were quelled following the War of 1812, Michigan's population growth was stagnant. While there were several factors contributing to this, some scholars have noted that the reports and policies of certain U.S. officials may have stifled migration to the territory. In the following document Tiffin reports to U.S. Surveyor General Josiah Meigs.

November 30, 1815

The surveyors who went to survey the military land in Michigan Territory have been obliged to suspend their operations until the country shall be sufficiently frozen so as to bear man and beast. Knowing the desire of the government to have the lands surveyed as soon as practicable, and my earnest importunities to urge the work forward, they continued at work suffering incredible hardships until both men and beasts were literally worn down with extreme suffering and fatigue—the frost set in early, and the ice covered nearly the whole country, but broke through at every step, and the pack horses could not be got along with them, they were therefore obliged to submit to the climate and its attendant rigors, and desist for awhile, intending to attack them again as soon as they think it possible to proceed.

. . . I think it my duty to give you the information, believing that it is the wish of the government that soldiers should have (as the act of congress expresses) lands fit for cultivation, and that the whole of the two millions of acres appropriated in the territory of Michigan will not contain anything like one hundredth part of that quantity, or is worth the expense of surveying it, perhaps you may think with me, that it will be proper to make this representation to the president of the United States and he may avert all further proceedings—by directing me to pay off what has been done and abandon the country—congress being in session other lands could be appropriated in lieu of them and might be surveyed as soon as those in Michigan—for when the ice is sufficiently strong to bear man and beast, a deep snow would still embarrass the surveyors. I shall therefore wait to hear you answer to this communication before I proceed any further thinking I should be unfaithful to my trust if I had lost any time in communicating the information received.

The country in the Indian boundary line from the mouth of the great Auglaize river and running thence for about 50 miles is (with some few exceptions) low wet land with a very thick growth of underbrush, intermixed with beech, cottonwoods, oak, etc., from thence continuing and extending from the Indian boundary line eastward, the number and extent of the swamps increases, with the addition of numbers of lakes from 20 chains to two and three miles across. Many of the lakes have extensive marshes adjoining their margins, sometimes thickly covered with a species of pine called "Tamirak," and other places covered with a coarse high grass, and uniformly covered from six inches to three feet (and more at times) with water. The margin of these lakes are not the only places where swamps are found, for they are interspersed throughout the whole country and filled with water as above stated, and varying in extent. The immediate space between these swamps and lakes, which is probably near one-half of the country, is, with a very few exceptions, a poor, barren, sandy loam land, on which scarcely any vegetation grows, except very small scrubby oaks. In many places that part which may be called dry land is composed of little short sand hills, forming a kind of deep basins, the bottoms of many of which are composed of marsh similar to those above described—the streams are generally narrow and very deep compared with their width; the shores and bottoms of which are (with a very few exceptions) swamp beyond description; and it is with the utmost difficulty that a place can be found over which horses can be conveyed. A circumstance peculiar to that country is exhibited in many of the marshes; by their being thinly covered with a sward of grass, by walking on which evinced the existence of water or a very thin mud immediately under that thin covering, which sinks from 6 to 18 inches from the pressure of the foot at every step, and at the same time rising before and behind the person passing over. The margins of many of the lakes and streams are in a similar situation, and in many places are literally afloat. On approaching the eastern part of the military lands towards the private claims on the strait and lake the country does not contain so many swamps and lakes, but the extreme sterility and barrenness of soil continues the same, taking the country altogether so far as has been explored and to all appearances together with the information received concerning the balance, is as bad—there would not be more than one acre out of a hundred, if there would one out a thousand that would in any case admit of cultivation.

With great respect I am your obedient servant,
Edward Tiffin

Edward Tiffin to Josiah Meigs, *MPHC*, vol. 10, 61–62.

Views of the Michigan Territory

A Gentleman in Detroit

February 6, 1824

Dear Sir:

You requested me from time to time to advise you of my views of the western country, and I cheerfully avail myself of a leisure moment to comply with your wish.

While at Buffalo I heard much said of the Michigan Territory, and, finding the tide of emigration rolling in that direction, I determined to float with the current. I embarked accordingly on board the steamboat, and in three days, traversing the entire length of Lake Erie, arrived at Detroit. I was much surprised to find upon this lake (which a few years since was considered almost too remote to explore), a steamboat perhaps inferior to no other in the United States. The accommodations are excellent, and our voyage was exceedingly pleasant, its monotony being relieved by the frequent stopping of the boat to stand and receive passengers at the little villages along the border of the lake. I regretted that evening prevented from viewing the scenery upon the American and Canadian shores as we ascended the Detroit Straits.

Detroit, which is already an incorporated city, is beautifully situated upon the bank of the straits, about eighteen miles from the lake, and presents an imposing and handsome appearance.

Being fond of nature, as you know, and somewhat an agriculturalist by profession, I remained at Detroit but one day, and then started to explore, in company with some gentlemen who had arrived in pursuit of the same object with myself. And here I cannot but remark how incorrect are our ideas in New England respecting this Territory. I find the land rich and luxuriant, generally heavily timbered, and interspersed with numerous streams of good, pure water. It is a limestone country, and level, but in few instances too much so for cultivation. After a tour through the country north and west of Detroit, we turned our attention to the south part of the Territory, where a new Land District has been established and a Land Office just opened upon the River Raisin. Upon this river, you will recollect, was the disastrous defeat of Gen. Winchester during the late war.

A map, which I had the good fortune to obtain, indicated in this part of the Territory peculiar advantages, and here I determined thoroughly to explore. Being directly at the western extremity of the lake, which is only an extension of the Great New York Canal, the facility to market must be great, and I am informed that the distance from Detroit to New York City may now be traveled in nine days. Near the mouth of the River Raisin, which is about forty miles south of Detroit, in an extensive bay, almost land-locked, arrangements are now making for the erection of a wharf, and at this point are anticipated important commercial advantages. Near the mouth of the River Raisin is a small settlement, consisting principally of French, excepting the immigration now going in. I was much surprised at the appearance of the farms, which, I am told, have been cultivated for a long period without the use of manure or any of the improvements in husbandry which have been so successfully adopted in the Eastern States.

We traversed entirely beyond the settlement upon the river, and slept one night in the woods—the earth our bed, our saddles a pillow, a blanket and the canopy of heaven our covering. But for every inconvenience we were richly repaid. So fine a country I have never seen. The river is extremely circuitous in its course, its meanderings constituting the richest bottoms imaginable, heavily timbered and many of them similar to the "Ox Bow" upon Connecticut River. The timber is very large and of the best kinds: it consists of black walnut, hickory, maple, elm, white wood, bass wood, sycamore, oak, beech, ash, etc. I have not seen tamarac in this part of the country.

The latitude is about the same with that of Connecticut, but the climate must be milder, for I am informed that horses subsist during the whole winter without being fed, and that cattle are easily kept upon the wild grass cut in the prairies. There is an abundance of fruit in the settlement to which I have alluded, and, although no attention is paid to the orchard, the apple possesses a flavor I have seldom tasted.

But I cannot go into too much detail; suffice it to say, that, taking into view the price of public land, one dollar and a quarter the acre; the quality of the soil; the facility of the market to which will be offered by the New York Canal; the salubrity of the climate, and the resources of the country at large, I have never seen greater inducements to immigration presented, either for the purpose of agriculture or speculation.

I forgot to state that the political institutions of the Territory are rapidly changing, and it is believed that, in four years, the banners of sovereignty will be unfurled and the Territory will become a State.

"Letter from a Gentleman in Detroit," February 6, 1824, *Detroit Free Press*, reprinted in *MPHC*, vol. 7, 74–75.

The Toledo War

An Account from a Militiaman

1885

"Yes, I was a soldier in the Toledo war," he said in reply to his questioner. "It is so long ago, however, that the whole affair seems to me now just like a dream. It was a time of great excitement in Michigan, and when we won our 'glorious victory' the Territory was wild with enthusiasm. The whole Toledo war may seem very funny to look back at, but most of us went down expecting to risk our lives. Every one expected bloodshed, and Gov. Stephens T Mason, Michigan's boy Governor, meant business when he ordered out the Territorial militia for the invasion of Ohio—or, rather, for the protection of the Michigan frontier, for so we then regarded the strip of territory in dispute. The militia then consisted of all men, capable of bearing arms, between certain ages. We paraded and drilled on the Campus Martius, before Andrews' old hotel, a week after we were called out, before we started for the front. Some of us were armed with guns, but the great majority carried long broom handles, and with these on our shoulders we went through the military evolutions. Crowds turned out to see us and the town was in full excitement. There was no sort of uniform even among our officers, and the only attempt in that direction was that some of the 'invading army' stuck different colored feathers through their hat bands. It was about this time, in August, fifty years ago, that we started for the front. We were, as well as I can remember, something over two hundred strong. The advance on Toledo—then Ashtabula, Michigan—occupied four days, and was through a country not comparing favorably with its settled condition now. We camped the first night a short distance this side of Monroe. We had reached a point not far beyond that city the second night, some time being spent at Monroe, where we were joined by about thirty more men. Monroe then one of the largest cities in the Northwest. Its population was a few thousand and it was nearly as large as Detroit, while Chicago did not then have over three hundred. The third night we reached Tremainsville, and the fourth night we pitched our canvas on this side [of] the Maumee River, opposite Ashtabula. We had a vast amount of fun on the march down. The farming people *en route* generally welcomed us enthusiastically because we were 'fighting for Michigan.' They did a great deal for our creature comforts, giving us mush and milk and cooking us regular meals. We returned these favors by stealing pigs and chickens—of course we called it foraging. These we would carry along and get cooked at the next farm house. Sometimes we got them cooked on the very farms where we stole them. But, even if they knew this, the good-natured farmers endured it without complaint, because we were on our way to fight for Michigan. But, as much fun as we made, we were all very much in earnest and expected bloodshed. . . . There was a great excitement in Ashtabula when we came up against the city. The town—which did not have a population exceeding 1,500—was astir. A company of the Ohio militia, in arms, occupied the place, and gory times were anticipated on both sides. The first night passed away without hostilities, however, and the next morning the city surrendered. I don't know as you would exactly call is a 'surrender,' but they called out to us that there had better be no disturbance, and that is we would come in peaceably there would be no opposition to our entrance. Under this arrangement we entered the town, and were very finely entertained there. We got acquainted with each other and established many lasting friendships. . . . We occupied the city for four days and then, matters being temporarily adjusted, we returned to Detroit."

"Were there no casualties during the war?"

"The only person hurt, to my knowledge, was a Frenchman from up the Maumee Valley. The only firing done was by some rowdies not belonging to either 'army,' and he was wounded by one of these. It is claimed that he was shot because of an old grudge."

"Were you in the second capture of the city?"

"Yes. That was a couple weeks later. We had an easier time on that occasion, but didn't enjoy it too well for it was sort of an old story. This time it was a naval advance on the city. We went down by the little steamer Argo, stopping at Monroe. We took the city without trouble, and returned as we came. There were about as many as were in the march.

"The Toledo war was of great importance," said the veteran in conclusion. "The stiffness of the Michigan back gave us the Upper Peninsula—worth a dozen Toledo strips."

"How They Fought: Personal Recollections of the Contest with Ohio Fifty Years Ago," 1885, *Detroit Free Press*, reprinted in *MPHC*, vol. 7, 69–71.

CHAPTER 5

A New Frontier: The Pioneer Era

Once the awful rumors about Michigan were dispelled, the population grew rapidly. Facilitating this growth was the opening of the Erie Canal in 1825. These new arrivals found themselves in the wilderness and sometimes interacting with people they had only heard of—Indians. Stories of these "pioneers" are an interesting way to understand the hardships they faced in their relocation and their perceptions of the original inhabitants.

Pioneer Days

W. L. Coffinberry

Although I hardly feel myself entitled to the honored name of "pioneer" in this glorious State of Michigan, yet I am inclined to claim some rights in the State, having lived in the State as my home ever since June, 1844; and notwithstanding my personal absence from your present reunion, I am with you in heart and spirit. . . .

In the year 1829 I was a single man, living with an older brother who was married and had one child, and lived in central Ohio. My brother was ambitious, but poor, and wanted, as many other young men do, to make a strike for himself; and with that desire uppermost in his mind, he made up his mind to go to Michigan territory, get a hold and grow with the country. I concluded to try my luck in the same direction, and we left Ohio in the latter part of November, 1829, passing through Detroit and Lake St. Clair and landed at Cottrelville [near Port Huron] in a severe snow storm, and were obliged to remain there for the winter. We had intended to go to Saginaw; but the ice was now running in the river so we could not go any further.

We stayed in Cottrelville until February, and my brother and his wife and a sister of hers all became dissatisfied to stay there any longer, and there was no possible means of getting away from there but to go on foot on the ice of the river. So we made up our minds to that, and like the "prodigal son" of Scripture, we concluded to "arise and go to our father," who was then living near Mansfield, Ohio; and for the purpose of carrying what little baggage we had, I built a small, light hand-sled, wide enough and long enough to lay a small-sized straw bed on it, so that the wife and child could sit on the sled and ride, the sister walking most of the time; and with sufficient preparation and some provisions to keep soul and body together, we started on the ice to make our way in mid winter from Cottrelville to Sandusky City. We averaged about twenty miles per day, my brother and myself drawing the sled by hand, passing through Detroit and Pleasance Bay by the lighthouse, to within a short distance of Maumee Bay, and there we learned, to our dismay, that we could not pass the bay on account of a large breach or crack in the ice which we could not pass.

We then, for it was near night, made the best arrangements we could for a night's lodging on the icy beach of Lake Erie, without fire, matches being unknown, and our Indian spunk, or punk, having given out, and the night growing cold, we began to feel somewhat discouraged; but it does not do, when prospects before us begin to look blue, to throw up our hands, and say we can do no more; but I remembered an old story in Dilworth's spelling book, with an illustration of a man with his shoulder to a carriage wheel stuck in the mud, and the moral was—"put your shoulder to the wheel, and then call on Hercules."

We passed a long dreary night on the beach, and when morning dawned we aroused us from our "downy bed"; yes it was down on the cold ground, with very slight covering; but we, like people of that age of the world, were hardy, robust people, and although our supper was very small and our breakfast less, we kept up our courage, hoping for better days to come.

On the beach where we stayed that night was a strip of timbered land, from ten to fifteen rods wide. We were on the west shore of the lake, and immediately west of this strip of timber are extensive marshes; and at this time the water in the marsh had fallen sufficiently to let the ice break down and the water was above the ice, so that, looking across the marsh, it had the appearance of a lake of half a mile wide, bounded on the west by extensive grassy marshes. The snow had left the ground, having several clear, sunny days, and we had to leave our sled and go . . . on foot, and standing on the east side of this wide, and partly water-covered marsh, we could see a small house on the west side of the marsh, which appeared to be about a mile and a half from where we stood, and the first half mile all water; but judging from the make of the surrounding country, we thought the water was not very deep, so we concluded to start for the house.

I led the way, for I could swim, and if I should get past wading deep, I could swim back and the others need not come in where it was so deep. My brother carried the little boy, eighteen months old, on his back, and each of the women carried small loads of our bedding, etc., and we all waded through that water for about half a mile, which was three feet deep on top of the ice. We all reached the house in safety without the loss of a man.

The Frenchman, who lived in the house that we came to, received us very cheerfully, and then proposed to take his horse and cart and bring our baggage which we had left behind, and take us up to the State road, leading from Toledo to Detroit, and leave us at a hotel on the road, which he did. I left all at the hotel and started alone for my father's home.

There were many incidents in that little trip that might be interesting to relate, but I have already exceeded my intention, and beg pardon for so long a story without much in it.

"Pioneer Days," W. L. Coffinberry, *MPHC*, vol. 4, 55–56.

A Farmer on Hard Times

C. Dibble

February 27, 1840

I have been to meeting today. It is warm and pleasant as summer. It will be dry enough to go ploughing in a few days if this weather continues. I have just killed a mosketo so you may know that it is warm . . . I am contented to stay here. We have a farm that we can raise any kind of grain on it without having it drowned half a dozen times a year. I broke up five acres of new land last summer. We have 18 acres under improvement and 7½ acres of wheat on the ground and the remainder for spring crops. Our wheat was full of insects but we expect considerable damage from them. You [his brother, Horace Dibble] requested me to write to you how much I raised and whether I went to see the girls any or not. I will. We raised about 35 bushels of wheat from 6½ acres. The reason we had no more was the insects destroyed it. About 30 bushels of corn,

40 or 50 of oats, 28 of barley from one acre 80 or 90 bushels potatoes, 80 of rutabaga, 50 pounds of flax, and broom corn for 70 or 80 brooms, 1¼ bushel beans and onions I did not measure them but I guess about have a bushel. We fattened between 6[00] and 700 pounds of pork.

Hard times. Hard times is the complaint of most everyone we see. Money is scarce and produce is very low. There is but little money in circulation. I believe there is but too [few] banks in the state that is good. We are in hopes of better times. We have a new set of officers and I think they will manage better than the old ones. Our tory officers having voted our state for internal improvement and to them which never will pay the interest of the money. We shall have heavy taxes for many years. Our tax this year was $6.88. I suppose you have heard that father and I voted the whig ticket, and I think you would have if you lived here. I have voted the other ticket for the sake of the party, but hereafter I intend to vote for those that I think will make the best rulers.

C. Dibble to Horace Dibble, February 27, 1840, Bentley Historical Library.

Reminiscence of Travel to West Bloomfield

Asa S. Whitehead

I came into the territory of Michigan when but six years old [ca. 1831] and have never been out of the state since. My parents were pioneers in New York before they came to Michigan. When we came to this state we settled in the town of West Bloomfield, Oakland County, two miles south of Orchard Lake, which was said to be the home of the great Indian chief Pontiac. If it was not his abiding place it must have been a grand resort for him as it now is for the white man, on account of the numerous lakes swarming with fish, and the forest filled with game of all kinds. When the country was wild and new there was but one house between us and the lake and only two houses at the lake. With these exceptions it was an unbroken wilderness. The five years we lived near the lake were enjoyed by the boys on account of a delightful place to fish and swim. At that time there was only one row boat and an old scow on our side of the lake. The scow was used to carry apples from the island, which would produce 400 bushels some seasons. One could not penetrate the woods far before a deer would be started up. . . .

We came up the Erie Canal to Buffalo and there took a steamboat for Detroit. The wind blew a gale all the time we were on the lake. My father anticipated rough weather while we were on the canal, so he, being an old soldier, having served in the War of 1812, thought he would guard against all probable danger. So when the boat stopped he went into a place where they kept fortifications. I did not know what fortifications was, but he had them in a great big bellied two quart glass bottle. It was made of white glass and as clear as a crystal. I thought it was just a nice bottle. It was labeled DeWitt Clinton Bust, and DeWitt Clinton and the Grand Canal was blown in the glass on the opposite side. DeWitt Clinton was the originator of the Erie Canal and once governor of New York. Sure enough when we got on the lake the wind was blowing a gale and the boat rolling and pitching and nearly everybody became sea sick. Father thought it time to begin to fortify and get behind our entrenchments, and I guess he must have fortified me a little too for we were the only ones I seen on the way from Buffalo to Detroit but what were sea sick, but we two were so well fortified and entrenched, we were never sea sick the least bit. You must not think by this that my father was a drinking man; he was the most temperate man I ever knew who ever drank at all.

We were six days going from Buffalo to Detroit. We lay up in the Erie harbor three days and should have stayed there three days longer, but the passengers thought they knew more about the wind, weather, and running a steamboat than the Captain, and they never gave him a minute's peace until they were off. They were all going to the new territory of Michigan that promised land, so they would not wait, but changed boats and started. They changed from the Niagara to the Superior, which was called the fastest and safest boat on the lake at that time. But as soon as we got out of the harbor the waves rolled mountains high, and then they all wished themselves back in the harbor. But there was no turning back and everybody thought we were all going to Davy Jones's locker and that right soon. But we had a good captain and he knew all the routes and how to manage a vessel in rough weather, and attended to his business, but all hands had all they could do to keep the old craft afloat.

They used wood in the furnaces to make steam, but they could not make steam enough with wood to keep the boat from going back[ward] so they throwed barrel after barrel of tar, pitch and resin into the furnaces and then they could not make much headway against such a head wind. The boat was loaded with emigrants going to the new territory of Michigan and they all took desk passage, and they all ate and slept on the deck. The deck was covered with beds at night, laid down on the deck, and the sparks and cinders from that tar, pitch and resin was falling thick and fast all over the deck all night and every little while somebody's bed would be on fire; and someone crying my bed is on fire, your bed is on fire or someone was crying fire! fire! all night. Women were screaming, children crying, some praying, but more cursing and swearing. Men, women, and children were casting up Jonah all over the vessel, and I tell you the boat was a sorry looking place in the morning. But after a while they got the deck cleaned up and the beds put away, and things began to look a little more ship shape and cheerful. Along towards night, the sixth day from Buffalo, the wind began to go down and we landed in Detroit just as the sun was setting and glad to set foot on dry land once more. All I can remember of Detroit at that time, was a row of low, small, wood-colored buildings along the river and quite a number of old looking, and quite large, but not very thrifty pear trees. We stayed in Detroit overnight, and began in the next morning, bright and early, to look for a team to take us on our journey home, which was 18 miles from Detroit. I do not think there was a mile of railroad in Michigan at that time.

We were quite lucky in finding a good team and a good man. We had an awful road eight miles out of Detroit to Birmingham. It was corduroy all the way from Detroit to Birmingham, or had been once, but there were sections of the logs rotted out, and then we came to one of them the fore wheels would drop off and go so far down that the mud would run in the fore end of the wagon box. Then when we would come to the next section of logs they would have to pry the wagon up to get it on the logs again. The roads were so bad that we all had to walk who could. We only made 10 miles on the first day out from Detroit. It was about noon the second day when we reached our home. I remember we ate our dinner on boxes. We had some cold chicken and provisions left, so we did not have to make any fire to get the first meal ready. How they could have anything left after being on the road eight days, I never could see, but I remember it was stored in a very large chest and I suppose it was full. We had no chairs or tables nor much of anything else to do with, so we had to live in this way for about two weeks, as we could not bring much on the first load. Finally, in about two weeks we managed to buy an ox team on credit by buying two odd oxen and breaking them together. I suppose we got them on that account, but they were all the ones to be had. So when we got our breaking done we got one of our neighbors to go with their ox team back with us and bring in the rest of our things, and when they went after them the roads were even worse than when we came in with the first load, but when they got stuck in the mud they would have to double up both teams and help one another out, which they had to do quite often.

It was in the fall of the year when we got to our new home and winter [was] fast approaching, with nine in the family, the oldest child a boy 13 and the youngest of all a boy about 3 years old. We were set right down in the woods. The land was bought unsightly and unseen, but the man we bought off told us there were three acres all cleared ready to go onto, but when we got there we found a little old shell of a log house and not a stick cut, only what had been cut to burn in the old log house. After paying the man for bringing us in from Detroit, and paying for a cow, we had just 50 cents in money left, and I have heard my father say he did not know how he was going to get through the winter. But after we had got all settled down, and the rest of our things down from Detroit, he started out to see who he had for neighbors. It is not always the one who lives the nearest to you that is your neighbor. They were all neighborly, kind and helpful, both far and near.

Asa S. Whitehead Papers, Bentley Historical Library.

Reminiscence of Flint

Mrs. George M. Dewey

I came here [to Michigan] from Batavia, New York, in 1842, when I was about fifteen years of age. We came by stage from Buffalo to Detroit, and from Detroit to Birmingham by horse cars; then by stage from Birmingham to Flint. The roads were fairly good except during the spring and fall, when they were always bad and muddy.

On arriving at Flint, we stopped at the Northern Hotel, an old hostelry located at the corner of North Saginaw Street and Third Avenue. The Indians were living here at that time, and where the large factories are now it was then all solid woods of oak. The Indians camped there a great deal. The underbrush had been burned off, and it was that they called "Oak Openings." One day while we were stopping at the Northern Hotel, suddenly everybody rushed out of the Hotel—there was not a person left. Of course, we went outside also. There was an old man outside who was sawing wood, and we asked him what was the matter. All he would say was: "The pig squeal." It developed that a bear had entered the enclosure of Mr. Thayer, who lived not far from where the Catholic Church is now, and taken a pig out of his pig pen. This was close to the Hotel where we were. It shows you what Flint was at the time I first came here. Now this part of Flint is all built up, and even the place which was solid woods then is now covered in factories. My brothers used to kill wild turkeys and deer right at the place where the factories are now. There were plenty of deer around here then.

The Indians used to camp a great deal on what is now First Avenue. They used to put up their wigwams, and, of course, moved around from place to place; but at certain times of the year they lived around here. You could never tell when Indians were in your house. They walked right in without knocking, or any ceremony whatever, and, of course, having moccasins on, we could not hear them, until you would hear a sound of "Wooh! Wooh!" and you would turn around and see half a dozen Indians in the room. They were very curious about the things they saw in the house. Everything was new to them, of course, but they never did us any harm, and we never felt that they helped themselves to anything. My mother was told, the first New Year's that we were here, that the Indians would come for fried cakes, and sure enough, every New Year's day they would come, saying "Happy New Year, Happy New Year." There were a great many Indians during the first years that we were here. They brought berries and baskets.

There was a stage every day from Detroit, and one from Saginaw. After a time, I cannot tell just when, there was a plank road built all the way through; but not at the time we came. This was done some time afterward. When we first came here, the roads were pretty good, but sometimes in the spring and fall it would be impossible to get through except on horseback, the mud was so deep. The mail would be taken care of in this way. If they attempted to go through with a carriage or stage, they would sometimes have to stop and take the rails from the fences, or take logs which had been cut, and put them in the roads, in order to get through. Later they built what they called a corduroy road over portions of the stage road, which was used until they built a plank road, which they did later, through from Pontiac.

Mrs. George M. Dewey Reminiscences, Bentley Historical Library.

The Indians Visit Us

William Nowlin

Some three or four years after we came to the country [ca. 1837–38] there came a tribe, or part of a tribe, of Indians and camped a little over a mile southwest of our house, in the timber, near the head of the windfall next to the openings. They somewhat alarmed us, but father said, "Use them well, be kind to them and they will not harm us." I suppose they came to hunt. It was in the summer time and the first we knew of them, my little brother and two sisters had been on the openings picking huckleberries not thinking of Indians. When they started for home and got to the edge of the woods they were in plain sight of the Indians, and they said it appeared as if the woods were full of them. They stood for a minute and saw that the Indians were peeling bark and making wigwams; they had some trees already peeled.

They said they saw one Indian who had on some sort of crown, or wreath, of feathers in it that waved a foot above his head. They saw him mount a sorrel pony. As he did so the other Indians whooped and hooted, I suppose, to cheer the chief. Childlike they were scared and thought he was coming after them on horseback. They left the path and ran right into the brush and woods, from home. When they thought they were out of sight of the Indian they turned toward home. After they came in sight of home, to encourage his sisters, my little brother told them, he wouldn't be afraid of any one Indian but, he said, there were so many there it was enough to scare anybody. When they got within twenty rods of the house they saw some one coming beyond the house with a gun on his shoulder. One said it was William Beal, another said it was an Indian. They looked again and all agreed that it was an Indian. If they had come straight down the lane, they would have just about met him at the bars, opposite the house, (where we went through). There was no way for them to get to the house and shun him; except to climb the fence and run across the field. The dreaded Indian seemed to meet them everywhere, and if possible they were more scared now than before. Brother and sister Sarah were over the fence very quickly. Bessie had to run so hard to get home and was so scared that in attempting to climb the fence she got part way up and fell back, but up and tried again. Sister Sarah would not leave her but helped her over. But John left them and ran for his life to the house; as soon as they could get started they ran too. Mother said [John] ran into the house looking very scared, and went for the gun. She asked him what was the matter, and what he wanted of the gun; he said there was an Indian coming to kill them and he wanted to shoot him. Mother told him to let the gun alone, the Indian would not hurt them; by this time my sisters had got in. In a minute or two afterward the Indian came in, little thinking how near he had come being shot by a youthful hero.

Poor Indian wanted to borrow a large brass kettle that mother had and leave his rifle as security for it. Mother lent him the kettle and he went away. In a few days he brought the kettle home.

A short time after this a number of them had been out to Dearbornville and got some whisky. All but one had imbibed rather too freely of "Whiteman's fire water to make Indian feel good." They came down as far as our house and, as we had no stick standing across the door, they walked in very quietly, without knocking. The practice or law among the Indians is, when one goes away from his wigwam, if he puts a stick across the entrance all are forbidden to enter there; and, as it is the only protection of his wigwam, no Indian honorably violates it. There were ten of these Indians. Mother was washing. She said the children were very much afraid, not having gotten over their fright. They got around behind her and the washtub, as though she could protect them. The Indians asked for bread and milk; mother gave them all she had. They got upon the floor, took hold of hands and formed a ring. The sober one sat in the middle; the other seemed to hear to what he said as much as though he had been an officer. He would not drink a drop of the whisky, but kept perfectly sober. They seemed to have a very joyful time, they danced and sang their wild songs of the forest. Then asked mother for more bread and milk; she told them she had no more; then they asked for buttermilk and she gave them what she had of that. As mother was afraid, she gave them anything she had, that they called for. They asked her for whisky; she said she hadn't got it. They said, "Maybe you lie." Then they pointed toward Mr. Pardee's and said, "Neighbor got whisky?" She told them she didn't know. They said again, "Maybe you lie."

When they were ready the sober one said, "Indian go!" He had them all start in single file. In that way they went out of sight. Mother was overjoyed and much relieved when they were gone. They had eaten up all her bread and used up all her milk, but I suppose they thought they had a good time.

Not more than two or three weeks after this the Indians moved away, and these children of the forest wandered to other hunting grounds. We were very much pleased, as well as the other neighbors, when they were gone.

From chapter 11, "The Indians Visit Us: Their Strange and Peculiar Ways," *The Bark Covered House, or, Back in the Woods Again: Being a Graphic and Thrilling Description of Real Pioneer Life in the Wilderness of Michigan* by William Nowlin (Detroit: Herald Publishing House, 1876), electronic version available through the Library of Congress at https://memory.loc.gov.

Discovery of an Indian Grave

Bertha Adams Dawson

This narrative takes place at Ripley's Rock in Marquette, circa 1850.

On the top of the highest rock . . . a discovery was made by my father one Sunday afternoon when a few of the men and women went out for a little row and a picnic. It was rather a test of skill and courage to make the attempt to reach the top of the almost perpendicular wall, and gain the old gnarled pine tree that sprung from the hollow recesses of the big Ripley Rock. However, Papa was the victor. Under that gnarled tree, to his great surprise he discovered a grave. Just how many years ago that grave had been made and that last long sleep begun, there was no telling, but there was the last resting place beneath the kindly shelter of the little old pine tree, that seemed to stretch out its arms to protect the grave from the Summer's sun and rain, and oh, how many times had this same little tree bent low, almost breaking, when the high, angry waves dashed and rolled over it. And how it clasped in its arms the grave, stretching its branches out protecting against the snow and ice all Winter, and in the genial Spring when the warm South wind blew, and the sun melted the snow and ice, how it straightened up its head toward Heaven as if in thanksgiving, and seemed to smile at the lazy-winged sea-gull screeching overhead.

Maybe it was just a day like this and early dawn, how many years ago no one knew, that Indians dressed in their best, war-paint and feathers, and in their birch-bark canoes, silently bore the dead to its last resting place. Could it have been a Chief whom they wished to honor with such a high and stately burial, or was it an enemy whom they laid away out of their midst out in that lonely spot to be buried and forgotten?

Father stooping down, and looking over the rocks into the boats called out eagerly: "Come up—come up and see what I had found. I claim it—it is mine," and the eager voices came from below: "What is it—what is it?" An Indian's grave. Two other men succeeded in gaining the top, and after resting a few moments gazed in wonder toward the hallowed spot. Father said: "I have not touched a single leaf so that you might see the grave just as I found it."

Stretched over the grave were two long wide pieces of birch bark, sewed round the edges with porcupine quills, the ends being laced together with strings made from the cured deer hide. The piece was worked from top to bottom in the finest and most beautiful manner with the Indian hieroglyphics done in porcupine quills, and was slightly stuffed in the center giving it the appearance of a pillow, though my father did not know at the time the name of this Indian pillow which is [blank in MS.]. These pillows are highly valued, our Government paying large sums to possess them and putting them in the National Museum, which is the Smithsonian Institute. This Institute was then in its infancy.

Carefully lifting up this beautiful coverlet, as we might call it, Father found underneath it a wooden bowl from which to drink, the long cooking ladle of wood, beautifully carved with a bird's head on the handle, a wonder in wood carving; also a platter representing a fish, deeply and exquisitely carved in wood, but upon attempting to pick these treasures up, lo! they crumbled in his hands to fine dusts, and there they lay, a little heap of brown dirt, not a piece large enough to carry away remaining.

Next came another covering of plain birch bark. Lifting this carefully brought to the light of day a marvelous old gun barrel. The wooden shoulder piece had long ago gone to dust, and the screws and a few little steel ornaments were so badly corroded that all Father could save was the gun barrel, which was almost as long as father was tall, and with such a peculiarly small bore, that I can barely put my little finger into it. Days afterwards when Father polished it up, there were marks visible upon it, but he could not determine whether it was of English or French make.

Later that summer, the same party again visited the grave that lay under the shadow of the gnarled old pine tree, and dug it up, and a Mrs. —— who is still living here had the beads, or a few of them that were around the Indian's neck. The skull and crossbones are treasured by the —— family. Mr. ——, a lawyer long dead, kept a little copper cup. There were a number of other little mementos distributed among the party, my Father treasuring the pillow bearing the beautiful hieroglyphics, the loss of which in later years, he mourned until the time of his death.

"Bertha Adams Dawson Recollections," Marquette Regional History Center.

Indians of Michigan

A. H.

March 17, 1860

It may be interesting to some of our readers to know, that in the State of Michigan, there are now about 7,500 Indians. They belong to five different tribes, and speak so many distinct languages; many of them understanding no language but that of their own tribe.

Mr. A.M. Fitch, is the United States agent for all the Indians in this State. They receive from the General Government about $50,000 annually, in gold and silver, and about the same amount is annually expended for their benefit in some other way; in presents of goods, tools for farming purposes, the establishment of blacksmith shops, the support of schools, etc. etc.

When, once a year, they receive their payments, all are paid alike; male and female, old and young, healthy and sick, married and single. In the distribution of *presents*, while all receive something, those known to be sick or poor, are remembered more liberally. The writer was present at Paw Paw, Feb. 14, 1860, when the Agent paid 260 of these Indians, who met him there to receive their annuity and presents. Some preliminary questions relating to a debt against the Indians, was discussed and settled by them before payment. Several of them engaged freely and zealously in the explanation and discussion of this question, and when sufficient had been said, they voted, and all appeared perfectly satisfied with the decision of the majority. The orderly and friendly manner in which they discussed and decided this question, was worthy of much praise. White men, high in office, do not always discharge their duty with such deference, fairness, and propriety. And when they received their presents of shovels, hoes, axes, hatchets, augers, gimlets, planes, knives, blankets, ready-made clothing, shirting, calico, &c., &c. it did one's heart good to see how rich and thankful they seemed to feel.

The tribes are not so distinct and separate as formerly. They are considerably mixed. The number of Indians in the State has not diminished much for several years; but the real *Indian character* is slowly and steadily fading away. Many of them are learning the language and adopting the dress and habits of the whites. A few of them cultivate land and appear to live comfortably. Quite a number of them profess religion, and seem to me perfectly sincere and somewhat intelligent in their profession. Some of them, of course, are lazy and intemperate; but it is said, and no doubt truly, that there is not half the intemperance among them that there was ten years ago.

On the whole, they are a peculiar, and comparatively, a harmless and inoffensive race of people. They are not much given to stealing or any kind of crime or mischief. The writer has known Indians for many years, and has witnessed among them, acts of humanity, kindness, and liberality. If the whites would always be honest, fair and kind with them; if half the money spent in fighting them, were spent in providing for them, and in being just and generous with them; there might be very little trouble with the *Indians*, and much might be done to advance them in the road to civilization and happiness.

"Indians of Michigan" by A. H., March 17, 1860, *Wolverine Citizen* (Flint, MI).

The Burning of an Indian Village

Matt O'Reilly

This event took place in 1900.

On the west shore of Burt Lake there extended an arm of land containing about four hundred acres, and Indians have lived on it years before the White Man came.

Here they lived in peace and to us whites was known as a "Reservation." Their spiritual needs was looked after every month by a Priest from Harbor Springs, one of Father Marquette's early land marks. [Their] chief . . . called them together by ringing of the bell for prayers to sing in Latin or to ask for alms for some of their aged ones. Everything went peaceful until the resort boom came in the [eighteen] nineties and the White Man schemed to get them off. But it being a reservation signed by Governor Cass and the chief at that time, Kish-e-go-we. After the convent at Harbor Springs had opened up in 1831, the youth of the villages was sent there to be educated, and to my surprise was better educated than the whites I was mixing with. They could sing in Latin, play the organ, serve as altar boys, besides doing the many things that belong to Indian life.

The leaves had turned to their beautiful fall colors, an odd Indian could be seen here and there, digging potatoes, while the real aged man sat outside his hut or tent smoking away in peace and comfort. When in looking up two men drove in to one of the yards. One was the County Sheriff and the other was the man who bought or bid in the Tax Titles for which the land was sold.

At once they tied their rig to a small tree and proceeded to the house, one of the resort cottage type. After reading the necessary papers for removal of the contents, they proceeded with their work in removing stove, bedding, chairs and everything movable, and as soon as empty, one went in with oil can sprinkled oil in each room, set a match to it, and instantly it produced volumes of black smoke. As this went on sobs and curses rent the air, and in all directions Indians could be seen running, not knowing yet but what it was from stove-pipe or some other cause.

But when they all got there and found out the real news, just one word would had those two men going home dead with their boots on. On they went to the next house and repeated their actions, and the whites over the south shore of Burt Lake were wondering at so many buildings ablaze, all inside of two hours. When they came to the church, their heart failed them, and it alone stood there surrounded with the burning of poor Indians' homes, while tears and curses flowed freely from the afflicted ones. After those men done their work, they drove home satisfied of the job and proved to the world that the White Man turned savage, Michigan's last tilt with Indians.

I was not there at the time, and thank God I was not, for knowing my temper as it is I surely would put up a fight even if it cast me in jail. But I was there the next morning and witnessed the smoking ruins with the contents of all houses out on the road, while here and there they were aged Indians laying on their mattresses or bales of hay.

One afternoon after the four o'clock train passed, I noticed a priest coming to my home, and at once went and met him, and this is what he said, "Matt, I have some bad news. Here is a letter a lawyer in Cheboygan sent me." And it read as follows:

Dear Sir, this letter is to notify you to remove the contents of the Burt Lake church, or take the consequences.

And I answered, "Father, he cannot touch our church for there are no taxes on it." When he answered me, "For Pete's sake, go over with your two teams and bring everything to your home, not forgetting the bell tower."

"Father, let us fight it. They cannot touch church property on a tax sale," when again he answered "Matt, you see what they did [to the Indian village]. Please do as I tell you."

And as I looked at the priest in Franciscan robes, with the beads and crucifix hanging by his side, I answered "Father, I'll obey."

Next day I went over with my brother, my wife, my mother with two teams and loaded it up. But while we were loading it was sad to see the Indians stand and think of their past when that same bell called them to the chapel for prayer, alms, weddings, or death, in the past, and to think how the White Man could do such a thing with a sheriff by his side, but they did it, and got away with it.

Matt O'Reilly Papers, Bentley Historical Library.

CHAPTER 6

Coming to America: Immigration to Michigan

A fter Michigan achieved statehood in 1837, officials began a rigorous campaign to entice foreigners to settle in the state. They were indeed successful, as people of numerous nationalities made Michigan their home, and this success is presently evident with cities such as Frankenmuth and Holland, and there are many residents of the Upper Peninsula with Scandinavian ancestry. Large numbers of English, Scotch, and Irish settled in the state, notably the English in northern Michigan and the Irish in Detroit. Today, Dearborn maintains the highest percentage of Arab Americans. Certainly, large numbers of immigrants entering the region sparked tension, as some of these documents demonstrate. Even so, Michigan has a long history of appealing to foreign immigrants that continues even today.

The Emigrant's Guide to the State of Michigan

E. H. Thomson

1849

From no other State in the Union have emigrants from Europe received as much attention as from the Legislature of Michigan. In the Annual Message of the present Governor of the State, at the meeting of the Legislature in January, 1848, the attention of the members was directed by the Executive to the "valuable class of foreigners" arriving in the State. The interposition of State legislation was invoked "so far as to extend to them the benefits of an organized township government, and of such opened and constructed highways as would afford them access to mills, merchants, mechanics, and post offices."

Accordingly, laws were passed giving to the Holland and German settlements nearly 20,000 acres of land for the purposes mentioned in the Message of the Executive. Commissioners have been appointed under authority of law, to see that the wishes of the Legislature are strictly complied with. Roads for their accommodation, as well as bridges, have been built, and they exhibit as healthy and prosperous a condition as any colony on this side of the Atlantic.

The soil of Michigan is various. It may be divided into heavily-timbered, oak openings, and prairies; and the growth of the vegetation indicates the character of the land. The heavy-timbered land, covered by the largest class of forest-trees, indicates a soil of clay, a wet muck, or a dry, black, sandy loam, based on sub-soil of reddish earth. The last two species of soil are highly productive, yielding, with the careless tillage of new country, from twenty to thirty bushels of wheat to the acre, and they bear an abundance of every kind of grain which is produced in the State of New York. This soil is the most difficult to clear, but it has one advantage to an emigrant with small means: after the timber is cut down, the soil *does not require ploughing*; a harrow drawn by one yoke of oxen will render it fit for cultivation, as the surface of the land is exceedingly mellow.

In travelling along the main roads in Michigan, the emigrant will be struck with the miles of prairies, thick forests, and oak openings; village after village springs up, all indicating a remarkable freshness and vigor in their inhabitants. Wagons, loaded with household furniture and the families of emigrants, are constantly met at numerous points during the season of emigrating; and in looking away from the roads, you will see clearings through the woods, and the curl of the smoke from the prostrate trunks of smoldering trees shows that the emigrant is there with his axe.

The emigrant goes into Michigan for the purpose of practicing agriculture. When he has made the selection of his lands, his neighbors for miles around assist him in building a house of logs. His cattle feed upon the grass and herbage which surrounds his new home. He clears and ploughs his land, puts in his wheat and other crops, and the next year, or two at most, finds him an independent freeholder with a neighboring market for his produce. Every emigrant must expect to grapple with more or less hardships; but under ordinary circumstances, by the exercise of industry, the second or third year will find him in comfort and independence: for he derives a threefold benefit in his labor—an annual product from the soil, and increase in the actual value of the land cultivated, and also in that of the surrounding land by his improvement.

From "The Emigrant's Guide to the State of Michigan" by E. H. Thomson, agent for the State of Michigan, 1849.

A Response to Know-Nothings

Theodore Foster

Foster was a newspaper editor from Ann Arbor and a cofounder of the Signal of Liberty, *one of Michigan's abolitionist publications. His views on many issues during his time were considered quite radical.*

The wide diffusion of this mysterious organization [the Know-Nothings, a fervent anti-immigrant political group], and the success which has thus far attended its efforts demonstrates that it has its origin in some of the strongest principles of human nature. The order exists in a state of profound secrecy: the members affect to conceal their individual connection with the order: and no authorized exposition of its objects and principles has ever been vouchsafed to the rest of the community. But through the papers devoted to the advancement of their cause it appears that they seek mainly the repeal of all laws of the United States by which foreigners become naturalized citizens, and the exclusion from office of all foreign born persons, and of such native citizens as profess the Catholic religion. An organization for such purposes is unworthy the support of American citizens.

1. [Know-Nothings are] opposed to the principle of equal rights for all the Caucasian race on which our laws profess to be founded. A foreigner, who leaves his native country forever, and emigrates to America with his family and effect, becomes a permanent settler, and . . . [he who] is willing to renounce his allegiance to a foreign government is practically an American citizen. His interests, and those of his American neighbors, are precisely identical. Justice demands that after a reasonable time to become acquainted with our institutions, he should have an equal voice in the administration of that government under which himself and his posterity are to live forever. A residence of from five to ten years would seem to be sufficient for that purpose:

yet by the plan proposed by the Know Nothings children of foreigners brought here in infancy might live amidst out institutions for fifty, eighty, or an hundred years without any participation in the public affairs of their adopted country.

2. There is no occasion for the exclusion of foreigners from the rights of citizenship, inasmuch as they have never manifested any feeling hostile to our institutions. They have never attempted any rebellion; and in the Revolutionary war, and in our subsequent national contests, they have been foremost among the military and naval defenders of our country. The only offence alleged against them is that the Catholic portion of them are now united in striving to attain the establishment of separate public schools in which the Catholic religion may be taught by Catholic teachers paid from the general school fund. However untrue or impolite their project may be, they prosecute it only through the same means by which the friends of other national measures pursue their objects—by voting for candidates for office who are favorable to their realization. The plan of the Catholics may be opposed in the same way; it may be discussed and rejected without tumult or violence on either side; and its proposal by the Catholics is no excuse for Protestants who would therefore seek to deprive them of the right of suffrage in all cases because, in a particular instance, Catholics had failed to exercise it in that manner which Protestants seemed most advisable and judicious.

3. Neither are the institutions of America in danger from the numerical preponderance of foreigners. The total foreign emigration to the United States, according to recent statements, from 1820 to Jan. 1, 1853 was 3,204,848, being an average of only about 100,000 per annum. The number of persons of foreign birth in the United States in 1850 was 2,210,839: whereas the white natives were eight time as numerous, amounting to 17,737,578. Of the former, a large portion are Protestant. Besides, all the descendants of these foreigners, born in this country, are native born citizens, and swell that body much faster than the emigration augments the total aggregate of foreigners. This, if emigration be considered an evil, it provides its own remedy in the increased number of American citizens which results from it.

4. The exclusion of foreigners from citizenship, after the privilege has been enjoyed by them for three quarters of a century, would be felt by them as injury; and its inevitable tendency would be to stigmatize them as a degraded and inferior class of the American population. The natives would despise the foreigners; and the latter, in return, would dislike and hate those who kept them in degraded condition.

Such are the objections which may be urged to the proposal of the Know Nothings to exclude all foreign born persons from citizenship. But we have reason to believe that their paramount and ultimate object is to exclude all Catholics, both native and foreign born, from any participation in the administration of the government, by preventing foreign Catholics from becoming citizens, and by excluding native Catholics from every official station whatever. The Protestant clergy, almost without exception, cherish a hostile feeling toward the Catholics; and thereby inflamed the prejudices of their readers, and prepared them for any act of injustice against their religious enemies, which might be decently covered by pretenses of zeal for religious freedom or for national prosperity. Ambitious leaders, in organizing a warfare upon Catholics sought to enlist the influence of the most profligate as well as the better portion of the community. They hoped to draw into their secret society the class of devoted patriots, who were apprehensive of the evils of Catholic ascendency: those who disliked, or rather hated the Catholics purely on accounts of their religious tenets: those who disliked the manners, habits, principles and language of foreigners: those who entertained a contempt for the degraded condition of a large part of the foreign emigrants; and a large and influential class of citizens who were indignant at the base trickling of foreign votes every where envied by politicians. The original element of the whole movement was religious hatred, which sought to accomplish its ends by enlisting in its favor all the forces of national antipathy. Through these, they hoped to be able to overcome the strong attachment of the American people to the principle of religious freedom which had been widely cherished since its first manly assertion by Roger Williams two centuries before: and to establish a system of intolerance unworthy of their age and country, and which had always been discarded by the letter and spirit of their constitutions and laws.

From "Miscellaneous Thoughts," Theodore Foster Papers, Bentley Historical Library.

Speech to the Legislature

Governor Russell Alger

January 6, 1887

Another great problem that must be solved in the near future is the one of immigration. Two years ago I recommended the continuance of the Commissionership of Immigration, but the Legislature saw fit to abolish the office, and I am now satisfied that they were much wiser than I. An examination of the records of our asylums, prisons, poorhouses and jails, will startle you when you find the great percent of inmates that are foreign born. Bad people of all classes and conditions, criminals, paupers, partially insane, cripples, aged and infirm, are dumped upon our shores, having been sent from foreign countries here because it is much cheaper to pay steerage fare for them across the waters than to keep them, and they spring up in our jails, prisons, poorhouses, and asylums, and are supported by the tax payers of our State. While I believe it is for the best interests of this country to invite people, no matter how large the numbers, to come here from foreign lands, provided they are healthful in body and in mind, capable of earning a living, and of making good citizens during time of peace, and who would be willing in time of war, should that ever come, to take up arms to defend this country, yet I would not allow a person to immigrate to this country who cannot present a consul's certificate as to soundness of body, mind, and character. As I said before, this land of ours should not be a dumping ground for these paupers, nor should disturbers of the peace, such as Nihilists and Anarchists, from other countries be tolerated here. These are the disturbing elements, and an element that is growing in strength in our midst. I recommend that a joint resolution be adopted, asking our congressmen to urge that laws be enacted to carry out these views.

Russell Alger, Speech to the Michigan Legislature, January 6, 1887, in *Messages of the Governors of Michigan*, vol. 3, edited by George Fuller (Lansing: Michigan Historical Commission, 1927), 559–60.

An Arab American Grocery Chain

Jack Hamady

Dearborn currently has the highest percentage of Arab American residents of any city in the United States, but people with Middle Eastern backgrounds reside throughout Michigan. Lebanese cousins Michael and Kamol Hamady began Hamady Brothers grocery, headquartered in Flint, in 1911. Later, they hired their nephew Amin, who went by the name "Jack." This interview took place in 1997 between Jack and Lily Hamady and his nephew, Hani Bawardi.

1997

HANI BAWARDI [HB]: What do you remember Ammo [uncle], about the 1930s, the depression and the sit down strike? As far as business goes?

JACK HAMADY [JH]: Well, I think as far as the depression is concerned, this is where our company made a great deal of progress, because we were hard workers, the management was [hard-working], and the employees were good employees; we made sure we had employees who appreciated their jobs. And I think, we were able—naturally that is the only way we could make money—competing with the chains, because we had a warehouse within a very short area of the stores, we had to unload the cars right on the trucks and have the trucks go to the stores, and you can see how much saving there is in labor, and consequently combined a great deal of success and we profited by it and so did the community.

HB: And during the sit down strike, a lot of people were out of work, did the Hamady chain . . .

HB: We did not suffer much as far as the sit down strike, in fact; to tell you the truth; we sent food into the sit down strikers, we appreciated General Motors, but on the other hand, these people were our customers, and worked to help them having food to eat.

HB: To their houses, or to the . . . inside the factory?

JH: To the factories, to the factories.

HB: And eventually, the Hamady chain workers, was it unionized or no union?

JH: There was no unionization as far as we were concerned at that time, but our organization was unionized later, mainly because the union was trying to get into the stores, and the chains were all unionized, finally our company joined the union.

HB: [Can] you tell me about the community, the Arabs in general, where they congregated? What did they do in their free time, who were they? I remember for instance that there was a coffee shop that someone told me on Industrial Avenue . . .

JH: [The coffee shop] was run by the Riziks, I believe he had a restaurant there, and he used to tell people how wealthy his family was and how fortunate he was, he had six children, and he was always telling people he was a millionaire, and finally, of course, they realized he was kidding. [People said to him] "you're always telling us you're a millionaire, what do you got to prove it?" So one day he got his children all fixed up nice, and dressed well and everything, and he said, here's my six million; million number one and he introduced his children to the group that he had six million dollars because he had six children. But to tell you the truth, we people that are from the Middle East, we were hard workers, and they were good people, they were hard workers and they were committed, they were honest and honorable, made a good name to themselves. The Arab people that came here, the Middle East people that came here were people that had dignity, they were hard workers, a number maybe were not educated, but they had what it takes in character.

HB: How many of the people worked in the factory, auto factory, how many had their own business?

JH: Well, this is a good question, and I wish I knew exactly, but I can remember that many of them worked in the shops because they could make good money and they were hard workers, and a number of them of course opened their own businesses and became successful.

LILY HAMADY [Jack's wife]: I don't know how they learnt the language, believe me, that must have been terrible, because they couldn't explain anything, he couldn't speak a word of English, neither did his mom and dad could write and read, because in the mountains, they had no schools, there was no cars, no schools, nothing.

JH: This is the one thing why they call this country the land of opportunity; if the person is willing to work and be honest about it, and be true to the people he worked for, he did well, many of them came and went back and stayed, and number of course stayed right here.

HB: So your involvement with the Hamady chain began as soon as you arrived?

JH: Yes it did.

HB: And how long did you last?

JH: All my life, all my life, I stayed with the company, within the Hamady Brothers company, 55 years.

HB: Can you give us a summary of the history, what positions have you had and for how many years and how many stores?

JH: . . . I started working, sweeping the floor, sorting out rotten potatoes, because we used to buy them from farmers and we had to do inspection at that time, I cleaned out the lavatories. Perhaps my success in the company was that I worked with people and as I advanced, people respected me and people knew that I was a good person, and worked with them so my promotions in the company was earned, it wasn't just because I was Mr. Michael Hamady's, you know, relatives. It was a good company, my uncle was a great leader, he was a person that was not educated, academically, but God gave him a computer up here (pointing to his head). Good mind.

HB: What was his name?

JH: Michael, Michael Hamady. Mahmoud, Mahmoud was his name and he called it Michael.

HB: Did you know how his name was changed?

JH: Yes, I think when they first came to this country, they realized Mahmoud was a name not known, and many people that came to this country in the early days changed their names to a name that could be pronounced better in English and Michael was a very popular name.

HB: Is Jack your original name?

JH: This is interesting, I'll tell you a story. When I first came to this country, it was my desire to learn the ABCs and learn the language, and I was quite ambitious trying to learn the language, I wanted to be a good American. So I had to have an average in school, and being eleven years of age at the time [ca. 1921], it was easy for me to learn. So, my name actually was Amin, Amin was a very popular name in the Middle East, it has to do with a person, that if he's Amin, he's trustworthy, something of that nature, so I wrote down my name on a piece of paper that was the mathematical questions and answers and the teacher said . . . "just write your names on the bottom of the papers and hand them in." When she got that paper, at the bottom it was spelled "Amen," in Arabic, you know every letter is pronounced, Amin, A M E N, very simple, and I didn't know the language at the time, but the word amen has a different meaning than Amin. So I told the teacher, that that was my name, it was a very great embarrassment to me. So on the way going home that day, I said "My name is gonna be something simpler than that, I don't want the teacher to think that I am joking and kidding." So the most common name in this country at the time was Jack, Jack Dimson [Jack Dempsey] was a great star, a great boxer, national boxer, so I said what could be better than Jack?" And that's how I took the name Jack Amin Hamady and that shows on my citizenship paper.

Interview with Amin (Jack) and Lily Hamady, 1997, Hani Bawardi Papers, Genesee Historical Collections Center.

A Call for Immigrants
Office of Governor Rick Snyder

January 23, 2014

Snyder: Opening Detroit to the World Will Accelerate Comeback of Great City

Governor Urges Increase in Employment-Based Visas

Detroit must harness the power of skilled immigrants to grow its economy, increase its tax base and reverse its population decline, Gov. Rick Snyder said today as he urged federal action on his proposal that increases employment-based visas for immigrants.

"We want the world to know that Detroit is open for business," Snyder said. "Legal immigration helped to build this great city and is just as critical to its comeback. Immigrants create jobs and Detroit is a great value opportunity in terms of business costs and overall quality of life. The city has so much to offer anyone willing to contribute to its future. Of course, Michigan has always been a welcoming state to those wishing to call it home. We're excited about the potential that this initiative holds for Detroit's turnaround, and look forward to working with our federal partners to make it happen."

Under Snyder's initiative, the federal government would secure an additional 50,000 employment-based visas for Detroit's skilled immigrants during the next five years. The emphasis is on immigrants with advanced academic degrees, or those with exceptional ability in the sciences, arts or business.

Immigration is a proven driver of job creation and economic growth. Nationally, immigrants founded 28 percent of all small businesses started in 2011. Immigrants also file patents at twice the rate of U.S.-born citizens. In Michigan, immigrants are helping to advance our state into the new economy by launching high-tech firms at incredible rates. During the last decade, immigrants created nearly one-third of the high-tech businesses in Michigan, at a rate six times the rest of the population and ranking Michigan third in the U.S.

The governor was joined by Detroit Mayor Mike Duggan, who supports the initiative.

"In order for Detroit to grow again, we need highly trained workers to move in, open businesses and raise their families," Duggan said. "The governor's plan opens the door for more skilled immigrants to thrive in Detroit's fertile ground for economic innovation. They will create jobs and employ Detroiters." . . .

Specifically, Snyder's proposal:

- Requests application of a National Interest Waiver under the Employment-Based Second Preference (EB-2) visas to 50,000 individuals over five years for employment-based visas. Detroit would be allocated 5,000 employment-based visas in the first year; 10,000 each year in the second, third and fourth years; and 15,000 in the fifth year.
- Requires skilled immigrants who receive an employment-based visa under this plan to reside and work in Detroit.

Snyder unveiled his plan at the Ideal Group in Detroit, a Hispanic-owned company delivering innovative solutions in construction services, manufacturing and indirect material management. As the grandson of Mexican immigrants, CEO Frank Venegas understands the importance of expanding opportunities for skilled workers from foreign companies.

"I have seen firsthand how the strong work ethic and diverse set of ideas migrant professionals bring with them foster innovation and creativity in the business community," Venegas said. "In order for Detroit to be successful we need more contributions from workers all across the world."

A strong demand exists for professionals in the fields of engineering, Internet technology, health care and life sciences. More than 50 percent of Ph.Ds in the science, technology, engineering and math (STEM) fields and as many as 40 percent of master's degrees in engineering, life sciences, computer sciences and physical sciences are awarded each year in the U.S. to international students. As a benefit to American workers, each international student retained in the STEM fields is associated with 2.6 additional jobs for U.S. natives.

Snyder pointed out that Michigan colleges and universities host more than 25,500 international students who contribute more than $750 million to the state's economy each year. More than 82 percent of Michigan's international students who use their student visa to work in the U.S. after graduation earned advanced degrees, making them the type of talent that Detroit and all of Michigan needs in this new economy.

Snyder, America's most pro-immigration governor, said this initiative is just the latest example of how Michigan has established itself as a prime destination for skilled immigrants.

In his recent State of the State address, Snyder announced that he is creating the Michigan Office for New Americans to attract more skilled immigrants to Michigan. He also is urging Washington to approve Michigan's application to become only the second state with a state-sponsored . . . regional center to attract investment and create jobs for Michigan workers.

In addition, the governor has testified before Congress regarding the need for common-sense immigration reform at the federal level. He also implemented the Global Michigan Initiative, designed to recruit skilled immigrants and make Michigan an even more welcoming state. Last year, the Michigan Department of Licensing and Regulatory Affairs issued online guides that explain many of Michigan's professional licensing requirements for individuals who were educated or have work experience in foreign countries.

"Opening Detroit to the World Will Accelerate Comeback of Great City," Governor's Office News Release, January 23, 2014, http://www.michigan.gov.

Syrian Refugees

Ali Harb

November 11, 2015, Arab American News

The White House briefed 34 governors "on the rigorous screening and security vetting process" for refugees amid security concerns about relocating people feeling the war in Syria.

Citing the deadly terrorist attacks in Paris, Gov. Rick Snyder said Sunday Michigan will suspend efforts to resettle Syrian refugees.

Relocating refugees is strictly a federal matter, but Snyder is one of 31 governors to say their state would not welcome people fleeing the war in Syria.

Snyder's decision was met with condemnation from Arab, Muslim and pro-immigration advocates. . . .

Snyder made [this] decision after State Rep. Gary Glenn, R-Midland, called on him to "reverse his call to relocate Syrian refugees in the state."

"Given the terrible situation in Paris, I've directed that we put on hold our efforts to accept new refugees until the U.S. Department of Homeland Security completes a full review of security clearances and procedures," Snyder said in a statement.

He added that residents' security is a priority to him.

In a 90-minute conference call, hosted by the White House, federal security officials explained the process of admitting refugees to 34 governors across the nation.

"The Administration officials reiterated what the President has made abundantly clear: that his top priority is the safety of the American people," the White House said in a statement. "That's why, even as the United States accepts more refugees—including Syrians—we do so only after they undergo the most rigorous screening and security vetting of any category of traveler to the United States."

Dawud Walid, the Michigan executive director of the Council on American Islamic Relations (CAIR-MI), said the governor's concerns about the screening process for refugees are "insincere" because he knows that the Department of Home Land Security has a thorough system in place.

Walid added that Snyder quickly bowed down to a few Republican state representatives without meeting with the community.

"This goes to show the weight of Islamophobia in our society," he added. "The poor Syrian people fled their homelands due to ISIS, and now they're being prevented from resettling in some places because of people making generalizations that they are ISIS."

Brian Stone, a Democratic candidate for the State House of Representatives, said Snyder is punishing the refugees for something they did not do.

"I think we need to call this what it is; this is Islamophobia," Stone said.

He added that fear of Muslims is driving the governor's policy.

"The governor needs to confront his own prejudice," he said. "To turn away refugees who are fleeing from the same terrorists that are causing these attacks in Beirut and Paris and Baghdad is to further victimize people who are already victims of terrorism."

Former State Rep. Rashida Tlaib echoed Stone's comments.

She said refugees are fleeing ISIS, and the governor is telling them, "Michigan doesn't want you."

"Gov. Snyder is allowing these murderous terrorist thugs to dictate whether or not Michigan will provide humanitarian relief to innocent civilians, many of them are families, women and children," Tlaib told The Arab American News. "It's a shame to let those attacks dictate who we are. That's not leadership."

The former state representative said Snyder's move brings into question his efforts to make Michigan a welcoming state.

"White House Reassures Governors on Refugees; Groups Slam Snyder," by Ali Harb for *Arab American News*, November 11, 2015, http://www.arabamericannews.com. Reprinted with permission from *Arab American News*.

CHAPTER 7

National Crises: Antislavery and Civil War

M ichigan's antislavery activity increased rapidly in just a few decades, beginning in the early nineteenth century. Slavery had been practiced in Michigan for hundreds of years with the original inhabitants; thus when Europeans arrived, their version of the institution was not wholly unfamiliar. Despite the Northwest Ordinance of 1787 forbidding slavery in Michigan, many residents continued to own slaves. However, as families moved to Michigan from New England, western New York, and Germany in the early nineteenth century, they brought with them a staunch opposition to slavery; accordingly, the practice in the Great Lakes state was eventually phased out. Michigan's antislavery activity became famous, so much so that Henry Clay of Kentucky dubbed the Great Lakes state the "hotbed of radicals and renegades." Michigan's opposition to slavery manifested in several forms, from the secretive work of the Underground Railroad to the outspoken Republican-majority state legislature in 1855, which passed laws that some people felt undermined the return of captured runaway slaves. Because of Michigan's antislavery sentiments, the state played an active role in the debates surrounding the controversial Fugitive Slave Law of 1850 and later the Civil War.

Quaker Abolitionist

Laura Haviland

The escape described in the following narrative took place in the 1830s.

Willis Hamilton, an emancipated slave, the hero of this narrative, who fled to Canada with his wife, Elsie, to seek for her the protection of the British lion from the merciless talons of the freedom-shrieking American eagle, was emancipated three years previous to the date of this chapter, together with nineteen others (the reputed goods and chattels of John Bayliss, a Baptist deacon, near Jonesborough, Tennessee [the narrative goes on to describe how Bayliss freed his slaves after some religious reflection]). . . .

Elsie, the wife of Willis Hamilton, belonged to a neighboring planter. She was sold to a drover for the Southern market, and was being torn from her husband and two little daughters. Willis, in his agony, went from house to house, imploring someone to buy her, so that she might remain near her family. Finally one Dr. John P. Chester, who was about opening a hotel, agreed to purchase Elsie for $800, if Willis would pay $300 in work in the house, and fare the same as the other servants in boards and clothing. With these conditions Willis gladly complied; but after they had spent a few months in their new home Deacon Bayliss examined their article of agreement and found it to be illegal. He told Willis that Dr. Chester could sell Elsie at any time, and he could establish no claim to her, even if he had paid the $300, which, at the wages he was receiving, would take him nearly nine years to earn, with the interest, and advised him to leave Dr. Chester and work for wages, as he had done since his manumission. This advice was immediately acted upon, Willis being permitted to spend his nights with his wife. Everything passed off pleasantly for a few weeks, until one of the house-servants told Elsie that she overheard Master John sell both her and Willis to a slave trader, who would the following night convey them to the river with a drove ready for New Orleans. Frantic as the poor woman was with the terror and grief at this information, she managed to perform her duties as usual until supper-time; and when all were seated at the table she slipped out unobserved, ran through a cornfield into the woods, sending word to Willis by a fellow servant to meet her at a certain log. The moment Willis received the message, he hastened to her with flying feet; and here the wretched husband and wife, but a few days before so full of plans for a pleasant future, held their council in tears.

Willis, in his sudden fright and excitement, could only exclaim: "What shall we do? Where shall we go?" Elsie, cooler and more composed, suggested going to Deacon

Bayliss for advice. This Willis quickly did, and soon returned, it having been arranged that he should bring Elsie there and secrete her in the attic until the excitement of the hunt was over. After this they assumed the names of Bill and Jane, a brother and sister who answered to their own description of color and size on Willis's free papers—the whole list of twenty slaves emancipated by Deacon Bayliss being recorded on each paper.

After five weeks hiding at the southern terminus of the "Underground Railroad," they took up their line of march for Canada. In a Quaker settlement in Indiana they found friends to whom they revealed their true relationship, and here they spent a year with a Quaker family named Shugart. But the slight protection afforded by the laws of Indiana did not tend to give them a feeling of security, and so they started again for the promised land with their infant daughter Louisa. . . .

As times were hard in Canada, Elsie consented to come to Michigan with her husband if he could find a Quaker neighborhood. In their search they found our house, and my husband, Charles Haviland, Jr., after learning their condition, leased Willis twenty acres of ground, mostly openings, for ten years, for the improvements he would make thereon. Here they lived for three years, when one day Elsie saw a strange man peering through the fence. Her first thought was "a Southerner," and snatching her two little ones she ran for our house, only a few rods distant. The man pursued her, and she called for help to a neighbor in sight, at this the skulking sneak took himself off to the woods. This incident so thoroughly aroused their fears that they took another farm, a few miles distant, for three years; then a farm near Ypsilanti for a few years; from whence they removed to Monroe, where they induced a friend to write to Willis's old friend and master, Deacon Bayliss, making inquiries after their two daughters, who were left behind in slavery. They received a prompt reply, purporting to come from Bayliss, informing them that their daughters were still living where they left them. He would see them, he said, by the time he received their next letter, which he hoped would be soon, that he might be the happy bearer of glad news to the children from their father and mother. He professed great joy at hearing from them, wished them to write all the particulars about themselves, but cautioned them to write to no one but him, and all would be safe. He requested them to inform him in what town they were living, as he noticed their letter was dated in one town, mailed in another, and he was directed to address them in a third. Their friend, however, strictly cautioned them not to reveal their definite whereabouts, but to answer all other queries. Willis wrote that as his farm lease had expired there, he would have to seek another farm, and did not know where he would be, but to address a letter as before and it would be forwarded to him.

Their next move was to return to their first Michigan home on my premises, a few months after the death of my husband, taking up their abode in the little log house built for them a few years before, and working my land on shares. Another letter was soon received from their friend Deacon Bayliss, as they supposed, and they urged me to reply; but I firmly refused to write to anyone in the land of the slaveholder, lest the message should fall into the hands of enemies.

From *A Woman's Life Work: Labors and Experiences of Laura S. Haviland* by Laura S. Haviland (Cincinnati: Walden and Stowe, 1882), 53, 55–58.

An Attempted Arrest of Fugitive Slaves

Signal of Liberty *(Ann Arbor, MI)*

February 6, 1847

Re-Capture of Slaves

Our village [of Marshall] was thrown into a fever of excitement day before yesterday, by an effort, on the part of four Kentuckians to arrest a family of colored persons, alleged to be fugitives from slavery, and take them back into slavery.

One of the Kentuckians was here a week or two ago, and on Monday night the rest of them arrived; on Wednesday morning about sunrise aided by constable Dixon, they proceeded to the house of Adam Crosswhite (a mulatto man) which they broke into and attempted to bring him and his family before a magistrate. A crowd soon collected; and some strong language and noisy demonstrations were made—the result of which was that the Kentuckians gave up the immediate pursuit of the object.

Meanwhile a civil action was commenced against them for breaking into Crosswhite's house. This was tried yesterday and resulted in a verdict of $100, and costs all against the Kentuckians.—Following it came an action of assault and battery on C. Hacket, a colored man, by one of the Kentuckians, which was in progress when we went to press.

The matter had induced a very considerable degree of excitement, and a great many stories are in circulation, which have no foundation. Crosswhite and his family left town yesterday, it is supposed for Canada. We understand that the Kentuckians do not propose to pursue them, but that they will prosecute certain of our citizens for damages, in preventing the capture of the colored people and aiding their escape.

Signal of Liberty, Ann Arbor, MI. This is available digitally through the Ann Arbor District library: http://signalofliberty.aadl.org/.

Abolitionist Resistance to Arrests

Signal of Liberty *(Ann Arbor, MI)*

April 24, 1847

Astounding News!
The Chivalry Aroused!
Michigan Abolitionism Used Up!!
The People of Marshall in Danger!!

We hasten to lay before our readers the following momentous disclosures, as we find them taken from the Kentucky "Commonwealth" of February 25th.

"For the Commonwealth

"At a meeting of the citizens of Trimble and Carroll counties, held at King's Tavern in the vicinity of Milton, [Kentucky] on Wednesday, the 10th of February, 1847, to take into consideration an outrage recently perpetrated by an abolition mob in the State of Michigan, upon the rights of an aged and respectable citizen of [Kentucky] . . .

"The meeting having been explained, addresses were delivered by Rufus King and Francis Troutman, setting forth in a concise and forcible manner, not only the grievances which this meeting has assembled to discuss, but the violence which is so frequently practiced on the rights of our citizens by the ultra abolitionists of Ohio, Indiana, and Michigan.

"At the conclusion of those remarks, the following preamble and resolutions were offered and unanimously adopted.

"Whereas, it is represented to this meeting that Francis Troutman of the county of Bourbon, and State of Kentucky, was employed and empowered as the agent of Francis Giltner, of the county of Carroll and the State aforesaid, to proceed to the town of Marshall [in the] State of Michigan, to apprehend and reclaim six fugitive slaves, who had absconded from the possession of said Giltner to the said town of Marshall: And where, the said Troutman, as the agent aforesaid, in company with David Giltner, Franklin Ford, and James Lee, did proceed to the town of Marshall and arrest said fugitive slaves according to law, and that said Troutman and others were prevented from executing the trust confided in them by an abolition mob.

"Therefore, be it Resolved by this Meeting, That a committee . . . [is] hereby requested to wait upon the Legislature of this Commonwealth, in company with Francis Troutman . . . and make known to said body the outrage and violence which was perpetrated upon . . . Troutman and others, by an abolition mob, while attempting peaceably and lawfully to discharge their duty as aforesaid; and to request the Legislature to memorialize, through their Governor, the Legislature of Michigan, upon the subject; and also to request the

Legislature of this Commonwealth, if they deem it proper and expedient, to instruct their
Senators, and request their Representatives in Congress to take the matter into consideration
and to insist upon the passage of a law by Congress, making the offence of engaging in such
a mob punishable by imprisonment, in addition to the present penalty; and to request the
Legislature to furnish all such aid and assistance as may be in their power to enable said
Giltner to obtain redress from said grievance . . ."

We cannot pretend to fathom, with our feeble intellect, all the mighty results which
may grow out of this indignation meeting of the chivalrous Kentuckians, held at "King's
Tavern."—Some of them, however, we will allude to. We dare say that the landlord of
the said "Tavern" where this mighty "meeting" was held, made more out of the affair
than any other person has done, or will do. There can be no question that this meeting,
composed probably of a dozen or two of neighboring loungers and loafers, was of a
most spirited character; and that the exalted character of the proceedings was mainly
derived from the inspiriting draughts of the bar room. Mr. Francis Troutman, also,
being by this meeting constituted ex officio a lobby member for the next Kentucky
Legislature, may thereby make something. Who knows but he may look up for himself
a snug office, that will compensate him for the shame and loss of his disastrous journey
to Marshall, and this make good to come of evil?

But let us look to the measures proposed by the Chivalry. The first is "to request
the Legislature to memorialize the Legislature of Michigan, through their Governor."
We should like to see that memorial, and note the action taken upon it by our Legislative Doughfaces. But we want to see a first rate spirited document—none of your flat,
stale, concerns. As an encouragement to the Kentucky Legislature to get up something
really respectable, we hereby promise in advance to circulate it through the State at
our own cost and expense. Is that not fair?

But something more stringent is contemplated; nothing less than "imprisonment"
of all northern men who may presume to interfere with a Kentuckian doing just as
he pleases with any "nigger" whom he can find! Yes, and the Kentucky members of
Congress are "to insist" upon the passage of such a law by Congress! Who can doubt
but it will be done forthwith?

Nor is this all. The Kentucky Legislature are to be requested "to furnish all such
assistance as may be in their power to enable said Giltner to obtain redress from said
grievance."

Does not this make the people of Marshall to tremble? Who can tell what schemes
of vengeance against them may be devised in retaliation for their infamous treatment
of Mr. "Francis Troutman"? Perhaps they would do well to call a public meeting,
and by denouncing and disavowing the "abolition mob," make their peace with Mr.

Troutman before the retribution of the Chivalry shall fall upon them, involving the innocent with the guilty. We shall forward a copy of this number of our paper to the Frankfort Commonwealth, and if, through that paper, any offers of mercy for the Marshall people shall reach us, we will apprise them thereof forthwith.

Signal of Liberty, Ann Arbor, MI. This is available digitally through the Ann Arbor District library: http://signalofliberty.aadl.org/.

Michigan Right at Last

Wolverine Citizen *(Flint, MI)*

February 3, 1855

The following are the Joint Resolutions of Instruction referred to in our Lansing correspondence [adopted by the Michigan State Senate, directed to the U.S. representatives and senators of Michigan]. They breathe the true spirit which actuated the founders of our Government; and speak out openly, unequivocally and nobly, the sentiments of Republican Freedom, and the sense of the people of Michigan.

Resolved, That the act of Congress of 1850, known as the Fugitive Slave Law, was, in the opinion of the people of this State, an unnecessary measure; that it contains provisions of doubtful constitutionality; that the mode of proceeding under it is harsh, unjust and repugnant to the moral sense of the people of the States, cruel and despotic toward the person claimed as a fugitive, and that we are in favor of its immediate repeal.

Resolved, That our Senators in Congress be, and they are hereby instructed, and our Representatives requested, to use their best exertions to procure the immediate repeal of the act of 1850, known as the Fugitive Slave Law.

"Michigan Right at Last," *Wolverine Citizen*, February 3, 1855.

Michigan and Massachusetts "Personal Liberty" Bills

Detroit Free Press

Between 1855 and 1860, Michigan enacted three "personal liberty bills," ostensibly to protect free blacks from wrongful kidnapping by slave catchers, who then might sell free persons into slavery. Northern Democrats and southerners vehemently opposed these bills, claiming the personal liberty laws were attempts to subvert the Constitution and

federal fugitive slave laws, especially that of 1850. Michigan's personal liberty laws were
patterned on other northern states' laws, particularly Massachusetts. The following
article refers to Joseph Hiss, a disgraced Know-Nothing leader from Massachusetts.

November 8, 1855

If the "personal liberty bill," the product of the legislature at Lansing last winter, is not in all respects as atrocious an enactment as the bill of the same title under which the good name of Massachusetts is smarting, it is because of the fact that Michigan fanaticism had not attained the same intensity as Massachusetts frenzy. The design of the Lansing confederates was as aggressive as that of the rascals among whom Hiss was a choice spirit, but they had not so sublimated the spirit of treason—they had not so refined the essence of rebellion—as to frame an act which would so fully do justice to the dark purposes they had in view as the older and more practiced Massachusetts malcontents were competent to do. But the framers of our "personal liberty bill" are apt scholars in iniquitous schemes, and would, at another trial, bound at a single effort up to the mark of New England resistance. Next year, with power, they would put up a "personal liberty bill" that would challenge the admiration of GARRISON himself.

The Massachusetts act is not more nullification than the Michigan act. Both have in view effectual repudiation of the constitutional requisition of fugitive slaves.

"Michigan and Massachusetts 'Personal Liberty' Bills," *Detroit Free Press*, November 8, 1855.

The Black Republican Party and the Fugitive Slave Law
Detroit Free Press

November 18, 1860

Some of the black republican papers through the country are declaring that their party has never nullified the fugitive slave law! The audacity of the declaration is unsurpassed by any piece of audacity on record. The whole and sole object of the "personal liberty bills" which have been passed in those States where the black republicans have had the legislative power has been to nullify the fugitive slave law. The legislation of Michigan in this respect is a fair specimen of that of the other black republican States; and we propose, now, that a time has arrived when we can perhaps induce the public to look at it, to make an exhibition of this legislation. We refer the reader to Act No. 162, on page 413, of the session laws of 1855, (that being the first year of black republican power in this State,) entitled "An act to protect the rights and liberties of the people of this State." We subjoin the act at length:

"Section 1. *The people of the State of Michigan enact,* That it shall be the duty of the Prosecuting Attorneys within their respective counties, whenever any inhabitant of this State is arrested or claimed as a fugitive slave, on being informed thereof, diligently and faithfully to use all lawful means to protect and defend every such person so arrested or claimed as a fugitive slave.

"Sec. 2. All persons so arrested and claimed as fugitive slaves shall be entitled to all the benefits of the writ of habeas corpus and of trial by jury. . . .

"Sec. 5. No person arrested and claimed as a fugitive slave shall be imprisoned in any jail or other prison in this State; and any person having the care or control of ay jail or prison, and knowingly permitting the imprisonment of such alleged fugitive slave therein, shall be subjected to the payment of a fine not less than five hundred nor more than one thousand dollars [adjusted for inflation, this penalty would amount to roughly $12,800 to $25,600 in 2015].

"Sec. 6. Every person who shall falsely declare, represent, or pretend that any free person entitled to freedom is a slave, or owes service or labor to any person or persons, with intent to procure, or aid or assist in procuring, the forcible removal of such free person from this State as a slave, shall be imprisoned not less than three nor more than five years in the State Prison.

"Sec. 7. Every person who shall wrongfully and maliciously seize, or procure to be seized, any free person entitled to freedom, with intent to have such person held in slavery, shall pay a fine of not less than five hundred nor more than one thousand dollars, and be imprisoned five years in the State prison.

"Sec. 8. In all cases arising under the provisions of sections six and seven of this act, the truth of any declaration, representation, or pretence, that any person being or having been in this State is or was a slave, or owes or did owe service or labor to any other person or persons, shall not be deemed proved except by the testimony of at least two credible witnesses, testifying to fact directly tending to establish the truth of such declaration, pretence, or representation, or by legal evidence equivalent thereto.

"Sec. 9. No declaration, pretence, or representation, that any person is or was an apprentice for a fixed number of years, or owes or did owe service mere as such apprentice for such fixed term, shall be deemed prohibited by this act; and no such declaration, pretence, or representation, that any person is or was such an apprentice for such fixed term, or owes or did owe service merely as such an apprentice for such fixed term, shall be liable to any penalty under this act.

Sec. 10. All acts or parts of acts conflicting with the provisions of this act are hereby repealed.

"Approved February 13, 1855."

The second section of this act is in direct conflict with the fugitive slave law, that law prescribing, with great particularity, the method of ascertaining whether a negro claimed as a fugitive be such or not, such method denying to him both a writ of habeas corpus and trial by jury.

The third section is equally in conflict with the fugitive slave law, since all the proceedings under that law are required to be had before a Judge or Commissioner of a Circuit or District Court of the United States, whose decisions in the case are final, and with whose proceedings State courts have no concern whatever. . . .

The fifth section cannot be said to be exactly in conflict with the fugitive slave law, but its design, to obstruct the execution of the law, is transparent. From the formation of the government until the passage of these personal liberty bills the jails of all the States had been granted to all the uses of the Federal government, and it is only to uses of the fugitive slave law that they are now denied by the antislavery States. And then observe the severity of the penalty for a violation of the section by any jailer. The spirit of the section is just this: If there can be no places in which alleged fugitives can be securely confined pending their examination, mobs will have an opportunity to rescue them from the custody of the Federal officers.

The remaining sections are of no consequence in this connection.

The act, altogether, is the most complete and effective nullification of the fugitive slave law that could be devised. . . .

The black republican party "has never nullified the fugitive slave law"! We wish we could say that it had never done anything else. It has nullified it so entirely in those States where it has passed these personal liberty bills that all efforts to execute it in such States have been abandoned. It is practically a dead letter in such States, made so deliberately and maliciously—made so as an act of aggression against the South—made so to fan the flames of antislavery fanaticism in the North and excite the South to the very state of feeling which threatens the most disastrous consequences to the country.

Nor is this all. Michigan has another statute which is something worse than mere nullification of the fugitive slave law. It is as follows, and may be found on page 526 of the session laws of 1859:

"Section 1. *The People of the State of Michigan enact,* That section twenty-five, of said chapter one hundred and fifty-three, be amended to read as follows:

"Sec. 25. Every person who willfully, and without lawful authority, shall forcibly or secretly confine or imprison any other person within this State against his will, or shall forcibly carry or send such person out of this State, or shall forcibly seize and confine, or shall inveigle or kidnap, any other person, with intent either to cause such person to be secretly confined or imprisoned in this State against his will, or to be sold as a slave, or in any way held to serve against his will, and every person who shall sell, or in any manner transfer for any time, the service or labor of any negro, mulatto, or other person of color, who shall have been unlawfully seized, taken, inveigled, or kidnapped from this State, to any other State, place, or country, *or who shall bring any negro, mulatto, or other person of color into the State claiming him or her as a slave, shall be punished by imprisonment in the State Prison not more than ten years, or by fine not exceeding one thousand dollars.*

"Approved February 15, 1859."

The atrocity of this statute will strike the reader at once. The southern man who enters or passes through the State with his negro servant commits a penitentiary offence! It marks slaveholding as a crime, and places the slaveholder upon a level with the burglar or horse thief. It is an act of hostility on the whole South, and the only marvel is that it has not produced acts of retaliation in every southern State.

Nobody need wonder at the excitement in the South. It is the political party in the North whose legislation this is which has elected ABRAHAM LINCOLN to the Presidency. With what potency the disunion leaders use this fact among the southern people, and how powerless are the Union men with such a fact staring them in the face.

And now, that Lincoln is elected, do the black republican leaders want to save the Union or do they not? If they do, a conservative Baltimore paper points out the way. "We say then," is the language of the Baltimore *Exchange*, "to the people of the North . . . simply this: The solution of the present crisis in in their hands—its peaceful, happy, perfect and final solution. If they would have the South to be moderate, let them be just. If they would be believed, let them seal their good faith by intelligible and unequivocal action. Let them repeal their obnoxious and unconstitutional legislation—let the responsible leaders of the republican party even pledge themselves to that repeal—and we do not hesitate to say that within a week there will be peace and rejoicing over the whole South—even where the banners of disunion rustle thickest. This is what the people of Maryland think they have a right to ask from the North. Is it not right? Is it not fair? No patriot can deny that it is both, and we will trust the patriotism of no quarter of the Republic which is not willing to carry it out."

From "Black Republican Party and the Fugitive Slave Law," *Detroit Free Press*, November 18, 1860.

Personal Liberty Bills

Cass County Republican *(Dowagiac, MI)*

December 6, 1860

While the Democratic press and Southern politicians are making so much fuss about "personal liberty bills," it is well for the people to understand fully what they are, and to what they owe their origin. It is for making of laws for a State, the Legislature is amenable only to the Constitution of the State under which they act and from which they derive their powers. If there be anything wrong in the Constitution the members of the Legislature are no more responsible than the man in the moon, as the people received the Constitution from the hands of the Convention which formed it, and by their votes to approve it, they have laid an absolute duty upon the legislatures which set under it, to fulfil its requirements. In this State, the Constitution was framed by the Democratic party—such men as Storey, McCelland, Goodwin, Butterfield, and their compeers having made it. If they put into it anything violative of the Constitution of the United States, it was perjury on their part, and the duty of the people to reject their work; but they having approved it, it became the guide of those who are elected to fulfil and act under its provisions and commands.

Article 6, section 26 of the Constitution of this State provides that "the persons, houses, papers and possessions of *every person* shall be secure from unreasonable searches and seizures." The next section, 27, says "the right of trial by jury shall remain." Section 32 provides that "no *person* shall be deprived of life, *Liberty* or property without due process of law." Article 13, sec. 11, provides that "neither slavery or involuntary servitude, unless for the punishment for a crime, *shall ever be tolerated* in this State."

Now the question arises, do those provisions conflict with the Constitution of the United States. Article I., sec. IX, subdivision 2, provides that "the writ of Habeas Corpus shall not be suspended except in the case of rebellion or invasion, the public safety require it." Article VI of Amendments provides that the right of trial by jury shall not be waived, and art. VIII, that "excessive bail shall not be required, nor excessive fines imposed, nor cruel and unusual punishment inflicted. Article 6, provides that *no person* shall be deprived of life, liberty or property without due process of law." Subdivision 2, of art. VI. provides that the Constitution and the laws *made in pursuance thereof* shall be the Supreme law of the land, and that *judges* in every State shall be bound thereby.

Now the question is simply is the Fugitive Slave Law Constitutional. It is not enough to say that it has never been decided unconstitutional. It suspends the writ of Habeas Corpus; it denies the right of trial by jury, and allows the taking of personal property without due process of law.

The personal liberty bill of this State was not passed to prevent the rendition of Fugitive Slaves, but it simply restores the guaranties provided in the Constitutions in both the State and the United States, which were torn down by the Fugitive Slave Law. We append the following abstract of the law of this State, and ask every reader to compare it with the provisions above cited. It will be found in the session of laws of 1855, p. 413, and in the compiled laws of 1857, title 37, chapter 77. Its title is "An Act to protect the rights and liberties of the people of this State," and is as follows:

§ 1, Requires State's Attorneys to set as counsel for fugitives.

§ 1, 3, and 4, Grant habeas corpus, provide for trial by jury.

§ 5, Forbids use of jails, or other prisons, to detain fugitives.

§ 6, Provides a punishment of not less than three nor more than five years, for falsely declaring, representing, or pretending, any person to be a slave.

§ 7, Provides a fine of not less than $500 nor more than $1000, an imprisonment in State Prison for five years, for forcibly seizing or causing to be seized, any free person, with intent to have such person held in slavery.

§ 8, Requires two witnesses to prove any person to be a slave.

This is a correct abstract of the law, and gives faithfully its whole spirit and intent. And is there anything that a free man of a free State should complain of? It simply requires that before a person, claimed as a fugitive, be remanded to slavery, the claimant shall prove before a jury that he is a slave. It throws the whole burden of proof upon the Slaveholder, and relieves the State from all agency or responsibility in the matter. She occupies a *neutral* position in slave hunting. . . .

The edict has gone forth that all the Northern States must repeal these personal liberty bills—must submit to this new, novel and unwarranted construction of the Constitution; must allow the Supreme Court to sweep away every vestige of State Sovereignty; must stultify their Constitutions; must make all their laws subordinate to the whims, caprices and convenience of the slaveholders, or they will blot out and destroy every vestige of the Constitution and the Union, which is as necessary to them as to us. Modest demand! Sensible men they who second and sustain it! Repeal our personal liberty bills? Never, till the South return to the observance and construction of the Constitution as those who made it construed and observed it. Never, till the South give up its insolent and insulting claims to the supremacy of Slavery over every other right or privilege pertaining to the Union of States. Never—until the unjust, oppressive, tyrannical and unconstitutional Fugitive Slave Law is modified. Never—until the rights of free speech liberty and life and the privileges of citizens, guaranteed by the Constitution, are allowed to Northern men in all the States of the Union. Never—while disloyalty to the Constitution breaks out at every attempt of the people of the North to use the right of suffrage in a proper and constitutional manner. Never—until the South respects all the compacts she voluntarily enters into, and give up her designs to plant and extend slavery into our Free Territories. Never—until the Counsels of Humanity, Equality and Justice enter more largely into the actions and conscience of the people of the slaveholding States. When these things come to pass, personal liberty bills will become dead letters upon our Statute Books, otherwise they will never be blotted out until every instinct of Liberty has died out of the human heart, and the Infinite Creator has ceased to create Free Men.

"Personal Liberty Bills," *Cass County Republican*, December 6, 1860.

Farewell Message

Governor Moses Wisner

January 1, 1861

You are asked [by Democrats and Southerners] to repeal certain laws upon our statute books, known as "Personal Liberty bills," which are claimed to be in conflict with the Constitution, and defeat the execution of the "Fugitive Slave Law," and deprive our Southern brothers the right of temporary sojournment in our State with their slaves. If these laws are unconstitutional, and in conflict with the provisions of the fugitive slave law, then most certainly they should be repealed. The Constitution, and the laws of the United States, made in pursuance thereof, are the Supreme law of the land, and as such, are entitled to our highest consideration and respect.

The [Michigan] Legislature of 1855, passed two laws which met the approval of my immediate predecessor. The first is entitled "An Act to protect the rights and liberties of the people of this State." At the time of its passage, Michigan contained more than five thousand free colored citizens, each of whom was liable to be seized and forcibly taken into some distant slave State and there sold into captivity. These citizens were as orderly and law abiding as an equal number of our white people in the same station of life, and it was the duty of the State to protect them in the free enjoyment of all their rights. This law was designed for their protection and not for the purpose of violating the Constitution or preventing the execution of the fugitive slave law. It never has interfered with its execution. The President [Buchanan], in his message, tells us that the fugitive slave law has been carried into execution in every contested case since the commencement of his administration. The fugitive slave law is to be executed exclusively from the Federal Courts and its commissioners and marshals, and not by the State authorities. There is no part in the statute of our State that contemplates interfering with the judicial proceedings of the Federal Courts in the execution of the fugitive slave law. . . . The law was passed to protect the free colored citizen from "forcible removal from the State as a slave" and to punish his kidnapper. True, the act prohibits confining in our jails. . . . Has not Michigan exclusive control over her jails? Neither the Constitution of the United States, the fugitive slave law of 1793, nor the amendatory act of 1850, makes provision for or contemplates that the fugitive shall or may be confined in our jails. The government of the United States has her forts, arsenals, custom houses and marshals at her command, and is abundantly able to guard the fugitive from rescue without resorting to our jails for protection. . . . The Third and last "personal liberty bill" upon our statutes, is the act of the Legislature of 1859, approved by me on the 15th day of February of that year.

This law has been in force in our State for the past twenty-two years, with the exception of two lines in the act, which prohibits bringing "any negro, mulatto or other person of color into the State, claiming him or her as a slave." It is against these two lines that our southern brothers take offense, and you are asked to repeal the law because it prevents them from sojourning in our State with their slaves. I deny their right to bring their slaves into the State and hold them here as such for one moment. . . . The decision thus far has been uniform, that slavery is local in its character and cannot exist in the absence of positive law. That where the master voluntarily takes his slave into a free State, that moment "his shackles fall," and he is no longer a bondsman. . . . Our fathers, in 1787, spread over Michigan an ordinance which declares that "there shall never be slavery or involuntary servitude in the said Territory . . ." and twice since Michigan came into the Union have her people adopted a Constitution containing the same sentiment. It is an organic law of the State, and who can doubt the right of the [Michigan] Legislature to pass laws punishing the violators of that instrument?

Farewell message of Governor Moses Wisner, January 1, 1861, in *Messages of the Governors of Michigan*, vol. 3, edited by George Fuller (Lansing: Michigan Historical Commission, 1927), 411–12.

The Rights of the State of Michigan
Governor Austin Blair

January 2, 1861

Of what acts do the slaveholding States complain? In what have they been oppressed? We have had an abundance of eloquent speech from them, and endless general complaint of aggressions upon them and their rights. But the charge still lacks speci-fication. I deny the whole indictment. There have been no such aggressions. No right of theirs has been denied or refused to them by us. Our personal liberty laws furnish an example of no such denial. They were enacted for the protection and safety of free citizens of the State against kidnappers, and with no view to defeating the reclamation of actual fugitive slaves, under the law of Congress. That law is so entirely wanting in the usual safeguards against abuse of its provisions, that there is constant danger of its being used as a cover for the most nefarious practices. Michigan is a sovereign and independent State, and her first and highest duty is to guard the rights and liberties of her people. This she has sought to do by the laws in question. It is altogether her own affair, and with all due respect to the States of the South, she does not hold herself under obligation to justify her conduct in this regard to them.

The state only seeks to maintain her rights under the constitution and laws of Congress.

Austin Blair, Message to the Michigan Legislature, January 2, 1861, in *Messages of the Governors of Michigan*, vol. 3, edited by George Fuller (Lansing: Michigan Historical Commission, 1927), 439–40.

The Female Spy of the Union Army

Sarah Emma Edmonds

Looking to offer more than what a woman was typically allowed in America's Civil War, Sarah Emma Edmonds disguised herself as a man and enlisted with the Michigan Second Infantry under the name Frank Thompson. In the army, she served as a nurse, mail carrier, and spy—her most effective disguise, some claim, was dressing as a woman. The following two documents relate, in her own words, how she broke her leg in the service of the country, just before the outbreak of the Second Battle of Bull Run. Her intended audiences of each piece may account for the disparities.

We started for the village, and had gone about five miles when we were suddenly sur-prised and fired upon by [Confederate] guerillas. Two of our men were killed on the spot, and my horse received three bullets. He reared and plunged before he fell, and in doing so, the saddle-girth was broken, and saddle and rider were thrown over his head. I was thrown on the ground violently which stunned me for a moment, and my horse soon fell beside me, his blood pouring from three wounds. Making a desperate effort to rise, he groaned once, fell back, and throwing his neck across my body, he saturated me from head to foot with his blood. He died in a few minutes. I remained in that position, not daring to rise, for our party had fled and the rebels pursued them. A very few minutes elapsed when the guerillas returned, and the first thing I saw was one of the them thrusting his sabre into one of the dead men beside me. I was lying partially on my face, so I closed my eyes and passed for dead. The rebels evidently thought I was unworthy of their notice, for after searching the bodies of the two dead men they rode away; but as I was making up my mind to crawl out from under the dead horse, I heard the tramp of a horse's feet, and lay perfectly still and held my breath. It was one of the same men, who had returned. Dismounting, he came up and took hold of my feet, and partially drew me from under the horse's head, and then examined my pockets. Fortunately, I had no official documents with me, and very little money—not more than five dollars. After transferring the contents of my pockets to his own, he remounted his horse and rode away, without ever suspecting that the object before him was playing possum.

Not long after the departure of the guerillas, our party returned with reinforcements and pursued the rebel band. One of the men returned to camp with me, letting me ride his horse, and walked all the way himself. The guerillas were captured that day, and, after searching them, my pocketbook was found upon one of them, and was returned to me with its contents undisturbed. It lies before me, while I write, reminding me of that narrow escape, and of the mercy of God in sparing my unprofitable life.

After returning to camp, I found that I had sustained more injury by my fall from the horse than I had realized at the time. But a broken limb would have been borne cheerfully, if I could only have pet my horse again.

From *The Female Spy of the Union Army* by Sarah Emma Edmonds (Boston: DeWolfe, Fiske, & Co., 1864), 294–96.

How I Was Wounded

Sarah Emma Edmonds

September 24, 1896

Dear Sir [John Wedderburn, who was most likely her lawyer]:

Your favor of fifth inst. came duly to hand, and in replying I can but reiterate my former statement, as it is simply impossible for me to obtain testimony from "eye witnesses" to the injuries which I received when thrown from the mule, as formerly stated. I was entirely alone, there was not a soul within miles of me, as far as I know, when the accident occurred.

I now make this statement under oath, that at the time of said accident to my left side and left lower limb, I was occupying a position of trust and responsibility and that I was then the bearer of mail and important documents to troops who were then in line of battle near Centerville, and was making every effort in my power to reach them before they became engaged in action.

I tried to save time by taking short cuts across fields, etc., and after overcoming many obstacles, leaping fences and ditches without much difficulty, I attempted to cross a very wide ditch, but instead of leaping across it the mule tumbled headlong into it, throwing one with such force as to render me helpless—then falling on me and almost crushed the life out of me. While in that condition, unable to get out of his way, I was trampled upon by the mule in his frantic struggle to extricate himself—which was difficult, the mud being deep in the bottom of the ditch.

How long I remained in that condition I do not know. The first I remember was the booming of cannon—then the thought flashed across my brain "The Mail! The Mail!" With almost superhuman effort I scrambled to my feet, but found I had no use of my left leg—I felt sure it was broken, and the intense pain in my left side and breast, made one feel sick and faint. I looked around and saw the mule standing a few rods distant, patiently waiting for me—with saddle and mail bags hanging underneath him, covered with mud. Slowly and painfully I made my way to him, and at once set about readjusting the saddle and mail bags—but how to get on the mule's back was the question; but after many exhausting and ineffectual efforts to remount, I bethought one of a long rope halter around his neck, of which I made a ladder, and fastened it to the pommel of the saddle. On that ladder I crawled up little by little, until I reached the stirrup, and once more got into the saddle. I then started for the battlefield with the utmost speed that I could endure, and after extreme suffering reached Headquarters, and delivered the mail, etc. But I made no report of the injuries received, except to state that the mule fell down with me, and hurt my leg. But when the battle was over and the troops went into Camp, I was obliged to ask Doctor Vickery for some soothing lotion for my wounds.

Thus, you see, being miles away from my Company and Regiment neither surgeons nor Comrades could give testimony as "eye witnesses," not to the extent of the injuries I received—especially as I took the utmost pains to conceal the facts in the case.

Had I been what I represented myself to be, I should have gone to the hospital and had the surgeon make an examination of my injuries, and placed myself in his hand for medical treatment—and saved years of suffering. But being a woman I felt compelled to suffer in silence and endure it the best I could, in order to escape detection of my sex. I would rather have been shot dead than to have been known to be a woman and sent away from the Army under guard as a Criminal.

Sarah Emma Edmonds to John Wedderburn, September 24, 1896, from "Sarah Emma Edmonds Pension" collection, Civil War Trust, http://www.civilwar.org.

My Escape from a Speculator

William Webb

Webb's account is an excellent look into attitudes of Michigan residents during the Civil War. It is very important to understand that even though most Michiganians were antislavery advocates, they were not racially tolerant.

The Yankee soldiers landed at Paducah, Kentucky. I went down to see them once in a while. My master thought I was going to run away and stay with the Yankee soldiers. A crowd of the slaveholders came and bound me with ropes and carried me down to the blacksmith shop, and put a shackle around my ankle and a six foot chain fastened to it, and he took me to a speculator nine miles from Mayfield. Those men that carried me to the speculator, told him to keep me bound tight, for I was a dangerous man, and if he did not mind, I would get away from him. We got there on Sunday evening. The speculator put me upstairs in his house, and what he was going to do to with me, I am not able to say. That night a voice spoke to me, saying "be of good cheer, I will be along with you." When the morning came, it come to my mind what I must do. I went down to breakfast and I said to the old colored woman, who looked as if she was seventy years old, to give me a small file. She got a file and handed it to me and I slipped it into my pocket. She said, you are that man I have heard so much about [Webb was viewed as a sort of prophet among slaves in and around his community], and I know you will not betray me. I told her that I would never betray her in the world. Then I called the speculator and told him I wanted to go upstairs again. He carried me upstairs, and I told him I would like some rags to wrap around that shackle, it was hurting my ankle. He gave me some rags, and I wrapped them around the shackle and some of the links. I did that in order to file the chain off, and if he came up, I could wrap the rags around and he would not notice it. I filed the chain, and got through about two hours before sunset, and when the chain parted, it appeared to me as if it opened an inch wide. I tied a rotten string around the chain, so that I could break it easy, and I wrapped the rags around it the same as I had them. I looked out the window and marked out my way to escape, when night came on. When night came, he carried me down to supper. After he carried me down, I told him I wanted to go out in the yard. It was dark, and when the speculator took me out in the yard I broke the chain and escaped. I had twenty-seven miles to go to Paducah, Kentucky, to get to the Union soldiers. The next morning by sunrise, I was in Paducah. . . .

I left [Peru, Indiana] and came to Detroit, and I went out Fort street west, five miles, and chopped wood all winter. The cemetery [Woodmere Cemetery] is on the spot where I chopped wood. While I was out there a riot occurred [Riot of 1863] in the city, and a great many colored people were fleeing out in the country where I was, and some came to the house where I was stopping to get shelter, both men and women. They said there was a great many bad feeling white people in the neighborhood, and they did not know whether they were safe themselves. I said to Mr. Robinson, we had better be on guard. He asked me what I thought it was best to do. I told him to fix what guns we had in the house, and get what we could in the neighborhood, and he did as I advised him. We put a guard around the place, so that if they saw any people coming, to give the alarm. We sat up and watched all night, but everything went off quiet. I came to the city the next day to see what damage they had done. The colored people were very scarce in the places I had been used to see them, and I found that some had run over into Canada, and some of them had run into the woods. A great many gentlemen said it was a great pity they had such a cruel riot, and I asked them if there was no law to prevent such a mob, and they said there was no laws for a mob. I said I think it is a very queer country that has no laws to protect people. They said yes, that is so. The next spring I came into town, and commenced whitewashing, and in working around, I whitewashed for the mayor of the city that spring [since this event could be in 1863 or 1864, the mayor to whom Webb refers is either William C. Duncan or Kirkland C. Barker]. We got into a little dispute about the work, and I talked to him with the best manners I could. He ran up to me and told me to hush, that he did not allow niggers to talk to him.

[This next section comes later in Webb's narrative, but it took place earlier chronologically.]

I made up my mind to get a paper when I arrived at Detroit. When I got here I put up at the North Star House. The next morning the boy came along with a paper called the Free Press. I had never bought a paper before in my life, and concluded to buy a paper that morning. I bought the Free Press, and hired a boy to read it to me, and the boy read it to me. I thought it was the most curious free paper I ever heard. . . . It seemed to me that it sided with the rebels, and being in a free State, I was surprised. I could not understand it. I thought the boy had made a mistake in reading it. I thought surely it must be a friend to the colored people, being named the Free Press. The next morning the boy brought around the Free Press again, and I thought I would buy it again. I hired another boy to read it to me, and told him to read about the colored people, but it talked so bitter against them that I could not understand it, yet I was not satisfied about the paper. I thought the boy had not read the paper right, for I thought by the name of the paper it must be a friend to the colored people. I thought I would buy another one next morning. That one I took to a lady, and asked her to read it to me so that I could understand it. I told her to read about the colored people. She read the paper to me, and after she had finished reading it, I asked her to tell me something about that paper, that I thought it was a paper that wanted everybody to be free. She told me it was not in favor of the colored people being free, and from that day to this, I have often wondered how it came to take such a glorious name, when it was so bitterly opposed to the colored people having their freedom, and wondered how an educated nation could be so opposed to an oppressed and ignorant people, when they were the cause of our being in this new land. I often thought it would take better views of the matter than it had done, because it makes dissatisfaction and hard feelings in the country when there is no necessity for it, brings mobs and violence on a weak class of people, when there is no need of it, and if they measure such as that out to the colored people, it will be measured back to them, again, and I hope hereafter they will take a more religious view of the matter.

From *The History of William Webb, Composed by Himself*
(Detroit: Egbert Hoekstra, Printer, 1873), 30–31, 38–39, 66–67.

Michigan's Boy Soldier

Corydon Foote

Foote enlisted with the Tenth Michigan Infantry in 1862 when he was thirteen years old. Because he was so young, his parents were obliged to consent to their son's enlistment. As one of the regiment's drummers, and perhaps because of his age, Foote avoided direct combat. Still, he witnessed devastations and horrors that come with war.

Nashville, Tennessee
January 28, 1863

Dear Parents, Having answered a letter that I received from George and now take the opportunity to answer your kind letter which I received last night and the night before I received one from George and have answered. The ninth Michigan is at Murfreesboro. I did not find out in time to see Del Parcels. I am selling news papers for an old man. He pays me good for it. I have [gone] in the other regiments and sell them for him. There is two or three of the boys writing by one candle and I cannot hardly see. . . .

My company is on picket tonight. I am glad that I do not have to stand picket for they will suffer tonight for it is cold now as we have had since I came down south. There was a fire in the town today. It did not amount to much. I was down to it. There was one engine there. They have got steam engines here. They are nice, I tell you. . . .

I had an accident while peddling my papers. There is a dog where I go sell my papers and I had just been in . . . and was just coming out when the dog bite me. It was a pretty good bite. I put tobacco on it and it feels better. I guess that it will get well.

Nashville, Tennessee
May 15, 1863

Dear parents, I now take my pen in hand to write you a few lines and as I had a few moments and I thought I would improve them by writing you a few lines and tell you what is going on here. You have heard I suppose that there was a man to be shot in our regiment. There was. And he was shot today. We all went over where he was to [be] shot. The whole division was out and it was like going on inspection instead of going to see a man shot. We went out on the Sally white Pike in a large open field and we were all in hollow square except one side then the Ambulance came in and they sat his coffin down and then he sat down and the priest stayed with him a while and then they blind folded him and then they gave the command fire and he threw up his arms and fell back. His legs was on the coffin. 4 bullets went through his heart and the other two was about 6 inches from his heart. He never stirred only put up his hands once. It looked hard to see a man set down on his coffin and see his grave and know he is to die there. I hope I may never have to see the same. You want to know of course what he done. He deserted three times, and this time he paid the penalty of the law.

Corydon Foote to his Parents, January 28 and May 15, 1863, as transcribed by the Perry Archives, Sloan Museum, Flint, accession numbers 1965.37.

CHAPTER 8

The White Pine Era: The Lumber Industry

Following the Civil War, Michigan's lumber industry boomed. The amount of timber produced by Michigan loggers for decades far exceeded that of other states. Michigan's logging activity gave rise to new inventions, such as Silas Overpack's "Big Wheel," manufactured in Manistee; it helped expand Michigan's railroad network, especially areas in northern Michigan after logging companies realized the benefit of shipping logs by rail instead of sled; and it gave rise to mythical figures such as Paul Bunyan and the lesser-known Silver Jack. Nearly every aspect of the industry was dangerous. Unfortunately, there were few efforts to sustain the industry. Great expanses were clear-cut, and by the turn of the twentieth century the industry was in rapid decline. It is possible, however, to witness today centuries-old tree stands by visiting Hartwick Pines near Grayling.

Diary of a Timber Scout

G. Olin Bignell

Timber scouts worked for lumber companies by surveying areas and its available tree stands. They would report that information back to the company, which would then make plans to cut those stands. G. Olin Bignell most likely scouted in the Muskegon area.

August 5, 1873

Breakfast bread hardtack and pork.

    We are off this morning goodly old shanty you have served as a good house but I hope never to see you again. Bought two pound sugar of [illegible word] Hooper. Went down to town line corner of 13 & 24 went north half a mile turned S.E. in a short time struck a swamp which was fearful. Chap lost his hatchet. Are camped in the swamp beside a creek no dinner today. Supper bread hardtack and pork.

August 6, 1873

After a breakfast of bread hardtack & pork we packed up and went for the swamp of which we took about half a mile it was not as bad as we went through yesterday being more free from underbrush. I find these swamps are wearing on my feet as I am not sure of my hold when I step. My feet will push through and catch on a root or limb and there is a continual strain on my ankle. We struck the state road and hung up our packs and divided the other. I taking part tying it up in a blanket and carrying it indian fashion we got started down the road at ten p.m. Eat our dinner of bread and water at the creek turned off the state road at the bridge [and] are camped on sec three 22.5 tomorrow we are going to try to book that land and start on our way back for supper we had bread and pork and the last of our hardtack which we were not sorry to see the end of it. Is failure for the woods I shall never carry any more if I can help it. It looks as though it was going to rain hope it won't.

G. Olin Bignell, Diary, 1871–1883, Bignell Family Papers, Bentley Historical Library.

The Strength of Lewis Sands

Manistee Democrat

February 28, 1890

Louis Sands is a native of Sweden, is 63 years of age, and came to this country in 1854, or when 28 years of age, settling in Manistee soon after. He shortly began taking logging contracts, in the pursuit of which he worked hard and prospered. There is a tradition current of the early days of Manistee and the prodigious physical strength of Louis Sands, that when one of his oxen fell sick while logging, Mr. Sands rigged the other end of his yoke so that he could take the place of the disabled ox, and the story goes that the work went right along without interruption. The narrative is well authenticated, and that he was able to keep up his end, all accounts agree. It is also related of his habits in those early days, that when it came to discharging supplies from vessels, it was his wont to disdain trucks and other artificial means of transferring freight, and would swing a barrel of pork or flour on to his shoulders and take it into the warehouse with the same ease that a man of ordinary strength would a box of crackers.

Title unknown, clipping in folder "Lumber Industry," Manistee Historical Society.

Reminiscences of a Logging Camp

A. S. Draper

My first job among the "river or camp men" was in the early spring of 1889. A friend of my father's wanted a chore boy to help the cook on the "run." The drive started near Morley and was to go through Muskegon, leaving some of the logs at Croton and Newaygo.

. . . I was permitted to go as a chore boy after a good deal of coaxing on my part and a lot of worry on the part of the home folks. The men had built us a shanty on a small raft, 18 by 24 feet that looked more like a large hen house with a place for a stove pipe than a cook shanty. The shanty had two rooms; the large room was the cook room and the small room was the store and bunk room; in the center of the cook room an old elevated oven stove was fastened to the floor, the legs set through holes in the floor, and the pipe fastened so that it could be changed from time to time as the wind changed. Big shelves were built in the wall, to eat and work off from. We served warm meals if the sailing was good; if not the boys had to eat canned goods. The cook did most of the serving. The men ate whenever they had a chance standing. When a man was at liberty he ran over to the cook shanty and got a "hand out" and away he went. One of my chores was to go to the farmhouses with two pails and buy milk, eggs, butter or anything that I could carry; or if the boys were near at meal time, try to buy them a square meal. We had a supply team, but what we could buy on the side was better liked.

About two years after my trip down the Muskegon I had another "whack at the woods" as we called it in those days. A new camp was going up; that is, the buildings were under construction and were getting in readiness for a winter "cut." If I remember right it was sometime the latter part of July. This camp was much farther north than I had ever been before. The camp was located north and east of Luther on the south branch of the Manistee River not very far from the village of Thorp. One of the rivermen that I knew said that he could get me a job for a month or so as a chore-boy or water boy "if I wanted to go." This time, thanks to good fortune I had no trouble at home or worry. . . .

In a day or so we started from Reynolds. I remember it was very early in the morning for the weather was very hot and the man wanted to get a good early start. We had two teams and a lumber wagon full of tools and supplies. One of the teams was hitched behind and whenever the team that pulled the load became fagged they were changed about; when we had to climb a long hill both teams were used. The roads were bad and we could not hurry. When we came to the bridge at Morley it had been condemned, so we found a place to ford the river and went on. There was but very little excitement along the way; a few times we had to get out and cut out a tree that had fallen across the road, and once we got caught in a thunder storm. We crawled under the wagon till the storm passed; as I was barefooted I rather enjoyed it.

We camped by the road at night and cooked our meals over a brush fire. The man I was with was very careful and would not let a fire be left burning when we went on. He said "the time will come when wood will be mighty skarce in these diggins." If others had been as thoughtful many bad forest fires could have been avoided.

In a few days we were on the job and were busy along with the army of workers. Anybody that could drive a nail or saw off a plank was a "first class carpenter." I was too young for that job so [I] became water-boy and chore-boy; then I went in the cook shanty as a helper. I waited on the tables, washed dishes, and peeled potatoes. I did not have to work all the time so [I] looked around and watched the men "put up the city." When we arrived the men were working on the men's shanty. I watched them notch long poles at the butt end and nail braces on the rafters. When the rafters were in place the roof boards were handed up and spiked on. The roof boards were one inch in thickness, as long and wide and light as could be found. The other lumber was as a rule two inches thick. When the last roof board was spiked, two layers of tar paper were tacked on. Nearly all the buildings were made of logs to the eaves; the gable ends and roof were made out of boards. Sometimes in a very large camp the men's shanty and cook shanty were made of boards and square timbers. The shanties were not well lighted for oil cost more in those days and daylight was cheaper. The floors were of two-inch pine, planed only for the dining room and boss's office. Auger holes were bored in the low spots to let the water off when the floors were scrubbed; a mop was never used around a camp. Stiff brooms, lye, water, and elbow grease were used well and often. If the floors were level the cracks did not count. The barns and blacksmith shop never had any kind of floor. Nearly all of the buildings were high and roomy. The filer's shack was the best lighted but was used only on very stormy days; a flat stump was better. The wagon shop and the blacksmith shop were together, for some of the horses were hard to shoe and two men were needed; other times the tires from the big wheels went wrong and two or three men were needed to set them.

But I am wandering; we must get back to the tar paper and the men's shanty. Inside of the men's shanty a number of bunks were built on each side of the room running up to the eaves and a few were placed crosswise in the further gable. A long bench was fastened to the floor and lower row of bunks on each side of the room. In the center of the floor was a frame 8 by 10 feet and about six inches high. This frame was spiked to the floor and filled full of sand or ashes. In the center a very large heater was set up and a number seven pipe ran up through a piece of tin that was nailed to the roof boards on the outside. Hanging from the braces were wires and small racks, for the men to dry their wet sox and mits on. . . .

When I finished high school, all but the last term, I responded to the call of the woods once more. . . . Late one fall I hired out to a lumber company. I was told that this special firm cleaned up everything as it went, and if I was no good at one thing I would be set at another. So I went out to their camp. I found the usual "city." I was given a green Swede as a partner. We had to go ahead of the sawyers and "fell" the trees for them, and if we got too far ahead we came back and helped saw the trees up into logs. The logs were cut in two different lengths, depending on the condition of the logs. . . . We tried to fell the timber so the gang following could get at it the quickest way, for a great share of the logs were cut by the thousand. We did not drop the trees just in the way they leaned but in the best places. To cut down a tree we cut a large notch in the tree with an axe, then sawed through from the other side to it, always starting the saw a little higher than the notch. If the timber pinched we used a wedge to force it over. Sometimes the tree went back on us and fell the wrong way and other times it would split up the whole length or to some weak spot, but as a rule we had good luck. After the sawyers came the swampers and skidders. The swamper cleared the way for the team and the teamster would hook onto the end of the log with a pair of large tongs and pull it out to the skidway; a skidway was a number of logs or poles laid in such manner that the logs for market could be decked across them off the ground; the logs were piled up as high as they would stick on. If the teamster could not get a log out with the tongs he wrapped a chain around the log and snaked it out. The runway used by the teams when it came to decking the logs was called "a cross haul." One time the boss sent a man that he did not like out to get him a cross haul. [The boss shouted], "where is that cross haul that I sent you after?" The man replied that it was frozen down and that he'd have to wait till it thawed out. The boss had to pay the man out of his own pocket. He did not try any more jokes that winter.

When logs enough were cut to start paying out money, the scaler and his helper, the "checker," started out and measured up the logs. I was transferred to the "checker" job and did that work nearly all that winter. The "checker" had to call the length and width of the log; the scaler put the "dope" in his little red book, also the number of feet the log scaled and called "next." When we had the logs scaled or were far enough ahead, the moving gang came with the big bobs and loaders, and the logs were loaded as high as they could be safely decked, anchored, and chained. One man stayed on top of the load; he was called the "top loader"; his job was a risky one, so was paid extra. He was the boss of the loading gang and as a rule the most popular man in camp. Before the teams were started the "man on the water wagon" had been over the road or runway. The runway was a glare of ice, but all the horses were sharp shod. The logs were "skooted" to the "drink" and again piled up and "checked" over again. This pile or row of skids was stacked at the top of a steep bank on a side of a hill, so the shoving would be easy in the spring. The logs were moving. "Daylight was in the swamp." I recall only one accident that winter. A teamster was killed, because the load was not properly anchored. When the men were paid off in the spring "the hard boiled ones" went to town and drank and fooled around till the "sharks" got all of their money; then they were kicked out in the alley and told to beat it. The rest of the men who were of different and wiser caliber went to work at something "springy" as cutting poles, peeling tan bark, or clearing land for farmers. . . .

The next fall I went to work in a hard-wood camp. This camp had all of the equipment that was required for an all-the-year-round camp, and a few other things as well; shacks for the married men; phone and fire protection. For a camp of the '90s it as considered number one. The company that ran that camp is still doing business. . . .

I was hired by the boss to do chores around the cook shanty. I was chore-boy about one week when the head cook and the cookie [head cook's assistant] got into a row over something or other; at last the cook chased his helper out of the shanty with a butcher knife. At dinner time the boss told me if I could do the work and get along with Al, I could have the job as "cookie." That was all right with me, so I was promoted to the job of mashing potatoes, washing white dishes, and waiting table; to wait on a table one had to be extra quick and watch every move. I progressed nicely both with the job and Al, till one morning I made a bad spill. That got "his Highness" badly riled up. He started the same butcher knife stunt on me that he always did when "crazy mad." I had just started to mash the potatoes for dinner. This was the first time he ever made for me. When Al got in good range I let the good four-pound masher fly. The flight was short and sweet. I had to bring him to with a pail of water. There was no head cook for dinner, but by supper time his head was all right, plus a large bump in the center above and between the eyes. No one asked a single question, but

I noticed more than one grinning face that night. From that time on I had no trouble in the cook shanty or elsewhere.

From "Reminiscences of a Lumber Camp" by A. S. Draper, Bentley Historical Library.

A Woman's Life in a Logging Camp

Lillian Haapala

An interviewer asked, "As I understand it, you married Neil in 1935?"

Yeah, in December. I went [to the logging camp] right away the first week that we got married, but I didn't—we had our own little shack that we stayed in. It was a hunter's shack that we stayed in until spring, and then we moved to Neil's dad's camp [near Escanaba]. There was an extra shack there that we could live in. [She worked as a cook after several years of living at the logging camp and raising her child.]

[In our logging camp,] the cook camp and the bunk house were about the same size, and they were side by side. There was a wooden walk between the two of them, so when the men would come to eat, they'd walk along that wooden walk. There was never no snow. The chore boy always cleared it. So, other than that, they were the same size. Of course we had two big long tables, and I think there were twenty guys to a table. . . . That's where the men ate. All they did in the bunkhouse was sleep. Yeah, that was their sleeping quarters, and of course they played their cards there or whatever they did in the evening. At the end of the bunkhouse there was a washroom built. When they come out of the woods, they could wash up a little bit—take a sponge bath even if they wanted to. But then we had the sauna, of course, all the time. It wasn't going all the time—twice a week, but in the summertime sometimes more often.

The [lumberjacks] stayed to themselves in the bunkhouse. They weren't out there in the cook camp; they weren't. The only time they come in there was for lunch or to eat. So, they weren't no bother at all. And we had a chore boy. He took care of the bunkhouses, anyway. [H]e had to keep it clean and scrub. He scrub[bed] it every Friday and clean out the spittoons. There was two big ones, one on each end of the bunkhouse, one of those big brass ones, and some coffee cans, too, for each one by the bed, even if—we didn't want him to spit on the floor. He was clean; he was clean. [T]he laundress did the blankets in the bunk house always, and the bedding. But then, when we washed the towels and stuff, we washed them in the cook camp. We did our own laundry, too. We washed the men's bath towels. We furnished them with bath towels, too. Every Saturday they got a clean towel, and they had to use it all week then. But at the end of it—at the end of the bunkhouse in the washroom there was handtowels galore, so when they washed their hands and stuff, they could use those, you know. They didn't have to use their bath towel only for bathing, you know, when they took a bath. Yeah, and those were washed every week, and they only had to use them whenever they took a bath.

I was a cookie when Neil's dad had the camps, and when he had two other cooks. So I was the cookie, which I had to do was wash dishes and peel vegetables and help with the scrubbing. And if—well, make a cake or something if she didn't have time to cook, or help her with the cooking even, a lot—fry the doughnuts and whatever I had time to do and always do the sweeping. I didn't know beans about a lumber camp until I ended up there. I learned [everything] through experience. [T]hat was the best teacher. I just learned by watching [the cook]. Oh yeah, she gave me lots of directions, and if I didn't know what I should do at times, she'd tell me what my job would be.

There was a little roothouse in the back of the cook camp [for storing food], or dug right out next to the cook camp to keep [food] better. Yeah, kind of a root cellar, but we had a door leading from the cook camp into that, so. Yeah, that's where we kept the butter and the potatoes and the other fresh vegetables—the carrots and cabbage and rutabegas and that kind of stuff. We used lots of [rutabagas] there. We had what they called a meathouse right—built on to the cook camp, too. But we had a go—had to shop more often in the summertime for the meat on account of the heat. There wasn't really no place—no refrigeration in them days there. So we just had to make more trips to the store then—to Nahma, too. That's where we had to buy all of our groceries from. They had a store in Nahma—it was the company—the company store, so we'd buy through them. [Despite the meathouse being screened-in,] flies got in anyhow. But we had the meats and stuff covered with cheesecloth—in the wintertime, we froze [food in the meathouse]. [As the cookie] I washed dishes, and the chore boy wiped. It was his job to wipe dishes then. All he had to do in the cook camp was—well, he'd have to carry the wood in, for both the heater and the cook stove, and then he'd wipe dishes and he'd help me peel the potatoes. And wipe the dishes—that was his job. And then help scrub on the days that we scrubbed, twice a week we scrubbed the cook camp—Wednesdays and Saturdays. [Changing from cookie to cook] didn't seem like too much of a change, only that I had more responsibilities than already, after worrying about all the—the whole works—the cooking. Other than that I had already learned from the previous cooks. [Interviewer: Was there ever more than one cook?] No, just one cook always. A cook, and a cookie, and a chore boy.

[What recipes did the lumberjacks particularly enjoy?]

Oh, they liked their meat and potatoes. Yeah, they were all meat and potatoes guys. If it was any size, form or shape, they liked them. Yeah, it was all so plain cooking, that. I'm familiar with several [Finnish recipes]. Kala mojakka [fish strew with potatoes, onions, carrots, cabbage, and spices], and this [*liha majakka*] is made out of meat, you know, meat stew. And [*vellija*] is like pudding. Yeah, and then this [*kovaa leipaa*] is hardtack, and we always had it there, too. And toast, because we had it sit on the lunch table always. We kept this on the table, you know. A lot of them wanted to eat hardtack instead of soft bread, too, you know, once in a while, regular. And the toast was always on the lunch table, a lot of them liked that with their coffee. We never monkeyed with [beer]. So, if they wanted their beer, they had to get it from town themselves. When we had the camps we didn't really allow them to haul too much of it there. When they start drinking like that, they don't accomplish anything either. They'd just party. [Alcohol wasn't allowed in the camp] but a lot of them brought it when they come from town. They had their bottles and stuff, anyway. But they couldn't start partying for days and days there—no way. Out they go if they think they can do that!

I learned [Finnish recipes] from my mother already at home and Neil's mother. Yeah, I liked to cook when I was a little kid even. I had to use leftovers a lot. I didn't like to waste. [If] I had no recipe, even, just slapped things together and taste it, see how it taste before—that's all. There was a lot of work there, all the bread and the cakes, and then the coffee rolls. We called them biscuits, but they were more like sweet rolls. And we made all those, and doughnuts once a week. Maybe fifteen dozen doughnuts, on a Friday, usually. That's a lot of doughnuts, yeah. Sometimes I'd make glazed doughnuts, and sometimes I'd make the cake doughnuts, and cake quite often. And bread—I had to make that several times a week. And then some of the guys sometimes, if they worked a little but father out of the camp, you know, on a strip, some of the cutters—well they wanted to take their lunch with [them]. So naturally you used more bread on account of that. One day, I baked—on the times that they were taking lunch I had to bake every day, for a while. Like one day I would make white bread, and the next day I'd make rye bread—fourteen loaves at a time. I don't know how I ever done it, but it didn't seem too hard, really, in them days. But it was still hard. We had a big monstrosity of a cook stove, and was that a good one, an old cast iron one. Yeah, it was a big one. My it was a good stove. I wish I'd have dragged it here [to my house].

We had breakfast at six-o-clock—well, they'd leave as soon as it started getting daylight in the wintertime, which was about six-thirty they'd take off to go in the woods then. I got up at four-thirty. The teamsters—when there was teamsters there, they came in for their early—before breakfast—coffee, after they had taken care of the horses and stuff. They had to take care of the horses before they took them out in the woods. Lots of them [came back in for dinner]. Even if a lot of them took lunch like the cutters that were far away, they still had to make the noon meal—three squares a day, yeah. They took [a dinner pail] in the morning. I set the lunch table—their big lunch table on the side, and pile everything on there—the meat and pies and breads and whatever, make tea for them. And they used to have lunch buckets. There were two compartments; on the bottom you'd put your tea or coffee—whatever you wanted to take—and then your top compartment you'd set—like a double boiler—then you'd put your other, sandwiches, or any other stuff on top there. So they'd heat it—that way in the woods it was hot. You had a hot meal! Anyway, they didn't have to eat a frozen meal.

[The jacks] were mostly Finns, they were most of them Finnish. I can't remember exactly. And the other nationalities—they were used to being with the Finns, anyway. They were all mostly like Finns, anyway. They ate what the Finns did and did what the Finns did! Yeah, they liked to be at our camp, anyway, I know, even the other nationalities. Not too often [were there serious injuries]. Oh, there was one guy working for Neil's dad. He lost an eye when a twig, or a branch hit him in the eye, and he lost his eye. But no other real serious ones, during our time, anyway.

Oral history (interview) of Lillian Haapala, April 18, 1991, Marquette Regional History Center.

To the Old Manistee, 1921

Tom B. Jones

As I stood on the banks
Of the old Manistee
And gazed at the waters below,
My thoughts wandered back
To the bygone days
Of some fifty years ago.

Oh, grand stream
You have history made,
It is written in prose and verse.
But not half enough
Of your fame has been told
And it's left to me to rehearse.

You waters flow on so peacefully now,
No log drivers yell do you hear—"Jam below, all lend a hand!
Look out there, boys, she's breaking away,
We have lost the key log clear!"

Your waters becalmed
Now and then a canoe
Glides swiftly on its way.
From source to mouth
They have no fear
Of a log jam causing delay.

An auto rumbles along your banks,
Where once an ox team plod.
Mighty dams now harness you power,
That once was controlled by God.

Man has stepped in and taken control
He sways you back and forth.
He lets you rush and roar as you will
Then shuts you off by force.

A log lifting crew with a gasoline rig,
Are lifting logs from your bed.
They are piling them high on your banks to dry.
And robbing you of your dead.

The living have gone, their deeds remain,
You soon will be left alone.
No one to break the silence,
As you smoothly glide along.

To you, old stream
I offer this toast,
As I stand on your scenic banks
And think of the boys
Who drove the logs
And played their rustic pranks.

The lumberjack you have served so well
Has long since passed his prime.
But you, old stream, do still flow on
Until the end of time.

From "Reminisces of a Lumberjack," a booklet, ca. 1921, by Tom B. Jones of Manistee,
folder "Logging," Manistee Historical Museum.

The Last Sawmill in Manistee

Grand Rapids Herald

January 24, 1926

Last Sawmill Going
Residents Saddened as Once-Great Industry Decays to Nil
Want Shingle-Making Days Back

The mouth of the Manistee River today: bare sand bluffs and the sand shores of the lake once dominated by pine forests, with the last commercial lumber mill being wrecked where once the pines and later the dozens of mills stood.

For with hunting gone, and even the last saw mills going out because there are not even poor saw logs left, the Indians are facing the necessity of leaving their ancestral homeland or starving there. Added to this, as recent news dispatches have indicated, is the suffering of those from large cities who have [been] sold homes by land sharks on the worthless sand that had once been a glorious forest of pine trees.

But to get back to Manistee lake. Today the last great commercial lumber mill is being wrecked, the last of dozens of mills which for seven years made this city the world's greatest lumber port.

"The Last Sawmill in Manistee," January 24, 1926, *Grand Rapids Herald*, clipping in folder "Lumber Industry,"
Manistee Historical Museum.

CHAPTER 9

Wealth from Underground: The Mining Industry

One of the conditions for Michigan's admittance to the Union was to cede its claim on the Toledo Strip (see the introduction to chapter 4). In return, Michigan received the remaining three-quarters of the Upper Peninsula. At the time, many Michiganians were unhappy: residents of the Lower Peninsula felt they received nothing more than a worthless wilderness of "perpetual snow," and residents in the Upper Peninsula were concerned they would be ignored by the rest of the state six months out of the year. Others remained upset because they were still convinced that Toledo would become the center of trade in the West, and they wanted Michigan rather than Ohio to reap those rewards. Arguably, the change paid off for Michigan.

Use of Michigan's copper resources dates back thousands of years with a group known today as Old Copper Indians. Despite not having advanced knowledge of metallurgy, Michigan's original inhabitants took advantage of the region's copper resources, using that which was relatively easy to extract, and they hammered it with rocks into tools such as knives, bowls, and spear points. Some of it was used for decorative or religious purposes. It was much later when Michigan residents implemented large-scale mining for valuable metals, including copper, iron, gold, and silver. Copper and iron, of course, were the most abundant. The exploratory expeditions were difficult early on.

The State's First Geological Expedition

Bela Hubbard

In 1837, the State of Michigan, then in the first year of its young but vigorous existence, organized a State Geological Survey; but the scanty appropriation sufficed only to enable its projector to accomplish, during that year, a limited reconnaissance. This extended, nevertheless, to some degree, into the almost unexplored portion of the lower peninsula.

Salt springs were known to exist, particularly in the vicinity of Grand and Saginaw rivers, and the few facts known of the rocks which constituted most of the coast lines, and made occasional outcrops in the interior, were sufficient to indicate the probability of the existence of coal and gypsum.

It was required, by the act of establishing the survey, that an examination and report upon the salt springs should be made at the end of the first season.

It is my intention to relate some of the incidents of a trip—or short campaign, if I may so term it—made in the fall of 1837, for the purpose of an examination of these springs, and such other geological discoveries as might be made, in the country traversed by those great natural highways, the streams tributary to the Saginaws.

The party consisted of four individuals: Dr. [Douglass] Houghton, the State geologist, and three assistants,—Mr. C.C. Douglass, the writer [Hubbard], and—a dog.

The latter was no inconsequential member of the corps, and had, like the rest, his appointed duties to perform. *Dash* was his name; indicative also of his nature.

This was before the days of railroads, although the young state had already projected its magnificent scheme of internal improvements, and for a considerable part of our contemplated route there were no highways but the streams. Our plan was to reach, by private conveyance, some point on the Shiawassee River, whence we could embark in a canoe and descend to the Saginaw.

Loading into a wagon at Detroit our few traps, which consisted of a tent, provisions, an axe and a gun, in the afternoon of Sept. 13, 1837, we proceeded as far as Royal Oak, where we encamped by the roadside, in the independent mode common to immigrants at that period. To the writer the situation had the charm which youth always finds in novelty.

I will not detail you with incidents, and will only mention the few villages through which we passed.

Prominent among these was Pontiac. The first settler, Mr. Williams, came to this place in 1817 or 1818, with an exploring party, among whom was Governor Cass. This whole region was then supposed to be an interminable morass, and so wild and dangerous was this expedition thought to be, that the party, before setting forth, took leave of their friends with all the solemnity befitting so grave an occasion.

At the time of my visit, Pontiac was a pretty, business-like place. It had been settled 13 years, but had just received incorporation by the Legislature. It has always retained its bustling character, while growing rapidly from a thriving hamlet into a beautiful and well-built city.

The surrounding country seemed to our eyes far enough removed from the gloomy morass which wild imagination had depicted it, 20 years before. It appeared to me the most beautiful the sun ever shone upon. It was of the character then beginning to be classed as "openings," characterized by a gravelly soil and a sparse growth of oaks and hickories. I speak in the past tense, because, though the rural beauty of the country is still unrivaled, little remains of the original character of the openings. This is a result partly of the process of civilization, and partly of the thick growth of small timber that has covered all the uncultivated portions since the annual fires have ceased, which kept down the underbrush.

Elevated 400 feet above Detroit River, broken into hills and knobs, which rise frequently 100 feet and more above the surrounding surface, with intervening vales and hollows, forming basins for lakes of the clearest water; in the midst of a park of nature's sole forming inimitable by the hand of art, this lake region of Michigan deserves its celebrity.

But at the period I allude to, no straight-fenced roads shut in the highway, and travelers might wind at will through the superb natural park, trampling down only flowers that in many places created glowing parterres; catching many a bright reflection from the limpid lakes, and sometimes stealing distant sight of a herd of deer, scarcely more wild than the peaceful landscape over which they roamed. Climbing a tree on one of the most elevated knobs I had a view over probably the whole of Oakland County; seven lakes lay at my feet; on the north and west undulations, like heavy swells of the sea, and on the east a level plain, stretching to the horizon like an ocean's verge.

Byron, in the south-east corner of Shiawassee County, was the termination of our wagon journey. The name had long occupied a prominent place on all the old maps of Michigan—at that time a decade was antiquity—held out to the newcomer the promise of a large and thriving village. The reality was disappointing. It possessed—all told—a mill and two houses . . .

At Byron, we exchanged our wagon for a canoe, and commenced a descent of Shiawassee River.

From Byron to Owosso, about twenty miles direct (but many more by the course of the stream), our way lay mostly through land more heavily timbered, but varied with openings and occasional plains. Through this part of the county, roads had been opened, and settlements had made rapid progress.

We were now to make our way by the aid of the current, but this meant not all plain-sailing nor luxurious enjoyment. The river was interrupted by numerous rapids, of difficult if not dangerous navigation, and over these shallows we had to drag the canoe. As this necessitated getting into the water, we were provided with water-tight boots, that turned up to the thighs.

At the approach of night a favorable landing was selected, and a new division of labor took place. While one cleared the spot and pitched the tent, another cut wood for the fire, and a third prepared the evening meal. Your humble servant, being installed into the ancient and honorable dignity of cook, had this duty to perform. Anyone who has sweetened his food with the sauce of hunger knows how little culinary art is requisite to satisfy famishing guests. Indeed, a piece of fat pork, fried upon a stick over the camp fire, after hours of labor in the wilderness, is a morsel sweeter than any which the pampered epicure knows. To this standard dish our one gun enabled up to add such small game as we chose to take the trouble to obtain.

From *Geological Reports of Douglass Houghton, 1837–1845*, edited by George N. Fuller (Lansing: Michigan Historical Commission, 1928), 20–23.

Annual Report of the State Geologist

Douglass Houghton

1841

As far back as 1831 and 1832, I had occasion to pass no less than three times, along the south coast of Lake Superior, as also to ascend several of the important tributaries of that lake, and during these years, I passed by three different routes, widely separated from each other, completely across to the Mississippi River. It is true that these journeys made through complete wilderness, uninhabited except by savages, were necessarily made under circumstances that admitted of only very general observations; but the result of these previous examinations have proved of immense service to me, in aiding the labors of the past season. I allude to these journeys and examinations at this time, in order to show you the difficulties by which a full understanding of the subject under consideration is surrounded, for I became satisfied at that time, not only that the subject was not understood by the mass of those who have traversed the country, but that even the natives of the country had no knowledge of the true sources from which the transported masses of copper had their origin. . . .

These observations soon showed me that this line of junction between the trap rock, and the south edge of the conglomerate, instead of pursuing a course parallel to the coast, only continued its parallelism for a few miles westerly from the extremity of Keweenaw point, after which for a long distance, it recedes from the coast rapidly. These facts served to explain in part, why the subject of the origin of the masses of copper had remained a mystery, for the country through which this line passes is hardly ever passed over, even by the Indians, and probably large portions of it have never been passed over by whites, but in addition to this, the obscure character of the metalliferous veins is such, that they would scarcely attract the observation of the traveler whose attention was not called especially to the subject, for many of the richest ores are so far from having the appearance of the pure metal that they would be the last suspected to contain it in any form. . . .

The extreme length of what I have denominated the mineral district, (within the limits of Michigan), may be estimated at a fraction over 135 miles, and it has a width varying from one to six miles; but it must not be imagined that mineral veins occur equally through all portions of it, for sometimes, for many miles together, none have been noticed, and the situation of the country is such to render it probable they never will be. The range and course of the mineral district has been so far defined as to render it unnecessary to say more upon this subject, to enable such persons as may wish to examine, to pass directly along its complete length.

I have thus far omitted to allude particularly to the large mass of native copper [the Ontonagon Boulder], which has been so long known to exist in the bed of Ontonagon River, less perhaps this isolated mass might be confounded with the products of the veins of the mineral district. That this mass has once occupied a place in some of these veins is quite certain, but it is now perfectly separated from its original connection, and appears simply as a loose transported boulder.

The attention of the earliest travelers was called to this mass of metallic copper by the natives of the country, and it has been repeatedly described by those who have visited it. The mass now lies in the bed of the westerly fork of the Ontonagon River, at a distance which may be estimated at 26 miles, by the stream, from its mouth. The rugged character of the country is such, that it is but rarely visited, in proof of which I may state, that upon my visit to it, during the last year, I found broken chisels, where I had left them on a previous visit, nine years before, and even a mass of the copper, which at that time had been partially detached, but which, for the want of sufficient implements, I was compelled to abandon, was found, after that interval, in precisely the same situation in which it had been left.

The copper in this boulder, is associated with rocky matter, which, in all respects, resembles that associated with that metal in some portions of the veins before described, the rocky matter being bound together by innumerable strings of metal; but a very considerable proportion of the whole is copper, in a state of purity. The weight of the copper is estimated at from three to four tons.

From *Geological Reports of Douglass Houghton, 1837–1845*, edited by George N. Fuller
(Lansing: Michigan Historical Commission, 1928), 531–32, 533–34, 557–58.

Deaths of Miners

Inspector of Mines for Marquette County

These are compiled reports of accidents resulting in death. The accounts of the accidents are quite lurid and sometimes horrific. The ruling of "accidental death" by a jury exonerated a mining company of any wrongdoing. Of the twenty-two deaths that occurred between October 1905 and September 1906, eighteen were ruled in such a way.

September 30, 1906

ACCIDENT NO. 1

John Aro met with instant death at the Section 16 mine, of the Oliver Iron Mining Co., at Ishpeming, on the first level at 1:25 p.m., on Oct. 4, 1905. Aro and his partner, Richard Gill, had blasted a hole before going to dinner, and on returning to their place, they had found that the hole had not thrown all of its burden. They decided to blast it again, also two big rocks of ore that the hole had thrown down. Aro was engaged in charging the hole and Gill was preparing to blast the rocks. Gill said they were ready to blast and they decided to light one of his holes first, then Aro would light his and Gill the other hole last. Gill set fire to his hole and he claims that Aro was in the act of setting fire to his hole when it exploded with the result above stated. Aro was a Finn, married, aged forty. Verdict of the jury was "premature blast."

ACCIDENT NO. 2

Joseph Uren received injuries at the Negaunee mine, of the Cleveland-Cliffs Iron Co., at Negaunee, at 1:45 p.m. on Oct. 18, 1905, from which he died at 5:30 the same afternoon. Deceased was employed as a motorman and according to his own statement made before he died, he leaned out too far, coming into contact with the drift timbers, receiving the injuries which later caused his death. Uren was of English extraction, single, aged nineteen. Verdict of the jury, "accidental death, no blame to any one."

ACCIDENT NO. 3

Arthur Jacobson was instantly killed on the 10th level of No. 6 shaft, Lake Superior Iron Ore mine, of the Oliver Iron Mining Co., at Ishpeming, at 5 a.m., on Nov. 7, 1905. Deceased, along with three partners, was engaged in stoping [making a series of steps] out the bottom of the tenth level. They had blasted about 4 o'clock and had been barring down the loose ground from the blast. Two of the men had gone to get some powder to blast again, leaving the deceased and his partner barring [removing loose rock]. They had finished barring as they thought, and were standing about twelve feet away when without any warning a chunk of ore fell from the hanging wall, striking deceased causing instant death. At this particular place the back was probably 35 feet high, but according to the evidence of the day shift boss, they had gone over this back some three or four days previous to the accident and had taken down all loose ground making it secure. I had visited this place on the 27th of October, and found it in very good shape. Jacobson was a Finn, single, aged nineteen. Verdict of the jury was "accidental death."

ACCIDENT NO. 5

Bengt Erick Dahl was almost instantly killed at Negaunee, at 11:30 a.m., on Dec. 8, 1905. Deceased was working on a diamond drill operated by the Oliver Mining Co., for the day in place of his brother. At the time of the accident, Dahl and his partners were engaged in taking up one of the sand pipes, when the hook of the block broke, the block falling and striking deceased on the back, killing him almost instantly. What caused the hook to break is a mystery as it was a clean break, no flaw of any kind in the iron could be found. The hook was one and three-eighths inches thick. This accident was a peculiarly sad one as deceased was not regularly employed by the company just filling his brother's place for the day. Dahl was a Swede, single, aged thirty-five. Verdict of the jury: "accidental death."

ACCIDENT NO. 9

Jacob Saurakka was instantly killed at 5:30 p.m., Feb. 27, 1906, on the sixth level, No. 2 shaft of the Lake Superior Hard Ore mine of the Oliver Iron Mining Co., at Ishpeming. Saurakka was a trammer [cart loader] and was attempting to ride in the skip [elevator] to surface in direct violation of the rules of the mine. The shift-boss and all the men with the exception of the skip tender and the deceased were on their way to the surface. Saurakka told the skip tender to get in the skip and the deceased went to the electric bell, located about ten feet from the shaft, and gave the signal to hoist. After ringing the bell he ran to the shaft and jumped in the moving skip, getting caught between the shaft timber and the skip, completely severing his head from his body, the body going to the surface in the skip and the head being found after the accident on the gate at the sixth level. Saurakka was a Finn, single, aged twenty. Verdict of the jury: "Deceased came to his death from being caught between the timber and skip; accidental death; no blame attached to anyone."

CLASSIFICATION OF ACCIDENTS [AUTUMN 1905 TO AUTUMN 1906]

BY NATURE OF ACCIDENT

- By falling down shaft—3
- By falling down raise—1
- By fall of ground—6
- By premature blast—1
- By dipper handle of steam shovel—1
- By being caught between motor and timber—1
- By being caught between motor car and timber—1
- By riding on skip—2
- By being knocked over trestle—1
- By running chute—1
- By being hit with block—1
- By falling timber—1
- By suffocation—2

GENERAL AND MISCELLANEOUS

- Total number of mines in operation in the county—31
- Total number of quarries—1
- Total number of explorations—1
- Total number of men employed in and about the mining industry—5840
- Total number of fatal accidents—22
- Percentage of fatal accidents per 1,000 men employed—3.76

From "Report of Inspector of Mines for Marquette County, Michigan," September 30, 1906, Marquette Regional History Center.

Fond Memories of a Mine

Jacob Houghton

Jacob Houghton was the brother of Michigan's state geologist, Douglass Houghton. He worked for the Cleveland Mining Company and accompanied William Burt in his explorations of the Upper Peninsula. Burt discovered northern Michigan's vast iron resources.

With a great deal of interest I have read the account of the celebration of the 50th anniversary of the Cleveland Co. Reading it brings me back to an early period in my own life.

In 1844 I was in a party of surveyors running the Township lines between the mouth of the Escanaba and where are now the cities of Marquette and Negaunee. There was not a human being living within the limits of Marquette County. From the time that we left Escanaba until we returned there in the fall we saw no human being.

The party was under the direction of Hon. Wm. A. Burt, inventor of the Solar Compass. His assistants were Wm. Ives, R. S. Mellen, Harvey Mellen, James King, and myself and two packers. I was the youngest one in the party, 17 years. My duty was to take barometrical observations for determination of heights.

On the 18th of September 1844 we camped at the east end Teal Lake. The next morning we started south to run the range lines between Ranges 26 & 27 (the east boundary of the Jackson Mine). On going up the hill the variations of the magnetic needle became very great and Mr. Burt ordered us to look around and see what we could find.

Harvey Mellen was the first to find ore. Each one broke off a piece and brought it with us and those pieces were the first specimens of iron ore from the ledge taken away from Lake Superior. I cannot vouch for its having been pure ore. The fact that the magnetic needle was affected is somewhat against it. We did not know any more about the ore than some of the early miners did. The specimen that I took disappeared long ago. Some eight years ago at Lansing where he was a State Senator, I met Mr. Harvey. He asked me if I had my specimen yet. I told him that it had disappeared. He said that he had his piece and was going to keep it. Two years ago he was killed at a Railroad crossing and I am going to try to get hold of that specimen. I am now the sole survivor of the party of 1844.

Respectfully yours,
Jacob Houghton

MM Duncan Papers, Bentley Historical Library.

Not Hazardous Work

George Eisele

George Eisele was the assistant superintendent for the Oliver Mining Company, which operated in the Upper Peninsula. This is an excerpt from a speech he gave for a Rotary club.

1923

Mining has always been looked upon and generally considered as especially hazardous work. Statistics do not show that this is true in iron mining. The average number of men employed at the Chapin mine in the past 20 years has been about 750; in these 20 years 19 fatal accidents have occurred, averaging less than one per year, and—with the exception of a very small percentage—have all occurred through some negligence or carelessness on the part of the injured man himself or some fellow workman and not because of working conditions.

George J. Eisele Address, 1923, Bentley Historical Library.

CHAPTER 10

Social Change: Women's Rights and Progressivism

Because of the unprecedented number of casualties, the Civil War highlighted the need for women's civil rights, especially suffrage. In 1867, the Michigan legislature passed a law that enabled taxpaying women to vote in school elections, and in 1908, Michigan's revised constitution enabled taxpaying women to vote on bond issues. While it was the Civil War that brought a great deal of attention to the issue, arguably the First World War launched the issue forward, and Michigan removed most restrictions for female suffrage nearly two years before the adoption of the Nineteenth Amendment. Still, the debate for women's rights had existed long before these wars, and while the early advocates of women's suffrage deserve much greater attention, it is equally important to include counterarguments.

Ain't I a Woman?

Sojourner Truth

May 29, 1851

I want to say a few words about this matter. I am a woman's rights. I have as much muscle as any man, and can do as much work as any man. I have plowed and reaped and husked and chopped and mowed, and can any man do more than that? I have heard much about the sexes being equal. I can carry as much as any man, and can eat as much too, if I can get it. I am as strong as any man that is now. As for intellect, all I can say is, if a woman have a pint, and a man a quart—why can't she have her little pint full? You need not be afraid to give us our rights for fear we will take too much,—for we can't take more than our pint'll hold. The poor men seems to be all in confusion, and don't know what to do. Why children, if you have woman's rights, give it to her and you will feel better. You will have your own rights, and they won't be so much trouble. I can't read, but I can hear. I have heard the bible and have learned that Eve caused man to sin. Well, if woman upset the world, do give her a chance to set it right side up again. The Lady has spoken about Jesus, how he never spurned woman from him, and she was right. When Lazarus died, Mary and Martha came to him with faith and love and besought him to raise their brother. And Jesus wept and Lazarus came forth. And how came Jesus into the world? Through God who created him and the woman who bore him. Man, where was your part? But the women are coming up blessed be God and a few of the men are coming up with them. But man is in a tight place, the poor slave is on him, woman is coming on him, he is surely between a hawk and a buzzard.

"Ain't I a Woman?" as transcribed by Marius Robinson and printed in the June 21, 1851, edition of the *Anti-Slavery Bugle*. Sojourner Truth's speeches are available at http://www.sojournertruth.org/Library/Speeches/Default.htm.

Notes on Women's Rights

Theodore Foster

The much mooted question of Woman's Rights may be stated thus: "Do justice and expediency require that women should be invested with all the rights and privileges, social, civil, and political which belong to men?" The argument in favor of the affirmative may be stated thus:

I. RIGHTS OF WOMAN.

1. Man claims a right to life, protection for his person, his property, and his reputation. He also insists on his right of self-government, and of promoting his own true and substantial happiness.
2. He claims that he derives these rights from the Creator: that they are inalienable; that they belong to his person; that they are born with him; and that he carries them with him through every part of his existence.
3. He claims the exercise of these rights, because they have never been taken from him, nor has he ever voluntarily surrendered them.

4. The rights of woman are precisely identical and co-extensive with those of man. She has the same number of physical senses to be gratified; the same brain and nervous organization; the same number and kind of moral and intellectual faculties; and her life, person, property, and reputation are equally valuable to her. Her rights are derived from the same source, and are bestowed for the same period; she claims the exercise of these rights, inasmuch as they have never been taken from her by Him who bestowed them, nor has she voluntarily surrendered them to any other being.

5. This equality of rights establishes the absolute equality of the sexes. Neither can assume any authority over each other. The lord of creation has precisely the same rights as the lady of creation; no more, no less.

6. Hence, it is impossible for man to claim and prove *his* rights, without indicating, with equal force, *hers* also. . . .

IV. CIVIL RIGHTS.

1. But in order that she may enjoy . . . social rights in their full protection, some provisions of the civil law need to be amended.

2. Women ought to have their separate estates, contracts, debts, and injuries. Whereas now the very existence of the wife is unknown, in many respects, during her marriage.

3. The subjection imposed upon her by the law should cease. Now a woman is bound to obey her husband in all things; and in case she is refractory, he may restrain her of her liberty, lock her in a closet, and bind her with cords; and if she make opposition, and in enforcing his commands, her arm should be broken. The law deems the act justifiable, and will give no redress to the wife. The subjection of the wife to the husband is maintained by all writers on common law.

4. An instance of this fact is found in the act regulating the acknowledgement of deeds. The woman acknowledges that she executed it without any fear or compulsion of her husband. This is a relic of barbarism, now entirely useless.

5. Another instance is found in the law by which a woman, committing theft or burglary, in company with her husband, cannot be punished, the law kindly presuming that she acted through fear or compulsion of her husband.

6. In many of the States, the property of the wife goes with the marriage, and the husband may spend it as he pleases.

7. The right of dower is also unequal. By our law, when the husband dies, the widow has *one third* of his estate during life: when the wife dies, the husband has *the whole* of her estate during life.

8. Women ought to have an equal voice in disposing of their children: and in case of separation, she should have the charge of them granted to her by law, in all cases where he has shown a moral or intellectual unfitness for fulfilling his paternal duties.

V. POLITICAL RIGHTS.

1. It is to be borne in mind that it is not proposed to force upon all women the duty of voting or holding office, but to confer these privileges on such of the sex as may desire to use them.

2. A woman has precisely the same interest in all the affairs of society that man has. She has the same rights, person, feelings, property, and reputation to be cared for: and she is as deeply interested in the questions of free trade, banking, railroads, or any matter of legislation that man has. A wife and her husband have interests precisely identical.

3. Women who have property have a special claim, inasmuch as they ought not to be taxed without their own consent.

4. Women who have *no* property, need right legislation for their personal security.

5. Very large numbers of women are sufficiently intelligent to vote understandingly and judiciously.

6. Her strength of moral feeling would affect legislation favorably. The influence of the sex would be most decidedly against war, intolerance, licentiousness, and every gross vice. The opponents of granting women the right of suffrage themselves acknowledge that she already exercises a powerful, although indirect influence upon legislation; and that this influence is invariably for good.

7. There is nothing strange or unusual in the idea of women exercising a direct influence upon legislation. In all ages, and in most countries, women have occasionally acted as sovereigns, invested with supreme legislative power: and the administrations of the Queens of the earth will compare, in ability and energy, with that of the Kings.' At the present time, we have the example of [Queen Victoria] who rules over a seventh part of the human race; and whose personal partialities, in the bestowment of titles of nobility, deeply affects the welfare not only of the present age, but of future generations.

8. The right of voting need not necessarily be extended to all women at once. It might be just granted to females who owned real estate, or paid taxes: and its exercise might be restricted to local elections.

9. It is sometimes objected that woman's mind is inferior and occupied with trifles, and that she is not informed on matters pertaining to legislation in a degree sufficient to qualify her to exercise a sound and accurate judgment. If the force of this objection be allowed, it will not apply to very many intelligent women: and woman will not complain of the establishment of a certain standard of knowledge or intellect as a test of fitness for the enjoyment of political rights, provided both sexes are equally subjected to it.

10. Again, it is objected that the purity of woman's character would be sullied and disgraced by being brought into contact with the scenes of profanity, drunkenness, and vulgarity which are common at the polls. To which it may be justly replied, that those scenes would cease to exist when women were present, because all experience teaches that the bare presence of respectable females exerts a restraining power upon the most abandoned men.

11. Again, it may be answered that the elections occur but once or twice a year: that in order to vote, it is only necessary to hand a slip of paper to a board composed of four or five of the most respectable men in the town: that this need not occupy more than two minutes: and that a woman whose purity of character is of so refined and delicate a nature that it would be sullied or lost by an exposure of this kind for two or four minutes in a year, possesses an article which is not worth preserving.

12. Once more: all experience shows that while the intermixture of respectable females into popular assemblies always improved their sobriety, decency, and courtesy, such intermingling has no perceptibly evil effect upon the female character, but rather the reverse. Women commonly attend theatres, circuses, fourth of July celebrations, and political meetings, without receiving insult or abuse, and with evident addition to the gratification of the male part of the audience.

13. In the conventions of School Teachers, held by the authority of the State, where several hundred teachers meet, a perfect equality of the sexes prevails: women vote, and fill all offices; and the result has been found highly favorable by stimulating the ambition of both sexes.

14. An objection is raised to the holding of office by women, that the greater part of them have families that require their attention, and they could not attend to political duties without neglecting their domestic affairs. To which it may be replied that many women have no families at all: that others have only a husband: and that those in the decline of life have families grown up. But if a

woman have a family of children needing her care, that is reason enough why she should not be a candidate; or if a candidate, why she should not be elected.

There is nothing chimerical or visionary in the idea that in the year 1956, female suffrage will generally prevail in the United States. Very great changes in the constitution of Society occur in the course of a single century. In 1756, not a single public man, or writer on political affairs, could be found, either in this country or in Europe, who advocated universal male suffrage irrespective of property. Yet that principle is now established all over the American empire, to such an extent that not even the most conservative politician dare risk his reputation by proposing a return to property qualification for voters. The change in the next century by which women would all become voters would be no greater than has already taken place in the right of voting within the last hundred years.

"Women's Rights," notebook in Box 1, Theodore Foster Papers, Bentley Historical Library.

An Objection to Women's Voting

Lyman Willcox

Lyman Willcox was a prominent figure in Michigan throughout the nineteenth and into the twentieth centuries. He was a newspaper editor in Pontiac and Bay City, a postmaster in Bay City, and an official in the Land Office in Traverse City, and he served in the Third Michigan Cavalry during the Civil War. As a respected citizen, Willcox was often asked to give speeches on numerous topics.

In this country the ballot has been adopted simply as a means of determining the public will and not as a "divine" right nor a "God given" right nor an "innate" right discovered in "this the nineteenth century and age of progress" as we are being constantly informed.

The ballot has been adopted as a means to an end by the same authority and for a similar purpose as that establishing a police force or a court of justice. Through the act of voting elections give . . . character to government. But it is not voting which gives to government its strength. Behind the so called social compact, behind the laws, behind the government there must be a power to enforce its decrees. The very existence of law presupposes a power . . . to enforce it.

Free government rests not only on the obedience of the citizen but also on his strength. Our military organization and the liability of every able bodied man to perform military duty; our police force organizations and the obligation of every able bodied man to assist them; our sheriffs; our municipal state and national governments; our courthouses; our jails and penitentiaries all attest to this fact. Man, it is said, may live for days without food but not an hour without government. There is a spirit of discord in the human breast which will rend society in pieces the moment restraint is removed and this is the only excuse for government at all. Is a city burned to ashes? The presence of a military is instantly required to protect citizens, and the strong arm of the citizen soldiery is alone able to preserve the peace. It is the ever present force of power which preserves society and secures protection to persons and property. It is this irresistible, ubiquitous presence of latent strength which may be instantly called into action which makes society tolerable. . . .

God in his wisdom has seen fit to create mankind with two different functions and powers and has imposed upon them different duties, tastes, and characteristics. Not that one is superior to another in their several lines of duty, but that they are simply different. These different characteristics are marked by sex. Sex in itself confers no intelligence nor imposes different moral obligations, but it does divide and mark lines of duty and separates mankind into two great and equal classes, the union of which, morally, mentally, and physically, is essential to the existence, welfare, and happiness of both. This union constitutes the family, each integrant member being equally interested in the other and bound by kindred ties and reciprocal duties to each other. . . .

The civilized man [looks to] his wife and children and scarcely any but them; they alone are his constant companions; they alone soften his sorrows . . . ; they alone are interested in all that concern him. . . .

It is to the progress, to the preponderance of domestic manners that women owe their happiness and influence in modern society. It is to the domestic family circle, to our houses that we owe our civilization; and our unparalleled progress in natural and scientific wealth and even our liberties flow from the same foundation.

Now I ask in all earnestness, will women throw away all their present advantages and remand society back to dissoluteness and anarchy, and themselves to brute force in a mad race after Pandora's Box? childishly grasping after political power and notoriety in competition with men, which necessitates their absence from the hearthstone, divides their attention and energies from home to politics and to all the coarser realities of life, and engages them in a debasing struggle with men in the arena of the outdoor world?

I have too much confidence in the intelligence and womanhood of our American ladies to believe it possible. We have the evidence of the best wives and mothers of the land. The most intelligent and virtuous women of our country send up remonstrances which ring as clearly and sweetly as the [illegible word] vote against the demand of those who from some strange aberration of mind or perversion of nature shriek for woman suffrage. The true woman, the representatives of the sex, those who are not only able but willing to perform their duties and do not ape the manners of men, those who are not ashamed of their womanhood, say "We are . . . opposed to giving the elective franchise to women. That while we admit the necessity of extensive reform, both in the political and social relations of life, we deny that the bestowal of the right of suffrage on woman would in any way hasten that reform. That woman's duty is distinct from man's and is well defined; and that as going to the polls forms no part of it, we still strenuously oppose this movement as an invasion of our right not to do man's work.

We are the advocates of woman's rights, and those of our sex who are clamoring for suffrage should call themselves 'the man's rights party' since they are grasping after duties, powers, and privileges that naturally belong to the stronger sex."

Here we have an expression from women themselves, and it is marked with a clearness and decision characteristic of those who understand their rights and duties and are willing to perform them.

An aged spinster becomes disgusted with her life and longs for change. She asks for a ballot when she really wants a husband. A married couple in default of children pet[s] cats, poodles. Their hearts reach out for something they do not possess and they waste their affections on dumb brutes till wearied with the mockery they take refuge in despair and add their voices to the fierce shrilling after so called woman's rights, in the meantime a husband taking advantage of the dogma of equality puts his wife to work in the fields or the work shop, just to develop her physical powers, while he carefully preserves his own energies in calmly contemplating his wife's manhood. A wife in whose bosom the milk of kindness is dried up and whose motherly instincts have been sacrificed on the altar of pride and selfishness, whose wifely love is turned to indifference or hate strikes with revenge on society and demands her rights. A husband tired of his wife, seeks a near affinity and being marvelously impressed with the servitude of women joins in the medley. Another discovers in his wife abilities superior to his own and at once takes a back seat and pushes his wife out into the world to trade on the curiosity of the public while he quietly and serenely eats the fruits of her labor, satisfied if it pays, she by becoming an agitator gratifies her vanity and his indolence and avarice. These are the classes comprising the small army of platform stampers who keep up such a din and clatter about woman's suffrage and its kindred schemes of demoralization. I will not speak of that other clan of female agitators who so shamelessly parade their virtues and their vices before the public and who are deliberately debauching literature and morality, but they want to vote.

The complicated cares and duties of civilized society, more than the wars and crimes of the Middle Ages, make necessary to mankind the quiet peace and happiness of domestic life. Our life is a constant struggle with each other, with the elements and with all surrounding circumstances in which the weak are crowded to the wall.

Cities must be built, states founded, and governments established; canals must be dug, seas navigated, railroads & telegraph must be constructed, machinery must be invented, constructed, and improved and operated, mines must be opened and all the varied industries of a complex civilization carried forward with ceaseless energy, requiring the best brain and muscle with which the Creator has endowed mankind. This is the proper field of labor for man. His endurance, his physical strength, and his mental power are here required in their utmost force. Success requires ceaseless energy, intense appreciation, tireless labor such as man never before performed.

To accomplish this labor men must be cordially and earnestly assisted by women. The coarse and heavy labor, the struggle, conflict, and confusion of business life wears upon the mental and physical powers of man to such an extent that is unaided and left entirely to his own resources he would break down before his task is half accomplished and the aberrations of the world would soon reduce him to the coarseness and brutality of savage life.

The necessity for rest—from the ceaseless turmoil of the business world, causes man to seek for peace and consolation in the family relation. Woman offers him asylum and becomes a help meet and comforter. She binds herself to him by this stronger [bond] and more sacred than those of consanguinity. His life becomes her life and her home his home. She opens to him a new world, a world in which she is queen and subject. She [fills] her house with love and is the willing subject of duty.

The poet has said

"Love is a silver link, a silken tie
Which heart-to-heart and mind to mind
The body and the soul doth bind."

Marriage is the emblem of that love and the family its fruition. The union of two hearts blended in domestic relation completes the man and enables both parties to face the world as a unit and this husband and wife are fully prepared to conquer success and procure happiness, each in lines of duty parallel but not the same. Whatever breaks in upon the proper performances of those duties mars happiness and brings disaster down upon both parties.

In the domestic family system the influence of women pervades all the best and most sacred interests of mankind. As is the house so is society and as is society so is the world. The domestic family system is the foundation of our civilization and the basis of liberty. Change its characters and you change society. The elevating influence of woman flows from it, and the farther women remove from domestic life the more nearly they approach the line of disrespect and lose that restraining influence upon society which is elevating in character. By elevating in characters I do not wish to be understood to mean that this influence is exerted by women only, or that sex gives or entitles women to any respect whatsoever. Domestic manners tone down the coarser tendencies of man and woman, and instill into society a respect for the good, which is lost the moment she passes into the masculine conflict. Woman is loved and lovable because she is good and pure and represents the domestic affections. What man remembers his mother because she was a stump orator or a virago? No! it was the kind look, the sweet voice, the tender loving hand that cheered him in his sorrows and ministered to him in his afflictions, which have impressed her image on his soul and causes him to revere her beyond expression. It is this remembrance that the young man carries with him when he enters the business world to buffet the tides of fortune. It is this which preserves him from the paths of vice when the siren of pleasure would inveigle him into her snare. . . .

For woman to engage masculine occupations (and those occupations are masculine which are incompatible with a proper performance of domestic duties) is debasing. Whenever a woman strives to do that which is incompatible with the peculiar characteristics of her sex she weakens herself.

We object to women's voting because her true field of labor is in the domestic circle. She is not physically competent to become a part of the law enforcing power of the country. Our politics are already too vacillating and to extend the right of suffrage without at the same time strengthening the government would be suicidal. To allow her to participate in the duties of government would place her in a position where she would consider children an encumbrance and lead to a vivid realization of the calamity so tersely expressed by Horace Greeley in his deathbed delirium when he exclaimed that he died before he was born.

It will add bitterness and venom to our already too bitter political contests, and carry the conflict into the bosom of our own families and involve father, mother, and children in the whirlpool of discord.

"Woman's Right to Vote," folder entitled "Speeches, Woman's Right to Vote," Box 2, Lyman G. Willcox Papers, Genesee County Historical Collection.

No Benefit to Women's Suffrage

William Webb

Another matter I have often though about this question, that has arisen in the land, with respect to women voting. I myself am opposed to it, I cannot see where it would be any benefit to them in any way at all. If I could see any benefit it would be to the land, I would be in favor of it. I have talked with a great many learned men, and asked them if they were in favor of it, and they said a woman that has no husband had just as much tax to pay as if she was a man, and they said they though she ought to vote. I told them if that was all the reason they could give, it could be mended very easily without voting, because where a woman has property, they always marry as soon as time will let them. They told me they could hold office and do business like a man. I told them I did not think any man would like to have his wife exposed to all kinds of abuse, and did not think any lady would want to vote. Then they said they had just as good a right to vote as the colored people had. Then I told them no person ought to wish to do anything through evil. I told them a man ought always to think before he speaks. I told them that was the cause of so much evil being in the land. I told them I thought it would be one of the greatest evils that could befall the land, if the women should be allowed to vote. I talked with a great many that were opposed to it, and I thought to myself they were about right on that subject.

The History of William Webb, Composed by Himself (Detroit: Egbert Hoekstra, Printer, 1873), 68.

Michigan Association Opposed to Woman Suffrage

Helen Keep

There was nothing odd about the formation of groups opposing women's suffrage in the early nineteenth century, but as strange as it might seem, the Michigan Association Opposed to Woman Suffrage was made up entirely of women.

February 13, 1913

Dear Sir;

You have doubtless heard of the new organization which we have formed because we do not believe the majority of women of Michigan wish to vote. Since we organized one month ago, we have enrolled names from all over the state. Would you kindly give us names of people in [Sault Ste. Marie] who would be interested in our association that we may send them literature? Also would there be sufficient interest to warrant us in sending you a speaker next month? Thanking you in advance,

I am cordially,
H. E. Keep

A Response to Helen Keep
Office of Governor Chase S. Osborn

Your favor of Feb. 13 addressed to Gov. Osborn is received here while Mr. Osborn is in Europe. The people of this section of the state are very progressive in their ideas and I believe the sentiment generally is in favor of woman suffrage. Governor Osborn, as you may be aware, is a believer in woman suffrage.

Both letters are from Chase Salmon Osborn Papers, Box 32, Bentley Historical Library.

A Governor's Legacy
Chase S. Osborn

Some have labeled Chase Osborn as "Mr. Progressive" for his beliefs and his work as Michigan's twenty-seventh governor (1911–1913). He ran a newspaper in Sault Ste. Marie in the late nineteenth century, and he later served as Michigan's game warden and railroad commissioner. Historians have claimed it was his role as railroad commissioner that convinced him that regulations were seriously needed. He was fervently against corruption, which explains why he exposed a bribery scheme that took place during the 1900 state Republican convention—Osborn was a Republican! In his autobiography, Osborn reflected on his dedication to issues such as women's suffrage, prohibition, and workers' compensation, work that was potentially dangerous for him and his family.

Very near to my heart I had the matter of a workmen's compensation law. I had given the subject considerable study in Germany and England and had talked it over often with my intimate associates and many others. The Legislature in regular session had empowered the Governor to appoint a commission to study the question and draft a form of a bill embodying a suitable law. The commission appointed, serving without pay, had given earnest attention to the important subject and had submitted a report of indubitable value. To obtain action upon this was my chief purpose for a special session. Also, I wished to utilize this meritorious measure to further define and stiffen partisan lines in the Legislature, so that I might feed in good measures that otherwise would not carry. The workingmen's compensation act passed [in 1912]. The Legislature empowered the Governor to appoint an Industrial Accident Board to administer the law. The success of the new law might largely depend upon the practical foundation laid for it in its earliest application and interpretation. I secured for the board the only two members of the commission that framed the law who could be secured for state service. By virtue of the understanding and administration of this law by the first board, it came to be recognized as one of the best compensation enactments in America. It has been copied by many other States. Gradually it will undoubtedly be brought nearer to perfection.

Police Commissioner Croul, of Detroit, an official of rare courage and capacity, had told me that of some seventeen hundred saloons in Detroit quite twelve hundred were owned by brewers and distillers. It was their practice to start a booze joint on every likely corner they could obtain and especially near factory doors. Brewery-owned saloons were the worst of all. I saw to it that a bill was introduced making it illegal for brewers and distillers to own or encourage saloons. Forthwith fell upon me the liquor people. The Royal Ark, an association of saloon keepers in Detroit, endeavored to intimidate members of the Legislature. Conditions of much bitterness arose.

I found the Michigan Bonding Company to be the most hurtful and the boldest source of evil in the State. It was organized under a law that gave it the practical control of all the saloons in the State. If a saloon keeper did not obey its behests, his bonds were refused. It charged big fees and was strong financially. It had one or more agents in every county and cleverly selected them from among the best-equipped attorneys. By means of a retainer it secured the services of lawyers who would not naturally line up with it. Thus equipped, the Michigan Bonding Company became a dangerous entity. Of it men were afraid. It was the core organization around which was built opposition to woman suffrage, prohibition and all related reforms. I asked the Legislature to repeal the law giving it existence and I made a fight against it that was nearly successful.

The fight at Lansing while these bills were pending became a vicious one, with enough bad feeling and personal passion almost to obscure reason for a time. I received as many as ten letters in one day threatening my life. To these cowardly messages I paid no attention. They only indicated the feeling that existed among the whiskeyites.

Dynamite was placed under my house but it did not explode. My residence was on fire twice mysteriously. One of these fires occurred at two o'clock in the morning. I was attacked on all sides. Throughout all the conflict I did not worry nor lose sleep. My wife stood it bravely but confess now she was deeply worried and wearied. But only words of cheer and courage came from her then. As for myself, I thought I was right and I think so now when the embers of thought are colorless from fire. Perhaps I took on some of the spirit of the crusader. At least I placed my trust in God and calmly asked divine approval and direction.

Those who were advocating woman suffrage were not united. Some of them, including most of the women propagandists who came to Lansing, were fearful that a measure submitting the question to the people could not pass the Legislature and that its failure would prove a setback. After discussing the matter with Representative Charles Flowers, a veteran partisan of the cause, and with several others, I decided to present the question. It carried nicely. Later, when it was submitted for popular consideration, it undoubtedly carried in the State. However, the liquor interests succeeded in obscuring and invalidating the result. Its next submission was in the spring, when the country vote is light as compared with that of the cities, and suffrage was then unquestionably defeated.

When the returns of the vote began to indicate that the measure had passed at the first plebiscite, those opposed held back the reports from polling precincts that they controlled, giving the impression that whatever totals were necessary to accomplish the defeat of the women would be supplied. There were signs of a sharp practice that was used by the vicious elements to obtain a momentary end. Apparently the only adequate redress for such is an aroused public that will finally act so decisively as to brook no resistance or trickery.

I do not say that all of those who oppose votes for women are vicious, but I do say that wherever I have been familiar with conditions, the management of the campaign against suffrage has been controlled either above the surface or below it by those who are inclined to lawlessness and who make it their instinctive business to fight anything that tends to improve the public tone or widen the zone of influence of those who would most likely, in the nature of things, to endeavor to cure those evils that are eating cancerously at the foundations of the human family.

Women are the matrix of the race. They occupy a sphere that man, a mere fertilizing agent, never enters. Consequently woman knows instinctively when her own is imperiled. Fundamentally this is the *raison d'etre* of the woman movement. All talk of liberty and equality is incidental. Nature, always operating to make life dominant over death, and in ways often most obscure and indirect so far as man's vision and comprehension are concerned, is the author of the activity that has for its purpose the bringing to bear of the powers of woman directly against the jeopardy of her children. The tendency may be delayed or misdirected but it cannot be defeated, any more than the precession of the equinoxes can be controlled by human agencies.

From *The Iron Hunter* by Chase Salmon Osborn (New York: Macmillan Company, 1919), 284–87.

Temperance

Roland Dunn

Michigan implemented statewide alcohol prohibition in 1855, but it was largely ignored and almost never enforced. As a result, it was repealed in 1875. That, however, did not discourage members of the Anti-Saloon League or the Women's Christian Temperance Movement, and other groups like them, from continuing their work to rid the land of "Old John Barleycorn." After nationwide prohibition took effect in 1920, Detroit became a center of smuggling booze into the country. At times, the federal government spent nearly a quarter of its prohibition enforcement budget in Michigan alone. Accordingly, officials encouraged citizens to help curb illegal activity.

Roland Dunn wrote this piece on prohibition for a speechwriting contest when he was a student. Later, he became legal aid to Governor Frank Fitzgerald.

1910

The annals of history record no nation without its crisis. These crises are not spontaneous outbursts of thought and sentiment, but the culmination of decades, even centuries, of accumulated conviction. . . .

As Americans, we are facing a situation of singular gravity. Never before have the problems that confront us been duplicated. Not a century and a half old we stand in the vanguard of civilization, with few exceptions, excelling the foremost powers of earth. But justly proud of our success we must reluctantly admit that vice and corruption have kept pace with our laudable achievements. The seriousness of this lamentable condition has lately been impressed upon the American Public. In our impetuosity we have allowed the reins of government to fall into the hands of political combines. A few have been benefited at the expense of the many. But now the submerged majority are protesting against the rule of the few and agitation is giving birth to a political revolution. Investigations are being demanded. "Insurgency sweeps the land upsetting politicians and parties, dethroning bosses and graters, heralding reforms in every line." Unjust rate-discrimination is leading to severe measures. Jackpots are being unearthed and the offenders subjected to the law. Interstate commerce regulations are enforced, and Lorimerism is denounced [William Lorimer was a politician from Illinois who was accused of bribery]. Social and economic reforms are being instituted; and the result is good. But while meeting these issues, we have neglected a paramount one, that evil known as Liquor Traffic. . . .

Note the appalling evils that confront us today. The Liquor problem; the Cigarette curse, the Desecration of the Day of Rest; Political corruption and that hidden sore of the world, the White Slave Traffic [prostitution]; which, with divorce and associate domestic evils, is the greatest curse the world has ever known. But of all these evils why attack the Liquor problem? Now there is no need of enumerating to an intelligent public the awful consequences of drink; it is enough that these facts be emphasized. This evil is one that may be attacked openly and directly and destroyed at its source; also every evil tends to make every other evil worse. You may purge this land from political corruption and graft; blot out that destroyer of the nation's youth, the Cigarette curse; prohibit that symbol of dishonesty, the Gambling evil; crush out the existence that polluter of society, the White Slave Traffic; destroy the whole Satanic combination and when you have finished you are still in the clutches of this modern Octopus, the Liquor Traffic.

How much corrupt politics can be traced directly to the liquor forces? How many vices under its patronage? Here is the answer then. By attacking it and totally destroying its influence, immediate help will come to thousands and thousands of homes: but which is better the foundation will be removed from the more subtle evils, thereby giving to this country's morale, upon which depend on future economic conditions, a tremendous uplift.

Speech of Roland Dunn, 1910, Roland G. Dunn Papers, Bentley Historical Library.

Public Involvement in Enforcement

U.S. Bureau of Prohibition

1930

In the Government's effort to stop liquor smuggling across the Canadian border, the railroads have aided materially. Until recent year the carriers touching the border were used extensively by liquor smugglers who brought loads of liquor across to the

American side in small boats and reshipped by rail to interior points for distribution through bootleg channels.

The most troublesome spot on the border in liquor smuggling is at Detroit. The peculiar conditions around Detroit made it easier for smugglers to operate, and they were more difficult to catch in that area than in any sector of the Canadian boundary.

When the Government began to build up its defensive lines in this border area it became necessary to negotiate with the railroads for aid in stopping smuggled liquor shipments in freight cars in that territory.

Public Cooperation in Prohibition Law Enforcement: Business, Civic, and Industrial Groups Aid
in Promoting Better Observance and Enforcement of the Law (Washington, DC: Department
of Treasury and Bureau of Prohibition, 1930).

CHAPTER 11

A New Industry: The Horseless Carriage

Although Michigan inventors were not the first to develop the automobile, the Great Lakes state quickly became the center of the industry, which began to take shape at the turn of the twentieth century. There were numerous reasons why Michigan came to dominate the automobile market, and the efforts of those such as Ransom E. Olds, Henry Ford, and William "Billy" Durant certainly pushed Michigan to lead the industry. On the eve of the Great Depression, Michigan companies accounted for roughly 75 percent of automobile production; after the Great Depression, about 90 percent. Despite the decline of Michigan's auto industry in recent decades, it currently leads the country in automobile production. These documents provide a glimpse into the early industry in Michigan.

The Founding of General Motors

Billy Durant

The True Story of General Motors
The place—Flint, Michigan, the "Home of the Buick."
The time—Six o'clock, evening, May 15, 1908.

I was dining with my daughter, Mrs. E.R. Campbell, when I was called to the phone. Chicago in the wire—[Benjamin] Briscoe calling.

"Hello, Billy, I have the most important matter to discuss with you, and want you to take the first train to Chicago."

"What's the big idea, Ben?"

"Don't ask me to explain; it's the biggest thing in the country; there're millions in it; can you come?"

"Impossible; too busy; sorry. But I can see you here. Why don't you take the ten o'clock Grand Trunk arriving at seven o'clock tomorrow morning. I will meet you at the station and we will have breakfast together."

"All right, I will be with you."

I met him at the depot, a hurried breakfast at the hotel, then to my office. Comfortably seated, Briscoe presented the following:

One of the partners of J.P. Morgan & Company had made a small investment in the Maxwell-Briscoe Company when it was first organized. Pleased with the progress the company was making and recognizing the possibilities, he asked me if a sufficient number of motor car concerns could be brought together to control the industry. How would the leading companies regard a consolidation? Would Briscoe canvass the situation and report (at that time trusts and combinations were the order of the day—promotions of all kinds encouraged by the big banking interests). Briscoe had no well-considered plan but wanted to get my ideas. He suggested calling a meeting of about twenty of the leading concerns, naming Packard, Peerless, Pierce, Arrow, Stoddard Dayton, Thomas, etc. What did I think about it?

I told him frankly that I did not believe the plan was workable. The proposition in my opinion was too big, too many concerns involved, too many conflicting interests to be reconciled.

Why not modify your ideas, Ben, and see if you can get together a few concerns committed to volume production in the medium priced class, all having a common objective, all heading for a highly competitive field: I named as my choice Ford, Reo, Maxwell-Briscoe, and Buick. I suggested that he first see Henry Ford, who was in the limelight, liked publicly and unless he could lead the procession would not play. Get Ford if possible, and then take up the matter with R.E. Olds. When, and if, everything is arranged to your satisfaction, advise me the time and place and I will attend your meeting.

Briscoe agreed. I then took him through the factory, showed him what we were doing, which quite surprised him, and put him on the Pere Marquette train for Detroit, feeling quite pleased with his visit.

About two weeks later I received word to meet him and the others in Detroit. The place appointed for the meeting was the office of James Danaher in the Penobscot Building. In the public reception room were gathered the principals, their close associates and advisers. The room was small, no place to discuss business. I sensed, unless we ran to cover, plenty of undesirable publicity in the office. As I had commodious quarters in the Ponchartrain Hotel and as the luncheon hour was approaching, I suggested we separate (in order not to attract attention) and meet in my room as soon as convenient, giving the number of the room and how to locate it without going to the office. This was accomplished and I had the unexpected pleasure of entertaining the entire party until mid-afternoon.

When we were once more together Mr. Briscoe made his little speech, saying that he had paved the way for the nucleus of a gigantic combination and it was up to those present to work out and submit a plan that might appeal to J.P. Morgan & Company. He simply repeated what he had already stated to all of us, referring to the advantages of consolidation, stressing the economies that would follow if well organized and properly financed.

Then came what might be called a "painful pause." Mr. Briscoe had no definite plan and the matter had not been seriously considered by the others.

At this juncture and to relieve the embarrassment, I submitted the following hypothetical question to Mr. Ford: If we were all agreed that a consolidation was a proper and wise procedure, and the Ford Motor Company's properties were appraised at $10,000,000 would he consider $6,000,000 a reasonable figure for the Reo Motor Car Company? My next question, addressed jointly to Ford and Olds: With Ford at $10,000,000 and Reo at $6,000,000, would $5,000,000 for Maxwell-Briscoe appear unreasonable? This question, evidently out of politeness, was not answered.

Mr. Briscoe, the prime mover of the project, having very different ideas, seemed slightly displeased and asked me what about Buick. To which I replied that the report of the appraisers and auditors and the conditions and terms of the agreement would be my answer to his question.

This opened the way for a general discussion: How was the company to be managed? Who was to be the "boss"? How were the different companies to be represented? Could anyone suggest a plan? Briscoe took the position that the purchasing and engineering departments should be consolidated, that the advertising and sales departments should be combined, and that a central committee should pass on all operating policies.

I took the position that this would only lead to confusion; that there should be no change or interference in the manner of operating, that the different companies should continue exactly as they were. In other words, I had in mind a *holding company*. Briscoe came back jokingly with "Ho! Ho! Durant is for States' Rights; I am for a Union." From that time and all through the luncheon, everybody except Henry Ford talked. Business conditions and the future of the industry were forecast, the hazards and uncertainties were gone into thoroughly, the desirability of a controlling organization agreed upon, the meeting breaking up with the best of feeling with a statement from Mr. Briscoe that he would see his people and report, and that, in all probability, we would be invited to meet in New York in the near future.

In due time, the call came and the manufacturers met with the representatives of the House of Morgan at the law offices of Ward, Hayden, and Satterlee, New York City (Mr. Herbert Satterlee being a son-in-law of J. Pierpont Morgan).

Following the introductions, the usual questions were asked:

What percentage of the industry did the four companies represent? Would it not be desirable to increase the number? Could anything be gained by a consolidation of the four companies? How much capital was employed by the four companies, and could additional capital be used to advantage? When and by whom were the companies organized? How were they capitalized and by whom controlled? Would a consolidation attract or discourage competition? What were the objections, if any, to a motor car combination?

The only reply to the last question was by Mr. Ford. He thought the tendency of consolidation and control was to increase prices which he believed would be a serious mistake. He was in favor of keeping prices down to the lowest possible point, giving to the multitude the benefit of cheap transportation.

What would the consolidated company be called?

Mr. Satterlee suggested the name "International Motor Car Company," and asked if there were any objections. He said that Mr. George W. Perkins, the active member of the Morgan firm was very partial to that name, and was very much interested at that moment in the International Harvester Company and the International Mercantile Marine. There was no objection to the name International Motor Car Company. Incidentally, it was agreed that the firms would defray the expenses of the appraisals and audits; before adjourning it was understood that the meeting called at the suggestion of Mr. Briscoe was purely informal; that there was to be no publicity and no commitment on the part of anyone present.

Leaving the meeting I took the evening train to Flint. I was satisfied that a consolidation was in the making, and began to put myself in position to act promptly when the time came. Upon my arrival, I went over the whole matter with my personal attorney, and friend, Mr. John J. Carton, and suggested that he draw up an agreement to be signed by the stockholders of the Buick Company authorizing me to act for them in an exchange of stock (Buick stock for stock of the International Motor Car Company to be organized), the exchange to be on exactly the same terms and under the same conditions as my own.

From *In His Own Words* by William C. Durant, collected and published in 2008 by Scharchburg Archives at Kettering University, Flint, 25–29. Reprinted with permission from the Scharchburg Archives.

Early Auto Work

Carl B. Parsons

I had been wanting to learn the wagon-maker's trade so, in 1900, I moved to Korset [Sweden]. The wagon-maker's name was Johan Anderson. He had a shop all alone and I was his only helper. I was to work for 2 years for nothing. Johan's father was supposed to keep house for us but he was an old drunkard—hardly ever sober. Johan was afflicted with epilepsy and had spells every so often, so, it was not a pleasant situation. But, what I did learn I learned well, and Johan was a fine man. I first built a wheel-barrow wheel and then a complete wheel-barrow, then a phaeton body complete with gear, wheels . . . and whiffle-tree. Here, I learned how to build a wagon from the ground up. . . .

Early in 1909 I was offered a position at the H.H. Babcock Company, Watertown, New York. They were bringing out a new automobile, which was more like a high-wheeled buggy, the wheels being about 36" in diameter. I had charge of the designing and building of the bodies. But the car did not go over which was easy to see—such large wheels and solid tires. Accordingly, I turned in my resignation which Mr. H.H. Babcock was very slow to accept. He wanted me to stay there and design carriages for them. I had for some time thought about the possibility of starting a shop building custom bodies, and here was my opportunity. So I organized the "Standard Limousine Company" renting space in a building on the northeast corner of Halstead Street and Briar Place in Chicago. We built up a very nice trade and had some of the finest people in Chicago as our customers, but I did not feel too contented because I realized, even then, that the custom-body business was not going to last—and we were watching what they were doing in Detroit.

We built a Touring body equipped with front doors, which was the first one that had ever been seen in Chicago. We also built the first Sedan body that was built anywhere. This was a custom body for Mr. J.C. Paul, inventor of the "Burnishine" metal polish. This body was put on a Marion chassis of Indianapolis, and was delivered to Mr. J.C. Paul on Thanksgiving Day, 1910, and displayed very prominently by the Marion Automobile Company of Indianapolis on the Automobile Row in Chicago. The next Sedan we were able to find out about was shown by the Stoddard-Dayton Auto Company at the Auto Show in February, 1911.

At this time I was offered a position as the manager of the Mitchell Motor Company's new Body Plant in Racine, Wisconsin. They made me an attractive offer and, under the circumstances, I accepted this offer. [My wife and I] had just been married and thought that Racine would be a nice place to live in. Here, I designed a complete line of bodies for the Mitchell Motor Company. Unfortunately however, about 6 months later Mr. Henry Mitchell, the general manager, died and the business was not in good shape financially. They borrowed 2 million dollars from the New York bankers who promptly stopped the finishing of the new Body Plant where I was hired to take charge. They did not put in more equipment, let the plant stand idle and continued to buy bodies from the W.S. Seaman Company of Milwaukee.

Accordingly, 30 executives were dismissed, and I was one of them, but when I went in to say good-bye to Mr. W.T. Lewis, Chairman of the Board, and his son William Mitchell Lewis, president of the Company, they tried to talk me into staying with them because they wanted me for other work, but I had already made arrangements to come to Detroit. They very kindly gave me one month's pay and an additional check for $500 as an expense check. Certainly they showed themselves as very fine people.

When I first arrived in Detroit everybody talked so much about the Ford Motor Company, so I wrote a letter to Mr. Henry Ford and took it out there (Highland Park) in person. This was referred to the Ford Information desk and upon receipt of this letter, Mr. Ford asked Mr. Maguire, then general manager, to talk to me about accepting a position to be in charge of their bodies. We had a long talk and Mr. Maguire told me that he did not think I realized that the Ford Motor Company is not what it is going to be. He stated that we are going to build 30,000 cars this year and 75,000 the next, and then only God knows where we are going. We did not discuss salaries at all and I think that if we had I would have been offered more than what I was getting. Mr. Maguire certainly was right as to where Ford was going. I did not accept the position offered to me but, instead, went to work for General Motors.

We came to Detroit the day before Thanksgiving Day, 1911. I started to work at the Cadillac Motor Company, under Mr. Henry M. Leland, immediately at their Body Plant, located on 23rd and Fort Streets. I was hired by Mr. Leland personally. They were building steel bodies. The Mullins Company of Salem, Ohio made the stampings which were hot stampings and no two alike. We made the best of it and did a fine job after using up about 55-lbs. of soldier on each body. We had to fit the woodwork to the metal.

After spending a year at the Body Plant I was called into a meeting at the Cass Avenue Office where Mr. Leland had gathered about 15 executives. He introduced me to them, some of whom I had not met before, and announced that I had made good progress with the Company and that I was just the type of man they wanted and I was to be the body engineer instead of Mr. Fred Keeler. And to a direct question by one of the executives: "What is Mr. Keeler going to do?" Mr. Leland replied, "He is going to assist Mr. Parsons," and that if we did not have room on the third floor of that building they would build a special building for me.

Shortly thereafter, I was offered a position with the Studebaker Corporation as chief body engineer at practically double the salary I was getting at Cadillac Motor Company. I talked this matter over with Mr. Leland and he told me that they could not meet the salary I was offered, so I left Cadillac and took the job at Studebaker.

From Reminiscence [undated], Carl B. Parsons Papers, Bentley Historical Library.

Factory Regulations
Imperial Wheel Company

April 1, 1906

Please do not accept employment unless you are willing to abide by the following regulations.

1. Working Hours.—6:30 a.m. to 11:30 a.m. standard time; 12:30 p.m. to 5:30 p.m., standard time, except on Saturday when the day ends at 4:40 standard time. First whistle blows at five minutes before the beginning of working hours. Second whistle on working hours. Over time 6 p.m. to 9 p.m.
2. Employees shall be in their respective departments prepared to begin work when second whistle blows, and if frequently or habitually late may expect dismissal.
3. Each employee will be given a number on the time clock. He will always ring same when he begins work, also when he ceases work, and he will not ring any earlier than fifteen minutes before the hour for commencing work, except by special arrangement with his foreman. Should he by mistake ring the wrong number or neglect to ring his own number he will at once report it to the time keeper. It is not expected that oversights of this character will occur often.
4. An employee known to ring in or out for another will be dismissed.
5. Employees will remain at their work until the whistle blows, and *all changing of clothing, washing, or cleaning up will be done after working hours.*

6. SMOKING in any buildings or about the yards is not allowed at any time except in the Boiler Room, and not there during working hours.

7. REGULAR PAY DAYS occur as follows: For work performed from first of month to and including the 15th, we pay the 23rd. For work performed from the 16th to and including the last day of the month we pay the 8th of the month following, except when the pay days fall on Sunday, in which case we pay the day prior. No money will be advanced between pay days.

8. All bicycles, clothing, shoes, etc., must be kept in places provided for that purpose in each department.

9. All persons, except those authorized, are strictly forbidden to use elevators and then for freighting purposes only, and all employees are warned against meddling with electric motors or any electrical appliances in any way, save as authorized by their foremen.

10. Each employee will attend strictly to his own work, and no one will permit himself to indulge in any loud talking, profanity or undignified conduct during working hours.

11. SUBSCRIPTION PAPERS. The passing of subscription papers throughout the factory in the interest of disabled employees will not be encouraged for the reason that every employee may protect himself against such a necessity by becoming a member of some association, which will provide for the payment to him weekly of a given sum of money in case of sickness, accident, or death.

12. All persons accepting employment may become members of the Flint Vehicle Manufacturers' Mutual Benefit Association upon signing an agreement to that effect.

We trust each and every employee of this Company will heartily co-operate with us in making the above regulations effective.

Imperial Wheel Company,
C.B. Hayes, General Manager
Flint, Mich., April 1, 1906

Imperial Wheel Company Factory Regulations handbill in John J. Carton Papers, Michigan Historical Collections, Bentley Historical Library.

The First Auto in Manistee

May 25, 1900

The first automobile to make its appearance in the city of Manistee arrived today on the M&NE [Railroad] from Traverse City where it has been on exhibitions for several days. The automobile is the property of Messrs. Swift & Company, the big Chicago packing house whose wares enjoy a prominent position in the markets of the world. It is an excellent machine of the best model extant. The motive power is electricity; the entire outfit weighs only 3500 pounds and was purchased at a cost of $2500. The engine is rated at six horse-power and the machine is capable of traveling 50 miles without recharging.

Mr. CE Cornwell is managing the entire tour of the automobile which will visit the principal cities in the neighborhood. The visit of the "fin de siècle" vehicle to Manistee is due to the enterprise of Cornwell & Sons who have built up an excellent business in Swift & Co.'s products.

The machine will be in town for a few days only and has already begun to draw very considerable attention. This afternoon it was taken to Brugman Bros. bicycle shop in order to repair the platinum electrodes of the bell which had become worn. The slight repairs were easily effected and the automobile will cruise around our streets without further delay.

From an unknown Manistee, Michigan, newspaper, printed May 25, 1900,
folder "Automobiles," Manistee Historical Museum.

Women in the Auto Industry

Automobile Topics

December 21, 1912

Women Form a Tire Supply Company

By its incorporation, the Essenkay Auto Sales Company, of Detroit, suddenly became known to the outside world through the fact that it is formed of women. Margaret Fellman is the guiding spirit and holds most of the stock, which Ruth and Frances Fellman are the other stockholders in the $10,000 company. The women have been operating at 809 Woodward avenue, Detroit, for several weeks, selling tires, fillers and rims.

December 21, 1912

Women in Automobile Plants, Too

The plant of the Ford motor Co., in Detroit, employs about 100 women in the magneto department, to wrap the coils, tin them, and the like. This department is the only one outside of the office where women are employed. A recent visitor to the plant, on being shown the women at work, expressed great surprise at finding the "fair sex" engaged in building automobiles. He apparently forgot the necessity for women when it comes to "sparking."

Henry Ford Weighs In

Automobile Topics

January 4, 1913

How Ford Parried Criticism

Henry Ford, on his last trip to Europe, bought a Rolls-Royce, in which he called on one of his British agents, according to a story now going the rounds in England. This man surveyed the lordly and aristocratic $8,000 machine, and turned up his nose, saying to Ford, "Your visit would have been more welcome if you had come in one of your own machines."

Ford got out of it very neatly by explaining that the first thing he did when he landed at Liverpool was to try to buy a Ford—but they were all sold, several months in advance.

"And so," he said, "I decided to buy the next best car that was immediately available."

February 8, 1913

Ford's View of the Future

As the biggest producer of automobiles in the world, Henry Ford, president of the Ford Motor Co., Detroit, Mich., sees no reason for anxiety as to the industry's future. In a statement dated from Los Angeles, Cal., he says:

"When I look toward the future and perceive what it holds for the automobile industry, my eyes are dazed with its radiant portent. To my mind the industry is in its infancy, and even the most sanguine expectations of what the coming years will hold are bound to be surprised by the actuality."

Authors unknown, *Automobile Topics*, vol. 28, 1912–1913, via google.books, https://books.google.com.

The $5 a Day Wage

Henry Ford

Many employers thought we were just making the announcement [in 1914] because we were prosperous and wanted advertising and they condemned us because we were upsetting standards—violating the custom of paying a man the smallest amount he would take. There is nothing to such standards and customs. They have to be wiped out. Some day they will be. Otherwise, we cannot abolish poverty. We made the change not merely because we wanted to pay higher wages and thought we could pay them. We wanted to pay these wages so that the business would be on a lasting foundation. We were not distributing anything—we were building for the future. A low wage business is always insecure.

Probably few industrial announcements have created a more world-wide comment than did this one, and hardly any one got the facts quite right. Workmen quite generally believed that they were going to get five dollars a day, regardless of what work they did.

The facts were somewhat different from the general impression. The plan was to distribute profits, but instead of waiting until all the profits had been earned—to approximate them in advance and add them, under certain conditions, to the wages of those persons who had been in the employ of the company for six months or more. It was classified participation among three classes of employees:

1. Married men living with and taking good care of their families.
2. Single men over twenty-two years of age who are of proved thrifty habits.
3. Young men under twenty-two years of age, and women who are the sole support of some next of kin.

A man was first to be paid his just wages—which were then on average of about fifteen percent above the usual market wage. He was then eligible to a certain profit. His wages plus his profit were calculated to give a minimum daily income of five dollars. . . .

It was a sort of prosperity-sharing plan. But on conditions. The man and his home had to come up to certain standards of cleanliness and citizenship. Nothing paternal was intended!—a certain amount of paternalism did develop, and that is one reason why the whole plan and the social welfare department were readjusted. But in the beginning the idea was that there should be a very definite incentive to better living and that the very best incentive was a money premium on proper living. A man who is living aright will do his work aright. . . .

In this first plan the standards insisted upon were not petty—although sometimes they may have been administered in a petty fashion. We had about fifty investigators in the Social Department; the standard of common sense among them was very high indeed, but it is impossible to assemble fifty men equally endowed with common sense. They erred at times—one always hears about the errors. It was expected that in order to receive the bonus married men should live with and take proper care of their families. We had to break up the evil custom among many foreign workers of taking in boarders—of regarding their homes as something to make money out of rather than as a place to live in. Boys under eighteen received a bonus if they supported the next of kin. Single men who lived wholesomely shared. The best evidence that the plan was essentially beneficial is the record. When the plan went into effect, 60 percent of the workers immediately qualified to share; at the end of six months 78 percent were sharing, and at the end of one year 87 percent. Within a year and one half only a fraction of one percent failed to share.

From *My Life and Work* by Henry Ford (Garden City, NY: Doubleday, Page & Co., 1923), 126–29.

CHAPTER 12

Hard Times: The Depression and the New Deal

The Great Depression affected Michigan greatly, especially in the manufacturing sector. At its worst, the state's unemployment rate in manufacturing jobs was nearly 50%. Even those who were fortunate in finding or keeping a job were faced with incredible difficulty (see chapter 13). The following documents provide a look into the everyday lives of some Michiganians who experienced the Great Depression and Franklin Roosevelt's New Deal firsthand.

Poor Farming

Lillian Haapala

I was born on a farm and I lived there until I got married. . . . Yeah, poor farmers— during the Depression. It was hard. But we had enough to eat, anyway. When we lived on a farm [we] had cattle and chickens and pigs. We had our own meat, and we made a lot of our clothes and bedding out of flour sacks. In them days they had flour and sugar even in sacks. That was a job getting them prints off of them when you washed them, but when you boiled them in lye water they came nice. So we crocheted [and] made fancy pillow cases out of them. So, we managed. It was better than none.

Oral history interview of Lillian Haapala, April 18, 1991, Marquette Regional History Center.

Farm Life Began on My Wedding Day

Beatrice Byrne

Life on the farm began Jan. 30, 1934 [her wedding day]. Spring on the farm brought 5 cows to milk. Planting—corn, potatoes. Garden as far away as we could get from the house. Harry Morris gave us 20 strawberry plants to plant. Uncle Frank McGarry gave us a lilac bush that he said wouldn't do anything for him. So, I took it apart and planted it and it is beautiful every year. Spring always had fences to fix and poison ivy for me. Ray [her husband] didn't get poison, but I sure did. Next you pulled weeds from morning to night. The cows made pathways through the woods and I would take a pail and go down to the Huckleberry swamp to pick berries. There were only 5 or 6 bushes, but they had beautiful berries and I loved getting away from the work. I saw the biggest snake while picking at my best bush, and you can bet the berries were still there for the next picking. Mary Jastifer and I loved to go down and pick.

There was a big black sweet cherry tree near the house and the cherries were always high up and I was scared to climb. But Ray made me climb and pick them. I was glad when the wind blew it down. It just missed our car that was parked near it. Two plum trees were by the windmill and there were peaches to pick and can in the fall. And apples, apples to pick. We had the best sweet cider. Ray had it made after the people had sweet grapes run, and that made it real sweet. Ray always had 4 or 5 barrels of cider in the basement.

I always had to take the babies out in their basket in the car when they were a month old, to turn beans or work in the fields. Corn had to be picked up and put in bunches of 4 each. Later we picked the corn off the shocks and put it in what was the playhouse and when he took it to the mill, I had to take the leaves off to have it ground for the cows.

When the children were big enough, weeds were pulled till dark by all, when they were 2 years old. Then he got a combine [and] I used to have to ride it. Beans were the only crop I hated. I had to go out, rain or shine, and turn the darn things. The kids loved it when the thrasher came to do them. One thing I will say, we were never hungry. We killed a beef and we had our chickens and eggs and potatoes and garden. Ray went to Grand Rapids once a week and bought 4 or 5 barrels of day old bread and sweets. And we had lots of good bread and sweets.

I hated to go grocery shopping with Ray. He followed behind me and put back anything I put in the basket, like dish soap which I needed, and soap to wash the clothes which was hard to get enough of. Wash day was a nightmare anyway. You pulled water from the cistern and heated it on the wood stove. I thought I was in heaven when [Ray] bought me a washing machine. He told me he got it so I could get done sooner and could help in the fields.

Oral history of Beatrice Byrne, Ada Historical Society.

Detroit during the Depression

Henry Biggs

I know Detroit quite well. Me being a native born of Detroit in 1911 and my father preached here in 1900. My father was Reverend Robert L. Biggs.

As a fair boy, I knew from Beaubien Street to Woodward. Unless you were working as a maid or houseman or chauffer, there were no blacks over there. When you come to Grand Boulevard, there was no police protection north of the Boulevard except mounted police. Of course the city wasn't extended as far then as it is now. They had to send a mounted police out to investigate, because they didn't have the transportation then. This is going back to the 1920s. . . .

[Southerners and immigrants] mostly came here because Detroit was the "Motor City" of the world at that time. Everybody wanted to get to Detroit where the big money was [Biggs mentioned earlier the allure of Ford's five-dollar-per-day wage]. People were renting out their basements, their attics. They were putting in partitions and sleeping two people in the same room. If you worked days and I worked afternoons, you would sleep there in the night, and I would sleep in the same bed during the day.

When the depression came in the early '30s, for three years as a young man I walked the streets of Detroit and couldn't find a job, couldn't buy a job. It just wasn't there.

Well, I shined shoes. I cleaned and blocked hats. At that time, people were burning a lot of coal. If I seen five tons of coal, I would ring their bell and ask them if they wanted it put in their basement. I didn't ask how much you'd pay. I'd just go ahead and put it in there with their approval, and whatever they'd pay me was acceptable.

I remember one time, it was near Christmas. I shoveled three tons of coal and the people gave me some food and three dollars; and I was all day doing that and part of the night. It was night when I went home. I was happy to have that money because I could take it to my sisters and they could buy food for the table. My mother and father were deceased. I was just in my teens at that time. . . .

I worked on the WPA for approximately a year and a half, during the depression, and I tried to get to be foreman on the job. That was when they made me a supervisor over the repair work—shovels, and picks, and so on. That was as high as I could go. I went to the GAR Building [Grand Army of the Republic Building, Detroit] to try and get a promotion. I protested, and I still couldn't get past that barrier that was there due to the color of my skin, not because of knowledge or what I could do.

From *Untold Tales, Unsung Heroes: An Oral History of Detroit's African American Community, 1918–1967*, edited by Elaine Latzman Moon (Detroit: Wayne State University Press, 1994), 44–45, 46, with permission from Wayne State University Press.

Giving Up the Practice of Law

Ernest Goodman

When the depression came and I was faced with it, I began to find out that the work I was doing as a lawyer, all of it, was on behalf of small retail stores that sold furniture and jewelry on credit to working people. Our job was to try to collect these accounts or repossess it if they couldn't pay, especially when they were laid off. The black community was particularly victimized by this practice. The more I did that kind of work, the more I felt that it was something I didn't want to spend my life on. I read and studied. I became aware that the Thirteenth, Fourteenth, and Fifteenth Amendments had utterly failed to provide any protection to black people.

Over the next five or six years, from 1929–1935, I made the decision to leave the practice of law or at least my kind of practice. Fortunately, as it turned out, all the different enterprises my partners and I entered into terms of making money didn't go very well, and we went broke. I heaved a sigh of relief. I had escaped this rat trap, this cage in which I had found myself enclosed.

Then I began to find something else to do on behalf of people individually—human beings, not companies. I joined a number of organizations—the American Civil Liberties Union, very early, probably in 1935; then the Professional League for Civil Rights; and the Civil Rights Federation.

I saw people, unemployed, walking aimlessly, doing nothing, selling apples on the corner. These were people who looked able and intelligent; they just didn't have any money. I saw my father losing his source of work, his little business. Then I began to read the sources and causes of the depression, and began to understand what was happening, not only in Detroit but over the entire country.

I began to understand that people were being destroyed for no reason I could see that was logical or necessary. I then began to understand what I had been doing as an individual, as a lawyer. I had been working on behalf of a system that was destroying the people around me. I began to realize that I was becoming a part of this system. I made a decision I didn't want that. I wanted to fight on behalf of the people who were being oppressed and do something to help them. The only thing I began to feel sorry about was that I had wasted all these years when I could have been doing something that was useful and constructive.

From *Untold Tales, Unsung Heroes: An Oral History of Detroit's African American Community, 1918–1967*, edited by Elaine Latzman Moon (Detroit: Wayne State University Press, 1994), 61–62, with permission from Wayne State University Press.

Getting By in Grand Rapids

Floyd Chaffee

Well, my father worked on the railroad as a section labor[er], the pay was low, he had to work 6 days a week and every third or fourth week he had to walk the tracks on Sunday for a couple hours, that was part of his job, checking out the tracks. I know that at one time he was bringing home about, I guess his pay, I don't know if he brought it all home, but about $17 a week. We were paying $15 a month in rent, which was the average rent at the time. We lived in the first house below the old Ada School, lived there for 7 years, starting in 1925, so we were living there when the Depression came about. [Mother] was taking in a few washings to do and she did some seamstress work for a few people that wanted a dress made or something. At one time her and another lady that lived 2 houses away from her made door stops. They sold them for $1 a piece. I don't know how many they sold, probably a dozen, maybe. Not a lot, but it still helped. Even though the Depression wasn't on [he was talking about his mother taking jobs before the Depression set in], my mother would take other jobs, too. This was working in towards the time of the Depression, getting close to where I'm talking about now. She also made baked goods on a couple days of the week, tarts and donuts and homemade bread. I would deliver it with a little market basket. I would go around to 4 or 5 different people that would buy the stuff every week. Then, at another time she was making pies for Lena Lou. Mr. Causey, who was running Lena Lou would come over and pick up the pies a couple times a week, or whenever she made them. Another time they had a telephone crew working in Ada and they had to find a place to eat and she served meals to them, dinners, just a dinner to them if they were working in the yard. There would be a crew that would come in there, Bob Morris, next door was in charge of the crew and they would come to the house at noon and they would get a good dinner, all the staples, nothing fancy. Cake or pie, roast beef and gravy, homemade bread, of course, and maybe some sliced peaches, whatever. It was a good meal, it filled them up, and it cost 50 cents. 50 cents was a lot of money in those days. I imagine you could go into a restaurant and get a meal for that, too. But I would say her meals were a little better. They were to me, because I never got in a restaurant. In those days, during my early years and during the first part of the depression, I never went into a restaurant to eat.

I wanted some of the money, of course, and I'd do odd jobs around and I even raised a little garden and sold radishes and stuff out of it, to make a nickel here and a nickel there. If you had a nickel, you thought you were rich then. If you had a quarter, you were a millionaire.

I started delivering the morning Herald, the Sunday paper, and the evening paper, the Press. On the Sunday paper I made 2 cents a paper, and there were between 40 and 50 papers, so I would get about 80 cents or a dollar a week. That was for the Sunday paper. The daily paper was half a cent and I had between 35 and 40 Press papers that I delivered, the Grand Rapids Press. In a week I would make, well if I had 35 I would make 17 cents or 18, say 20 cents a day. I would get around a dollar or a little over at the end of the week. And I had to collect for the papers too on Saturday and that took me quite a while getting [money] from all these people. Some of them paid up and I had trouble with a few. Most of them ended up paying, although I lost a few cents myself on it. I was working for Rex Anthony. If I wanted to keep delivering [to customers in arrears] on my own and take a chance on losing, I could do it, but if he told me to shut them off, I had to shut them off. I had to shut some people off.

Well, I saved my money and I put it in Grand Rapids Savings Bank. I had to put it under my mother's name because I wasn't of age. The Depression hit in '29. I had $54 or $53 in the Bank, and when the bank went [under], I got [back] $26.00. That's all I got at that time.

[The bank would later pay out a fraction of the remaining amount owed to Floyd, which was another $26. He received $2.50.]

Floyd Chaffee Oral History, Ada Historical Society.

The Bankers' Stranglehold on Money
Father Charles Coughlin

Roman Catholic Priest Father Charles Coughlin supported FDR early on, but as the New Deal took shape, Coughlin turned on Roosevelt because of the president's supposed change of heart toward banks. Coughlin was known for conducting a radio program out of Royal Oak, which was quite popular. Despite his popularity, Coughlin lost much of his support, and his program, for expressing anti-Semitic views.

April 11, 1937

I ask you farmers why is it you are unable to till your ground, raise your wheat, sell it at the market for a profit? Because there's no money extant or available. I ask you laborers why is it that you are always growling for higher wages, why is it that sometimes you are forced to sit in idleness in the ranks of those who have no jobs? Simply because there is no money in the pockets of the industrialists to hire you. I ask you industrialists why it is that at seasons you are forced to close your factories, that your belts of production are slackened, that your machinery becomes idle? Because, because the purchasing power, the money available in the pockets of the consumers of the nation is not there. Why is it that boats rust at docks in the ports? Why is it their hulls are empty of wheat, of cotton, of corn, and of products? Because there is no money, money for which trade can be implemented, money by which these things can be obtained by others. In other words the common denominator of all business, industry, farming, labor, and commerce is that vital thing called money, the vehicle, the medium of exchange. And yet despite the facts that Christianity has complained bitterly . . . that a group of individuals have so gained control of issuing and regulating money that the rest of us dare not breathe against their will, despite the fact that the Congress of the United States has specifically said that Congress, or the people, should issue and regulate the money, we Americans stand like dolts stupefied today after a four-year period of relief, a four-year period of "New Deal," a four-year period of reconstruction, worse off at this moment than when Herbert Hoover left the White House in nineteen hundred and thirty three. You question that statement? Dare not question it because I will use for you the latest government facts. Relief that does not relieve. Relief? Oh yes, turn back the page to nineteen hundred twenty nine to nineteen hundred thirty three when our streets were filled with the unemployed, when our farms were vacated, when property was being confiscated, and when little children and innocent women were living on the belt of starvation, I again repeat, in many senses we are worse off at this moment. What are the facts? Well, according to Mr. Green, the president of the American Federation of Labor, there are nine million unemployed American citizens at this moment. Do not take his figures. Take the figures of Harry Hopkins, the administrator of the WPA, and he admits that probably we have seven and a half million unemployed at this moment. And they are conservative figures. And more than that, seven and a half million unemployed, where are the employed persons working today? At present, there are three million jobless on the federal relief payrolls. Another million five hundred thousand on the pay relief rolls of the states, counties, towns, and hamlets of America. Four and a half to four and three-quarter million jobless managing to live without relief, and these are figures which our New Deal government admits. There's where we get our eight million unemployed. Or else look at it from another standpoint. Counting all the families of American citizens there are together twenty-five million men, women, and children in this nation after four years of the New Deal who are forced to eat the black bread of relief. Relief? Why, those figures surpass the figures which Herbert Hoover bequeathed to this nation in 1933. Relief? Relief that has failed to [relieve] although the federal government in these four years has spent ten billion dollars to correct unemployment, and all those counties, states, towns, and hamlets have spent three billion dollars on the same projects. Thirteen billion dollars over four years, three and a half billion dollars every year, to break the back of unemployment, to relieve a situation that grew out of the sins of modern capitalism, and as a result of it all we have accumulated more upon relief, we have accumulated approximately fifty billion dollars of debts of money poured down the rathole of civilization, and we have inherited a laziness and a laxity and a system of living off Uncle Sam on the part of one-fifth of our nation.

"Relief that Does Not Relieve," Charles Coughlin radio address, April 11, 1937. Numerous audio files of Coughlin's addresses are available at https://archive.org/details/Father_Coughlin.

CCC Camp Wolverine

John Cox

Like other New Deal programs, the Civilian Conservation Corps played an important part in lifting Michigan out of the Depression. Most enlistees in the CCC were young men who were sent to camps that were established throughout the country. Michigan would see a few hundred camps, though they existed at various times. CCC enlistees in Michigan worked on numerous projects, but perhaps most astonishing was refor-estation—over 480 million trees were planted in Michigan between 1933 and 1941. For their hard work, enlistees received meals and a small stipend, and some were able to take classes to finish their education.

March 30, 1936

Petoskey and Boyne City business men were entertained at Camp Wolverine last evening. They heard a number of fine speeches regarding the work of the CCC and the ECW [Emergency Conservation Work Act] but it was one of the enrollers, John Cox, who gave the men a glimpse of the greatest work of the organization.

Claude Pangbron, educational director at the camp, introduced the enrollee, saying:

"This man enlisted in the CCC at Chicago and was sent to the west. Later he was brought back to this camp. He had a fifth grade education but through diligent work won his eighth grade diploma last week. He has been learning to use a typewriter and this spring will start his high school studies."

"It isn't because I've won my eighth grade diploma that I appreciate the CCC," Cox began in a halting manner. "It isn't because for the first time in my life I've got money in my pocket. It isn't because I'm in better physical condition than ever before. It is because here I've been given a chance to show I'm as good as the next guy."

Deliberately the youth took a paper from his pocket and looked at his notes.

"Please pardon my mistakes in grammar and this speech," he said. "It is the first time I've ever tried to do anything like this."

No one doubted his statement as he proceeded slowly through his carefully prepared talk. When he sat down, the guests gave him the greatest ovation of the evening. In two minutes the young man had given a greater glimpse of the work of the CCC than all of the other speakers combined.

Captain Kuehne, commander of Camp Wolverine, told more of the young man in a private conversation later. Cox, he said, had been confined to a public institution for nearly all of his younger life because of a physical affliction, now entirely cured. Turned loose into the world, he faced insurmountable difficulties until given a hand by the CCC.

"Now he buys a government bond every month," said the Captain. "He sells various articles to the other campers and adds the profits to his $30 a month pay. Each month he sa[v]es away another $37.50 bond. In addition he makes beautiful watch chains and lanyards from horsehair and picks up a little change that way."

The rehabilitation of boys like John Cox is the greatest work of the CCC, but it seldom comes to public attention. Such an achievement cannot be measured in dollars and cents. But John Cox appreciates the assistance of the CCC and no man who heard him last night would doubt that he will pay substantial dividends in good citizenship to the government that invested in him.

From unknown newspaper, date written in margin March 30, 1936, *Family Search*,
https://familysearch.org/photos/artifacts/13595957.

CHAPTER 13

Organizing Labor: Unionization of Michigan Workers

By the twentieth century, labor organizations had been established in Michigan for some time, but to a small degree. However, the Progressive Era and the Great Depression seemed to carry the movement further than it had ever been. Most business leaders opposed labor organization, and tensions between workers and businesses were sometimes very high. Violence was not uncommon in these situations. The security forces of some companies used intimidation and strong-arm tactics to break up union activity—and some labor organizers used the same to achieve their means. Still, labor organization was an important issue, the debate over which continues to the present day.

Open Letter on the Contract System

C. W. Post

Michigan's food-processing industry flourished at the turn of the twentieth century, especially with the advent of cold cereals, such as corn flakes, invented by Dr. John Harvey Kellogg in Battle Creek. However, the cereal boom did not begin with Kellogg but with Charles W. Post, a businessperson from Illinois who became a patient of Dr. Kellogg in 1891. Post was attracted to Kellogg's idea of cold cereals, and in 1898 he marketed Grape-Nuts, which quickly became popular throughout the country. Because of the success of both Post and Kellogg, Battle Creek became known as "Cereal City."

March 25, 1903

Dear Sir:

If you have sufficient interest in your safety to wish to de-unionize your workers, or, if they are not already unionized, to prevent their becoming so, I feel quite justified in venturing the statement that you can obtain results well defined and satisfactory by adoption the form of agreement with each employee as laid down in the enclosed blank. There are well considered reasons for each paragraph.

If you handle your employees one by one and gradually get them under the contract system, as herein defined, you will discover that instead of belonging to a union and constituting a smoldering hotbed of hatred and opposition to you, they have become your friends and co-workers, because the element of injustice and avarice is eliminated when the contract is entered into. The fundamental features are that the employer and employee both are left to exercise their individual liberties absolutely, but the question of compensation is as absolutely fixed during the term of this contract. The employer may discover that he has contracted with a second-class man instead of a first-class one, or that the employee is filthy, abusive, drunken, careless, breaks up machinery or merchandise unnecessarily, or for some reason is an undesirable employee. It is possible, under this contract to dismiss him; but he cannot be dismissed for the purpose of filling his place at a lower wage. So on the part of the workman, he may dislike his employer, after having started, or may consider the works unsanitary, or the work itself detrimental to his health, or he may have other well defined reasons for disliking his employment. He is at liberty to abandon it, but is not at liberty to discontinue for the purpose of accepting higher wages elsewhere during the life of his contract.

My only excuse for bringing this matter again to your attention is that the labor question is before the manufacturers of America and calling loudly for solution. I know this plan does not solve the problem. The subject is, of course, of no pecuniary interest to me as related to yourself, but is the adoption of the plan works for the public good, the object will have been accomplished. You are at liberty to reproduce the blanks and make use of the plan without any charge whatsoever. I respectfully urge that you make a trial of this contract system with a few employees, and this demonstrate in a practical way whether or not it has value as applied to your work.

Respectfully,
CW Post

Open letter of C. W. Post, Box 3, Post Family Papers, Bentley Historical Library.

Proclamation of Freedom, 1905

C. W. Post

Why have the people come to despise the very term "labor union?"

The feeling seems universal and is held by the great general public and by probably more than half of the unwilling members of the unions.

Statistics show about ten "union" members to every eight hundred citizens and this small minority undertakes to rule the rest of us, if we don't obey exactly and quickly they slug, throw bricks, shoot, cut, dynamite, boycott and murder.

They must make trouble in order to feed their vanity by seeing themselves discussed in the papers, and also to show the "Union" that hires them that "there's something doing." So they order people about, interfere with business, stop street and R.R. cars, building operations, delivery of goods, serving of meals, delivery of bread, meat, or even milk necessary to keep babies alive, and we have been treated to the horrifying scene of their interfering with the sacred rite of burial of the dead.

They become criminals in order to force a few cents or dollars extra out of the public.

Then after they have forced their labor on some firms, they refuse to do the work as directed by the employer and a strike occurs. . . .

When a manufacturer cannot afford to pay the price asked for labor, the unions, in order to force him, go on a strike, picket, boycott, riot, and set up general disorder. Then the police are called in to preserve peace. There has been no disorder by the man who buys labor. It is only caused by the men who have labor to sell and who become outlaws, and bandits under the leadership of anarchists.

[The Anti-Injunction Bill] has been pushed hard before Congress by the Labor Leaders. It is a bill to take away from the courts any right to issue a restraining order to prevent the commission of crime. Under the present wise laws for the protection of life and property, when it seems clear that striking Union men, bandits, and out-laws plan to attack other men or destroy property, the court can issue and order of injunction commanding them to desist or refrain from doing such unlawful act. This has been a great preventative of crime and can never harm any peaceable person, but the "Unions" have the appalling impudence to ask Congress to pass a bill to tie the hands of every court and this allow the Union strikers full sway to assault, dynamite, burn and destroy without hindrance.

When Union men are caught assaulting, burning, or in murder, whose money protects them? Union funds.

If any merchant is coward enough to refuse to help defend his city and her people, preferring to lickspittle for the tyrannous "Unions," don't boycott him, just let the public know it and he will quickly find that 85 percent of the people are not "Union" and his cowardice and traitorous attitude toward his townspeople will bring its own reward.

"Proclamation of Freedom," Box 3, Post Family Papers, Bentley Historical Library.

A Response to the Proclamation of Freedom

L. J. Bodine

Dear Sir:

Permit me to thank you for your highly "instructive" and amusing "Proclamation of Freedom" printed in the Sunday Chronicle. It is really refreshing in these days of hypocrisy and cant, to see a man come forth and fearlessly state his position on such an important subject, regardless of what the cost may be. Not having been aware of, that your goods are being boycotted, and being a consumer of both Postum Coffee and Grape Nuts, it will perhaps please you to know that at least for the time being, I shall cease to use them, this, despite the fact that I am not one of your criminal unionists . . .

I fully agree with you that Americans are born workers, for in no other country on earth can you find a people who can so easily, systematically and thoroughly work the workers as the Americans, and I have no doubt, but that employers, and some of those who hope to be such, have an inborn sympathy for and a desire to help along every peaceable workman who does not try to encroach upon their profits. I blush with shame to think of the many harsh things I have said about capitalists, when I read in your article of how hard our employers work with their brain to get together money so as to pay those who work with their hands. It matters little, that is it was not for the "hand" workers producing the goods to sell, the "brain" workers could work their brains from now until doomsday without realizing a penny.

It is to be regretted that a strike cannot be won without the results you mention, viz: stopping of business and interfering with the delivery of necessities of life, but, what are the methods of capitalism when it wishes to attain its ends? They are always peaceful of course; always in accordance and never conflicting with justice and good morality. Rubbish! and you know it. The crimes of organized labor, though they may be many and large, are as nothing when compared with those of capitalism. Would you have the readers of the Chronicle believe that capitalists are losing any sleep because of the knowledge they have that there are babes in this country that have no milk? If you know anything at all of the condition of labor in this or any other country, you know that there are many places where labor receives so little in wages, as to be insufficient to give proper nourishment to mothers, and therefore are not in a condition to give enough, if any, of their own milk to their babes.

Bodine to Post, May 1, 1905, Box 3, Post Family Papers, Bentley Historical Library.

Copper Country

Judge Patrick Henry O'Brien

The working man had no show if he was hurt during the mine. They'd give him $500 if he were killed, and if he were working, they'd give him enough to live on. Nothing for his injuries. They had a rule that defeated a man if he tried to get it in all the states. Enforced to the letter in Wisconsin and Michigan. They were very conservative and very backward. There were 3 rules that defeated a man. One was if he was hurt through the neglect of a fellow workman—that was an easy thing to do if a man let loose his end of a chain or something. That might tumble one man down a shaft or down the drift, so that he might break an arm or fracture a skull. If he were hurt through the neglect of a fellow worker, he couldn't recover it. Another one was the doctrine of assumption of the risk. It meant that he would take the ordinary risk of the occupation that one is in. One of the risks of being in a mine was to be hurt from falling rock. Anyhow, you assumed the risk. The third one was the doctrine of contributory negligence. The rule was that if one contributed in the slightest degree to the accident you lost.

Miners' organization was what they called an Industrial Organization. That means to say, that everyone that worked in the mine was eligible to be a miner, regardless. Like the ARU—the American Railway Union. . . . That was the type. When the Butte, Montana mines were organized, they were a solid body. They sent organizers to the copper country. I never knew anything about it although I was a great liberal, but I had never heard a thing about it. I didn't know about the organization, until one morning in 1913, the year before the European war broke out, 10,000 miners marched by my office in Laurium [in the Upper Peninsula]. They marched from Red Jacket [now Calumet] to Laurium [which was called Calumet until 1895] and then right back again through the township. I was on the bench then. I had been elected and I was serving my second year. I was living in Houghton then. Mr. Reese came to me for an injunction. Mr. Reese was the general council for the Calumet and Hecla and all the big mining companies. The strike broke out in either June or July 1913. Reese came to my home in Houghton, and he had an injunction, one of the broadest ones prepared, that almost prevented a man from breathing if he was on strike. He was handling it because he was the brainiest one of the corporation lawyers. The injunction was very broadly drafted to prevent the miners from meeting, marching, or collecting on the streets or anything of that kind. It was a very broad injunction. I told him that was pretty broad. I asked him for a modification. The miners' lawyers were damn good; they came from Butte. They handled the thing with some local lawyer with them, but they did the work. They came in with a motion to dissolve the injunction. The injunction was issued and enforced for a couple weeks or so. The miners were madder than hell about it. I split the baby. I didn't dissolve it, but I amended the injunction so it did not include the prevention of marching and of meeting and that sort of thing. It merely prevented overt acts that had a tendency to create rioting and that sort of thing. I allowed the modification injunction to stand. I granted first the broad injunction, and then it was modified by the order I made about two weeks later. That injunction remained during the strike. When they came to be punished for a violation of the injunction, they would come in and they would want to send [500] to 600 men to jail for violating the injunction. I'd say "There was no right to put a man on probation for violating an injunction, but I put him on probation anyhow." I told him to go home and be good. . . . The mining companies wanted me to actually create a bull pen, as they called it. Put them all in jail, behind the fence. They couldn't find a jail that was big enough to hold them, but to create a bull pen like they did in Butte and other places. My family was ostracized because of my actions. My wife was fond of society; we went to all of the leading events in the social life of Houghton. On the 31st of December, we went to a New Year's party. Of course, that was after the injunction was modified, after the miners were allowed to go at large, etc. The papers lambasted me to beat hell. I was a member of the Houghton Club where this New Year's party was being held. That was the most exclusive club in Houghton. Just like the Detroit Club. We went in and not a soul spoke to us. We only stayed about a half hour. The ladies turned their backs on us when we would try to talk to anybody. So we sneaked out. Bessie came home and went into hysterics. I comforted her that that was nothing to worry about. I think that shortened her life. She was a Canadian, very proud and very fond of that kind of thing. All women like that type of thing. But they were particularly trained that way. She was more or less opposed to the stand I took. Anyhow, it made my fortune, the stand I took. I was invited to go here and there. Sort of a defender of the working man.

From Patrick Henry O'Brien Interview, October 16, 1957, Bentley Historical Library.

Governor Woodbridge Ferris

January 11, 1914

My Dear Children:

One week ago today I was planning my trip into the Copper Country. Today I am at home having taken the trip—notwithstanding my repeated announcements that I had no hope of settling the strike, the papers announce that I failed. I accomplished what I set out to accomplish. Many of my friends did not think it safe for me to go. To be absolutely frank, there is always danger in a territory where *everybody* sees "red." It would take pages, yes, a book to tell you all about the situation. There are as usual two sides to the dispute but as I have said one thousand times it is a fight for the recognition of the Western Federation of Miners. Indirectly, it is an effort on the part of socialists (in the Copper Country—"red" socialists) to further their cause—I met Burger of Milwaukee, Russell of New York, Steadman of Chicago, rampant socialists. What do they care about this strike? Just enough to use the strike for socialism. If you could only know what I know your blood would boil. The men of wealth (in all forms) are asleep over a volcano of discontent and anarchy. An industrial . . . and economic revolution is fast approaching. The socialist . . . press in the Copper Country should be put out of business. It fans the flames of the basest and most brutal passions. The mine owners are not angels. Too long they have waited. Capital and labor should be twins, should cooperate.

Woodbridge Ferris to His Children, January 11, 1914, Woodbridge Ferris Papers, Bentley Historical Library.

Samuel Pepper of the Michigan National Guard

July 28, 1913

To Hon. Grant Fellows, Attorney General
Lansing, Mich.

No particular change in situation.

Jurisdiction extended to Keweenaw County this morning on Governor's order. Some pumps started, without disorder. Newspapers here state tonight that all mines will start pumps today or tomorrow. Some parading by workmen today, but no hostile demonstrations. Troops in good shape. Pepper.

July 30, 1913

To Hon. Grant Fellows, Lansing, Mich.
Attorney General

Day has been comparatively quiet in the entire district; trouble last night confined to individuals, nothing serious except as reported. Crowds in Calumet in better humor; think situation improving, especially among resident strikers. A good deal expected of proposed arbitration. No open interference reported at shafts today. Pepper.

July 31, 1913

Situation continues about the same; report as to shooting by sentry proved untrue: C&H shops opened with small force today; men working certainly need protection; threats and assaults continue; no open disorder where militia stationed. Have Carew forward all my mail. Pepper.

Samuel D. Pepper Papers, Box 2, Bentley Historical Library.

A Statement on Collective Bargaining

Flint Alliance

This statement is intended to make clear the position of The Flint Alliance so far as collective bargaining is concerned.

The Alliance at no time has had any intention of becoming a party to negotiations between The General Motors Corporation and the United Automobile Workers of America.

It has no such intention now.

When the Alliance requested a conference with William S. Knudsen, Executive Vice President of General Motors, "for the purpose of discussing collective bargaining" it asked for that meeting at an hour when conferences between the union and General Motors would not be in session.

The chief purpose in asking for that conference was to urge that long and drawn out negotiations not be permitted to hinder Flint workmen from returning to their jobs.

It is an accepted fact by thinking persons that this request by The Alliance was merely seized upon by the union as an excuse to violate its agreement for conferences. Mr. John L. Lewis, the union's leader in Washington, had expressed himself forcibly, at the time plans for the negotiations were announced, that the union had no intention of negotiating until it was recognized as the "sole bargaining agency."

The Flint Alliance had not then and has not now any interest in the controversy between the union and the corporation.

We do have, however, a very vital interest in the situation which has been created by the union's methods.

The Alliance has but one purpose. That is to get men back to their jobs by lawful and orderly methods.

Let bargaining begin after that is done.

George E. Boysen
President, The Flint Alliance

From *Flint Alliance Bulletin*, ca. 1936, Burton Historical Library.

A Report on Union Activity in Flint

Captain Harlow Tubbs

Captain Tubbs is writing to A. D. Greene of Redford High School, Detroit

---

January 27, 1937

I'm replying to your request for information on the Michigan front. So far it has been extremely quiet but who knows when the lid will blow off.

The vast majority of people here in Flint seem to be opposed to the United Auto Workers and especially to the tactics used by the strikers. In fact any person who owns any property whatsoever should condemn the illegal seizure of private property. Many of those who voted for Murphy and Roosevelt are beginning to feel that the present administration is too weak to handle this definite attempt to make the labor racketeers dictators of American labor and industry.

We have undercover agents working throughout the city and they report that only about 10% of the G.M. workers are members of the Union. They also report that these strikers are well armed and in certain places are drilling as military units.

So far I have attempted to give my personal observations unbiased by personal convictions, but nevertheless I feel that this is only the beginning of a domestic situation which can only be stamped out by prompt and decisive action on the part of the government. If they are allowed to get away with it, how long will it be before the small storekeeper, farmer, manufacturer, and homeowner will be paying tribute to the labor racketeers? And again, how can we hope for a solution from the powers which owe allegiance to John Lewis. . . .

If I don't stop soon this letter will cover your next issue. Possibly it would be better to print extracts from it as my personal opinion may not be acceptable to you "hoodwinked" Democrats.

Sincerely,

Harlow O. Tubbs

Captain Harlow Tubbs to A. D. Greene, January 27, 1937, Box 1, Eva Marie Van Houten Papers, Bentley Historical Library.

From Inside the Flint Sit-Down Strike

Francis O'Rourke

December 30, 1936, 6:45 A.M.

Men waving arms—they have fired some more union men. Stop the lines. Men shouting. Loud talking. The strike is on. Well here we are, Mr. Diary. Two sit-down strikers. This strike has been coming for years. Speed-up system, Seniority, over-bearing foremen. You can go just so far you know, even with working men. So let's you and I stick it out with the rest of the boys, we are right and when you're right you can't lose. What a lot of talk. Confusion. Curses. Now the fellows are settling down. I never knew we had so many entertainers in this little shop. Some are dancing, other have formed a quartet, fair singers too. Now a snake dance, everyone is asked to sing a song, so a dance, or recite a poem. So the day is passed. It's 4 A.M. Time to go to bed. *What a night.* NOW I LAY ME DOWN TO SLEEP.

Thursday, December 31, 1936, 11:30 A.M.

Had a good sleep, was surprised for a minute to find myself here in the shop. What will happen today? I hope it will be over. Thinking of that party at my home this evening. I wonder is the basement is decorated for the occasion. Wonder how Sweet (the wife) and the children are feeling. Bet Mother is worried about me. I felt so sorry for Dick today—he wanted so to stay, but when you're feeling good it's tough enough to be here—when you're ill it's too tough.

New Year's Eve

Wonder if my company has arrived yet for the party—I bet they think I'm a swell host—they know I've never been a heel yet and I'm too old to start in now—Gee, I'm glad Chick and Junior are in with us—They're always clowning and able to say something funny. It's sure a help. Poor Ed over there looks blue—his chin will be dragging the floor in an instant. Never expected to spend New Year's Eve in a shop, but here I am, for which I'm glad.

There it is, twelve o'clock, whistles, cheers—1937. Peace on Earth—Why must men in the world's most perfect Democracy have to take such steps to survive? Well the wife and all my guests are out on the street celebrating with me. It's sure swell, but (somehow) a lump climbs into a guy's throat. My brother-in-law here beside me, feels the same way. I can see we'll have to kid each other out of it.

Prayer's and sleep—It's harder to sleep each night. Thoughts march in and out, in and out, until dawn chases them away and we sleep.

January 2, 1937

Won't we have any rest? Sheriff Wolcott was here with an injunction. Did you know we were breaking the law? Did the fellows at Kelsey-Hays in Detroit break the law in their sit-down strike? If so why didn't the Wayne County Sheriff serve an injunction on them? Are the laws of Genesee so different than those of Wayne County? I never expected Sheriff Wolcott and his law enforcement agents here.

We have done no harm. We're just honest working men that have been pushed so far and so hard that we can't keep it up any longer. They say we're lazy workers. Is a man lazy if he has not missed a day's work in two years, has not been late, and kept up with a line manufacturing forty-five bodies in an hour all that time? Most of these men have done just that and our employment records prove it. I'm glad the Sheriff is gone. Wonder if he will return? On guard against violence, watch, watch, watching all the time. No rest tonight. We don't want violence and yet we hear peace preached all the time by our strike leaders.

January 3, 1937

Well, the Sheriff never returned. Our prayers were answered, Thank God. Now we can have peace and rest. We need it. The boys are pleased that there was no trouble—the spirit is at the highest it's been since we sat down. Everyone is cheerful and all smiles. There is talk that we can return home without the danger of them scabbing our jobs. Home, Sweet Home. . . . I think I'll buy a couple dozen of those cards and hang two in each room of the house. I wonder if Patsy can ride the tricycle Santa Claus brought her, and Jerry the bike. I have some Christmas shirts I'd like to try on. Sweet probably want the basement cleaned.

January 4, 1937

In time I guess men grow used to anything. Let me see how many days have we been here. One, two, three, four, five long days. Gee I thought weeks had passed. The fellows are in a playful mood. Some have a ball made of rags and are playing basketball; using an old pail for a basket. We have a volunteer barber now—and boy is he busy? This has been a swell day. I hope the night passes the same.

January 5, 1937

The Flint Alliance an anti-strike organization has been organized. What a night of wild rumors—On your pins boys—here they come, up to the gate—they won't take us out, we're sincere. All through the night, no rest, no sleep—jittery nerves, strained morale. The time and the conditions are taking their toll. One brother is acting queer. Should we ask him to go home? Another is sick of body, but his heart is all there. We'll have a car take him home over his own objections. Some of the weak are giving up. Wonder if we can rest today. We ex-service men don't mind it much. The breaking point seems between 6 o'clock and 8 o'clock in the evening. My company was over this evening. Sweet and the children sure are loyal. They haven't failed yet. It sure helps to know the good wives are with you in thought and spirit, Thank God for that. Wonder if we can sleep tonight.

January 6, 1937

Another day, Diary, and a fair rest! Suspicion seems to have taken hold. Each of us watch the other. Is he one of us, or is he one that is paid by our opponent? Watch him! Watch out for him, I hear all day and into the night. Day time seems like eternity and nights seem like minutes. Sorry that Boysen took the stand he did. I always had respect for George, but I'm afraid it's gone now.

January 7, 1937

Well Diary, Fisher #2 gets pretty cold when the heat has been turned off. I'm glad we have those blankets from home—they sure come in handy, . . . Eat, no thank you. I'm not hungry. You don't have much appetite when all you do is walk back and forth—one end of the shop and back again—always thinking of what tonight will bring. Here it is evening again—evil always come in the night—be on your guard at all times men. Are the guards on each door? Watch the back of the shop. They could come across the railroad bridge and sneak up on us from the rear—be on your guard at all times men. They shall not take us out.

January 9, 1937

This has been a very peaceful day—had an invitation to dinner with the trimmers—they have a kitchen of their own and T-bone steaks were on the menu. These trimmers are real chefs. I'll tell their wives about it when we get out. The men can prepare Sunday dinners at home for a change.

This usually was Sweet's and my night out and we usually make our weekly trip to the movies. I hope she can go tonight, she's been so good since I've been here, and tomorrow I see the children. They think I've been working all this time. Here she is now. . . .

"Hello, Sweet, How's everything at home? Do you have coal? How are the children? That was a lovely dinner you brought down last night. Yes, we are feeling fine; most of us have colds, but nothing to worry about though. Well, I'm glad everything is O.K. We'll see you tomorrow. Good Night dear." Well might as well lay down now.

January 10, 1937

Sunday and I've missed mass. I'm sorry, but I missed mass during the World's War and this is war. Sunday always seems like a day of rest, but so many visitors are out in front. I wonder what they think. Some have sneers on their faces. Usually office workers. They know nothing of the working conditions in the shop. Others are here with encouragement. Would like to go down on the walk like the inquiring reporter and ask each one down there for their opinion on this whole affair . . . The fellows here seem more relaxed than they have been for days. Some are kidding the watchman. The men and the watchman are very friendly toward each other—after all, we all are just honest working men.

January 11, 1937

Had a good sleep last night, since our Governor has said there will be no violence we now rest better. I wish the Flint Alliance would disband. I believe they are only causing trouble. This issue is not an issue that can be settled in the City of Flint. It's a national issue. So the Flint Alliance. So what? Well I see the heat has been shut off again, and it's getting quite cold in here. Well let's wrap up a little warmer, we'll have no trouble about that. 6:15 P.M. . . . Here they come!—22 Factory Police, with their long night sticks going to take the ladders are you? Go ahead, but why carry those clubs. Surely you know you don't need them. We'll have no trouble over a ladder. Wonder why all the police are out front. See, there's another car of plain clothes men, driving up to the curb. Watch them report to those scout cars that are parked across the road. Do they think we would start trouble? Men don't start trouble when they have been preached to, that there will be no violence and it has been two weeks nearly. What! They have locked the doors and won't allow our dinners brought in. Why? Those hot meals those ladies have out there will be cold in a few minutes. Won't they let our dinners from union headquarters in either? You men stay upstairs and let our Police Chief and his men go down and ask for the keys to the doors from Peterson. If he refuses we'll have to open the doors anyway. You can be cold, you know, but cold and hungry is too much. Won't give them . . . we'll push the doors. Open, there they go.

    The doors are open to us for the first time since this thing has started. Men are shaking hands with their brothers on the outside. Everyone is laughing. Let's sing a song. "Hail, Hail, The Gangs All Here." Look out men, the Police—Bang! Bang! Tear gas bombs. Close the doors quick. Policemen in helmets with gas masks on. Why did they fire on us? Where did they come from so sudden? They have broken the glass in the front door. Bang! Tear gas fired through the broken glass. Get the fire hose. They say no violence then they attack those unsuspecting, peaceful men. Defend yourselves as best you can. They have broken their words, so let them have it. Bring up those hoses. Come on you pickets. Stones, bottles, bricks, hinges, bolts, flying through the air, not much for defense but that's all we have. Some of our men are down. Lousy, shooting a man when he has no gun. Over goes a car. There goes another of our men. More tear gas. Smarting eyes. Look out for that riot gun. Bang! Bang! Ahead men, they are retreating. Keep them on the move. Even policemen can't fight and fight with a heart, with all their guns unless they know there is a just cause. More gun fire. It's terrible. Wild shouts and women crying for the safety of their loved ones. Ambulance horns. Reports of a shotgun fired very close. Bottles breaking on the street thrown from the roof. Our men up there are doing their bit. Now all is quiet. We have chased them back at least. Take care of our wounded, open those windows, let that gas out. You men who were out on the street come and get warm. Put on some dry clothes. Boy those hoses sure came in handy. And was that water cold; look my pant legs are frozen stiff. Don't leave the hoses men they are coming back. Come on men let's go out and get them. To your posts, they are making another attack. Lord protect us. Who's that shooting from the bridge. Some coward that's afraid to come down close enough so we can reach him. We got them on the run again. Don't stop now. Heavenly Father stop this outrage. Now all is silent again. Is that all of this, I ask you? Now stories of the attack. Tears running down cheeks, tears caused by tear gas bombs. Swollen faces, bloody clothes. What a mess. No one can sleep after this.

January 12, 1937

All is quiet on Chevrolet Avenue. Streets are littered with refuse . . . broken windows, dismantled cars—all leave their story of the night before. We men are pleased, the Governor is in town. We are glad the State Troopers and the National Guard are here. We have faith in them, maybe we can trust them. We thought the same of the City Police and look. . . . We want no violence, and will not seek any. Maybe the State Troops and the National Guards will act as our protectors from another attack. Tonight maybe we can sleep.

January 13, 1937

Our good Governor seems to be doing everything in his power to bring our men and those of the General Motors together. If this man Boysen would have kept out of it I believe a settlement would have been reached by now. Captain Lyons of the Michigan State Police asked to visit us today and we escorted him and his men through the plant. He said he was really surprised that there was no destruction of property and that the plant was in such fine shape, after all these hours our men have been here. There can be no destruction when our men watch everything so close, and no rules have been broken. It seems to me that each day brings us closer to an understanding and when an agreement is made we are ready to return to our jobs. We are seeing to it that nothing will have to be repaired before production can be got under way. . . .

January 14, 1937

News! News! Wonderful news. Governor Murphy, Our [union] President, Mr. Martin and Mr. Knudsen [of GM] are to meet at 11 o'clock today at our State Capitol and we believe that something will come out of this meeting. The boys all feel good about it but most of us are out of cash at home and our coal bins are empty. You can't put much away when you are working at the pay we receive and the cost of living so high. Out of work two weeks and we are broke. Everyone seems to be passing the day crowded around the radio, listening to News Flashes from Lansing—hoping they might tell us to return to our homes.

The day is passed. We have had word that the conference at Lansing still goes on. We are tired and some of us are going to retire. All guards at their posts. It's after midnight so back to the cotton for me.

January 15, 1937

Extra! Extra! Men are to evacuate the plants—General Motors and our Union are to meet Monday, January 18th and to come to some agreement in a period of fifteen days. We men can go home—is that good news or is that good news? The agreement that led to their future negotiations as I understand them are that we leave the plants and that General Motors do not remove dies or parts and do not attempt to resume operations in any of the strike bound plants during the fifteen days of negotiations.

Fair enough I think and my mind seems at rest for the first time since December 30 last year. That's a long time. Well I'm sure I'll rest tonight.

January 16, 1937

We are to leave the plant, Diary. The boys of Cleveland first then Anderson, Indiana then to Detroit then Flint. There will be a celebration at each place and Sunday evening we will all be in our homes and are the boys pleased? I wonder how the furniture looks and the children's toys. I'll be so glad to be with them again. Boy, I'm even anxious to see Mike (Mike is the cat). Well here they come—newspaper reporters. Reporters from all over the world it seems. Ed Lahey of Chicago, Louis Stack of the New York Times, Paul Benton of the Washington Times, Edward Angly of the New York Herald Tribune, Associated Press, United Press. Where did they all come from and the questions they ask. Let's get a picture of this. We want a picture of that. All through the day and the early hours of the morning. Gee! They're a nervy bunch. But I guess their jobs call for a lot of nerve.

January 17, 1937

Clean shirts, faces that show marks of an early morning shave. Most of the fellows have neck ties on today. Everyone seems to be up early. Some are washing their clothes, others are trying to make their shoes shine, everyone is in a happy frame of mind. Wonder when they will take us out. The band will be here from Cleveland and we are to parade down to the Union Headquarters. What a celebration. Already people are gathering in front of the shop. What a crowd. They seem to be as pleased that we are coming out as we are of going. 1:45 here comes the car with the loud speaker. Here comes the band. Music, laughter. What is that announcement? We have been double crossed? We are not going to leave the plant? Gee! I feel dizzy. Not going home. Not going home after all these preparations. General Motors would not keep an honest agreement. Boysen and his Flint Alliance. This thing would have been settled long ago and we would have been back at our jobs were it not for them. Peace on Earth—who, I ask you, is preventing that peace. Were we not ready and willing to carry out our bargain? Discouraged men. Heart sick men. Men who had planned to go home. But who have decided to stay for our own interest. Again the long march from the front of the shop to the back of the shop. Back and forth until we are tired and then to bed.

January 18, 1937

Awake at the foot of the hill called disappointment. Men who were smiling yesterday have frowns today. Not much talking and no singing. These men are sick at heart. Now do you wonder why we trust no one? Can you tell us why we should? For the past five years we have been meeting one disappointment after another. Is it any wonder these good men rebelled?

Reds, I see they call us. Reds if you will but I wish I could take you down the aisles of this silent factory about midnight and see these men on their knees at their cotton beds, asking their heavenly father for protection and blessings and I know asking the father of peace to guide them right. Men on their knees in prayer.

January 19, 1937

Another day. The shock of Sunday's disappointment seems to have faded some. Some of the boys are greeting each other with cheery good morning—our police force seems to be better natured. Some of the fellows are humming as they get ready for their shower. Do you know, Diary, these men that are left . . . are the ones that were forever complaining and are the ones who had the most to say before. These men that are here now are in my opinion the better workmen—the men that have one or more children and they are all clean cut fellows that think for themselves. Many have told me that is they could only gain human conditions for their children this fight would not have been in vain. And so you know they don't blame Messrs Sloan, Knudsen or the Fisher Brothers, but their petty bosses who in their greedy way have been working for bonuses that they get at the end of the year and have forgotten that these good workmen are also human.

January 20, 1937

Just another Wednesday. I see some rabbits out the back window and would like to go hunting. Nice day for hunting too. We have a new radio and I know by heart when the news reporters are in the air. Listen all day. Sloan is to meet again in Washington, hope something comes out of this meeting. I hope this is settled soon. Kangaroo court this evening. We use the court to punish offenders. The main offense is not washing dishes as soon as they are finished with them and not cleaning up the smoking rooms properly. Two of the fellows were found guilty after a fair trial and sentenced to scrub the dining room floor on their hands and knees. A severe sentence but order must prevail. The day is done and no good news as yet.

January 21, 1937

A new day and good news. Were there any extras out? Sloan is to meet Madam Perkins [Frances Perkins, secretary of labor for FDR] today. Maybe some agreement will come out of this meeting. Why is it so important we leave the shops? He does not intend to run them anyway so he says?

Extra! Extra! Sloan walks out of conference. I wonder what his plans are now. I wonder what scheme he intends to use to get us out. I pray for no violence. Each time a conference is broken I have a funny sick feeling in my stomach.

January 23, 1937

Saturday. Up and shaved also had a shower, just as if I were going down town to do some shopping for Sweet, or maybe go to a movie. It's a lovely day. If I were out we would drive to Detroit to visit some of our relations but I'm not out, so what? We have a ping pong table in the shop now and it is in use continuously—it helps to keep us occupied and some means of recreation. Most of the fellows are between the ages of thirty and thirty-nine. I would say our ages average about thirty-five, so you see they are all quite active. You have to be active to keep up with the line. While we were working we had a lovely baked ham and some fresh rye bread donated to us today—and it was good. Our meals are sent in three times a day by the union and we have plenty to eat.

January 24, 1937

Sunday and my turn on the fire patrol. I never cared about working on the Sabbath but we must protect this shop from all damages. We have organized a fire protection brigade and it is our duty to see that there are no fire hazards and that nothing is destroyed for we feel that we have an interest in this shop as much as General Motors has. Haven't we spent from five to ten years here?—shouldn't we feel interested in it? What have we to show for those many years of hard labor—nothing but bills. Yes, we'll have them paid all right when the lay-off comes, only to get back in debt again. Why don't we save our money, you ask me? When we have finished paying the grocer, the landowner, the insurance man, the gas and light bill, buying some clothing for the children and a little change for church, we end up with a couple of dollars to run us until the next pay day. Could you save some money with that amount?

January 26, 1937

More news that's not so good. Mr. Sloan declines Madam Perkin's invitation. Another queer feeling in my stomach, just as if I had never eaten for a week and then gone for an airplane ride. Oh! God, won't this ever end. The boys are trying to keep their spirits up but here and there you can see haggard faces that show nerves are about to crack. So our good President has rebuked Sloan. Wonder how the outside world feels about us. I hope public sentiment has changed for our good.

January 27, 1937

Another Wednesday and the week is half over. Wonder how the children are—is Sweet feeling better? I know she's nearly a nervous wreck and Mother as well. Gee! It must be tough on our Wives and Mothers but they believe as we do, so they too are keeping their chins up. Today we read that legislation has been asked to hold conferences in strike situations of this kind. We surely hope it passes. Today one of the fellows wise cracked—"President Lincoln freed the slaves but we are forgotten." We have a new ping pong table today and the fellows are lining up for their turns. I suppose it will keep them busy for a couple of days and then it will have to be something different. Some of the fellows seem to read continuously but I can't seem to get interested. I can hardly wait for the daily papers and then read only the strike news—then for a walk, always walking, always in a hurry and not going anyplace.

January 28, 1937

Lieutenant Governor Nowiki of the State of Michigan paid us a visit today. He said that he came to see for himself. He was quite surprised that there was no destruction after all he had read and [he] said too that we men did not appear to be the violent characters that we were painted by some of the newspapers. We were glad to have him with us, and I feel better that some responsible person had come in as we have nothing to hide.

January 29, 1937

A new day and hoping for new and good news. I seem to feel better today. I believe my nerves were getting me down yesterday but a good sleep and a new day helped. Mr. Sloan has promised to meet Madam Perkins,—maybe something will come from this. Wonder what was said, wonder if they are friendly toward each other. Had a motion picture show this evening. You should have seen it and got some idea of the speed-up system. It's exaggerated of course but I'll swear on my word that our lines run nearly that fast and there are no relief men either.

January 30, 1937

Mr. Sloan breaks his promise—now what? Were those promises made? It does not seem possible that a man in his position would do that, or have they thought of another scheme to try? You will find that our union is a lot stronger than most people think and that we can call out more shops if it is necessary but I do hope we won't have to.

January 31, 1937

Today I'm going to try and forget strikes, forget General Motors, forget Union and pretend I'm home—Home with Sweet and the children. Well it's getting near 9 o'clock—better get cleaned up for church—come on sonny get your hair combed and have your prayer book ready. I'll get the car. Are you ready Sweet? Come Patsy, Daddy will carry you. Let's stop and get Mother and Dad, we don't want to be late. There are some of our friends—it's nice to see them. Seems like we have been away for a long time doesn't it? Well Mass is over and dinner time. That was a nice dinner Sweet. I'll help you with the dishes. All right, Sonny, I will take you down there but you will have to walk back but it will be good for you and it's not far and Daddy can rest this afternoon. 6 o'clock and time for lunch, had a nice rest, after lunch will read the paper and go to bed for tomorrow is labor day—every Monday is labor Monday. Just a day of make-believing but it helps my mind from thinking of this terrible mess and I'm glad I thought of it.

February 1, 1937

What's the trouble fellow—you say they are taking over Chevrolet Plant Four. Look at those men go. Men running, men climbing over the fence, men cheering the sound truck, men coming down the street with clubs. More blood shed, more tear gas, more riot clubs. Another riot and another shop full of sit-down strikers. You heard me say we had more strength. More blood shed. So men shed their blood if they think they could bargain with the company and make fair bargains through the company unions? So you think there are so many men that quit their work because they are lazy? Here comes the troops—now maybe we will have protection—now maybe we will have peace. Thank God they are here. We know the company police across the road and the many others in there with them will not attack us now. Tonight fellows we can have some peaceful rest. General Motors has asked for another injunction but we can worry about that tomorrow.

February 2, 1937

All is quiet on the Chevrolet front, the National Guards have taken over the street. Major Ed Carrier seems to be in command. We have sung a few songs to the soldier boys and passed out time watching them change guards. Injunction has been granted and Sheriff Wolcott is coming down to take us out. We're not coming out. Waiting, waiting, won't he ever come. We can't get news from the outside and can't get news out. It's nerve wracking. Just waiting for the Sheriff and wondering when we go into action. I do hope none of us get hurt. All good men they are and don't want violence. We're not coming out though. 8:40 P.M. Here comes the Sheriff—seal the doors, get the hoses ready—let them start it first. I'll talk to him. "I have an injunction, will read it to you"—Legal phrases, we don't understand. We have until 3:00 P.M. tomorrow to leave. O.K Sheriff we'll be here when you come again. Thank God that's over. More waiting, men walking back and forth. The expression on their faces show they are on the verge of a breaking point. No news—if we only could hear from the outside. 1:00 A.M. Meeting called, someone has to go through the lines. Will they be arrested if they go—can't go back. Signals arranged. We'll signal from top of the hill to roof of shop. One of our men is leaving in the early morning. Hope he gets through O.K.

February 3, 1937

Let's go to the roof and watch for signals. I don't feel like eating. See that white house on top of the hill, that's where he is to be. Look! he's waving his arms to attract attention. Here's the signal. "Hold the Fort" all day long the same signal. Crowds gather on the top of the hill, coming down to see us get shot I suppose. 2:45—five more minutes and our time is up. Help us Oh, Lord and protect us. 3 P.M. Governor Murphy has asked that the injunction be set aside until negotiations are over. Thank God. The tension is broken, men singing, men laughing, all is quiet on Chevrolet front again. You see smiles on men's faces. Again we can rest. Boy, am I tired.

February 4, 1937

Now how will we get news, nothing to eat this morning. Are they going to starve us out? Men on the roof of Plant 4 are calling to us. They have no heat over there and nothing to eat either. Day and night it seems something is always happening at Fisher #2. Why don't they go out to Fisher #1 and raise hell sometime? Are there too many men there for them? LOOK! Here comes our man we let out yesterday to signal us. He has a military pass, soldiers stop him, they let him through the lines. Boy, am I glad. Hello Buddy, Gee we're glad to see you. You can carry notes for us? God! I'll write to Sweet and the children. Hope they are well. Tell them I'm O.K. and not to worry. She'll probably write me. Will you wait for an answer? Gee, thanks a lot. I feel a lot better now. Our mail man will be back in the morning.

February 5, 1937

Had a dandy rest last night—first one for weeks. We feel a lot safer knowing the guards are outside and our good Governor insisting there will be no violence. Wonder when our mailman will arrive. Boy! he'll be a welcomed fellow. Here he is now. Any word for my Buddy? OH! Boy—thanks a lot. Sweet and the children are well and everything is lovely. Governor Murphy, Lewis, and Knudsen are in conference yet. Things look good on the outside. Maybe we'll get out soon. I guess I'll find something to do. Maybe the time will pass faster. Well I've got a black jack braided. Hope I never have to use it. Some of the men are making knives and they sure are fancy ones too. Time to clean up the shop and then a shave and to bed.

February 6, 1937

Friday has passed, pay Friday and no pay. Well maybe we will make it up at the end of the year. We usually are laid off six to ten weeks at the end of each year. Funny no one tells how much we lose then. But the papers are mentioning how much we are losing every day now. General Motors is worrying about it now. But when we are laid off no one thinks anything of it.

February 7, 1937

Sunday and here we are—39 days or is it 40? Oh well it doesn't make any difference, we're here and here we stay. Some of the boys are playing ping pong. It's an endurance contest I guess—hour after hour they play. I guess they have been out of pennies or they are tired of playing penny ante. Chick has a new game, he has a lot of squares numbered from 1–10—if your penny falls on the square you get the number of pennies it calls for but if it hits on a line Chick gets the pennies. It's a good racket for Chick and so the day goes. A few minutes here then there—I don't seem to be able to stay in any one place long. I met Major Geers and Lieutenant Colonel Wiesenhaefer of the 125th Infantry today. Seem like nice men. Had a talk with Major Ed. Carrier—I like him a whole lot.

February 8, 1937

The conference in Detroit is still going on. Boy! I hope they finish this thing soon. I have lost 26 pounds and it seems like I'm losing more each day. I'll probably gain it all back when I stop worrying and I'll stop when this is settled. Our Leader, John L. Lewis is reported ill. I do hope it is not serious. Wonder if they will continue meeting if he's not there? The boys are taking up a collection for flood sufferers and I'm surprised at the amount they have. Pennies amount to dollars alright. We feel so sorry for those poor people.

February 9, 1937

New plans for a settlement. I wonder what they are talking about. How I pray they won't break up. Always listening to news flashes. I wonder if the announcers really know what's going on—I sometimes think they don't. We're sure Governor Murphy is doing all he can and we know Lewis will be reasonable. Guess I'll go to the roof and back—my long walk in the fresh air. Gee, the side walk looks good from here. Wonder how it seems to ride in a car, and go window shopping. I seem to be sleepy all the time lately. Maybe it's because I can't find anything to do.

February 10, 1937

Conference still goes on. No news but the good Governor is smiling they say. Well no news is good news. It won't be long and the news reporter will be on again. Maybe we'll have some good news then. A short recess and back in conference again. All you hear is what do you think—are they getting any place, do you think it will end soon? How I wish I knew. I can't stand this much longer. I'm beginning to jump at little noises—the fellows say "look out, he's about ready to blow his top." I'm not that bad yet. Wish I could think of something to laugh about or even a smile might do some good. May as well go to bed. This has been a bad day.

February 11, 1937

5:45 A.M.—McIntyre of the Detroit News was down in front and said the strike was settled. The guards have chased him away. The fellows are awakening everyone up and having a parade up and down the aisles. If it's not true it's going to be terrible. Wish our man that carries the mail would come. Hope the guard doesn't stop him today. Here he comes and he's smiling. He has a newspaper. Here's the headlines—STRIKE IS SETTLED—Thank God. The boys are dancing with each other, everyone is laughing. At last we go home, Home Sweet Home. The boys have voted to accept the agreement and here comes Fisher #1 down the street—crowds of people, flash lights, flags waving, banners, shaking hands. Chevrolet Plant four is coming out and they are on their way to Little Fisher. Will be home soon now, deary and I've not deserted you after all. Two wars we've been through and this last one we knew what we were fighting for. Peace on Earth, Good-will Toward All Men.

Transcription of O'Rourke's diary, dated April 1937, Perry Archives.

Letters to Judge Edward Black on His Injunction against the Strikers

Judge Black issued the first injunction against the Flint sit-down strikers, but a severe conflict of interest emerged—the judge owned a significant amount of General Motors stock.

"A Friend of Labor"

January 3, 1937

I have just finished reading the specific article of the injunction handed down by you, against the striking auto workers.

I personally believe you should have your head examined. You are as fit to sit on the Circuit Court as a garbage collector. I further believe the above heading is in error: it should be changed to read "You lousy bastard"

Yours truly,
"A Friend of Labor"

George H. Corey

January 7, 1937

Sir:

A lawyer with decent ethical standards, a judge with a high sense of his official integrity, and a gentleman—knowing that he was the owner of 3,665 shares of General Motors stock—would have been sensitive enough to have referred an injunction application to a disinterested Court. That you used your high office for your personal ends earns the hearty contempt of decent men and women everywhere.

I presume nothing will come of it, but I hope that it may be possible to bring about your impeachment. Men like you, intellectually dishonest and utterly lacking in judicial temperament, should be driven from the Bench. Even without you the Courts lack the respect to which they should be entitled.

Yours truly,
Geo. H. Corey

Maud M. Jerome

January 7, 1937

Dear Sir: Some fourteen years ago, you handed down a decision that turned me, then an expecting mother, out of a home.

That decision I then felt most unfair. I shall be honest I felt it a purchased decision. I still think the same and only you and God knows whether or not I misjudged for the wealthy and pompous other party, I understand, is now dead.

Be all this as it may, it is now ancient history, and today you are placed in an unenviable position because you did, what I presume any decent citizen believes was your duty.

I wish to be among the first to tell you I admire you for issuing that injunction. You did your duty and rightly and I hope laws will be passed in this Country outlawing these Unions, intent only on stirring up strife and trouble and making hardships for [our] communities.

Thank you for what you did.
Sincerely,
Maud M. Jerome

Edward Davison Black Papers, Box 1, Bentley Historical Library.

Right to Work

Jack Lessenberry

November 12, 2012

[The] labor movement's enemies in the legislature are now calling for the enactment of a so-called right to work law, which would outlaw the union shop.

Currently, if a union represents workers at a factory, plant or other enterprise, the workers either have to join the union, or at least pay union dues, as a condition of employment.

That would be illegal if Michigan enacted a right to work law, as 23 other states have done. Unions could still exist, but membership would be strictly voluntary, and they would be greatly weakened as a force for collective bargaining for the workers.

In fact, union leaders believe with some justice that this would mean the end of the labor movement, and they will fight to the death to prevent that from happening. (Even without right to work, unions have been losing ground nationally and in Michigan for decades.)

Governor Rick Snyder doesn't want the legislature to pass right-to-work laws. He fears that would be unnecessarily divisive, might have a nasty backlash, and says right-to-work laws are not needed in order for him to accomplish what needs to be done.

Senate Majority Leader Randy Richardville agrees with him. But they are considerably less radical than many of their fellow Republicans in the legislature. And some of those, like Senator Jack Brandenburg of Macomb County, are pushing for lawmakers to pass right to work, right away, during a lame duck session.

While Republicans will still control both houses of the legislature next year, they did lose five seats in the house, and doing anything radical might be a little bit harder.

There is little doubt that the legislature can pass such a bill if that's what they want to do, though even one of right to work's biggest boosters, Senator Patrick Colbeck of Canton, says it would be probably be too complicated to pull off in a lame duck session.

What nobody really knows is if the governor would sign a right to work bill if one lands on his desk—though most people think the answer would be a reluctant yes. I don't know for sure, but I do know this:

Passing a right to work law could end up being a long-term disaster for the Republicans. It could give Democrats the needed rallying cry to punish them in the coming midterm elections.

The fact that voters didn't want to stick collective bargaining in the constitution doesn't mean that they are solidly anti-union. The collective bargaining amendment vote was closer than the other constitutional amendments. There's some indication that many confused voters just blindly voted against them all.

The chances are that many of the same voters who are against unions having special constitutional rights would also be opposed to having the rights they now have taken away from them.

The governor has a lot he wants and needs to get done quickly, from finding a replacement for the emergency manager law to his favorite cause, personal, meaning business, property tax reform.

The last thing he needs is for a legislative jihad against Michigan's unions to get in the way.

"Right to Work?" by Jack Lessenberry for Michigan Radio, November 12, 2012, http://michiganradio.org. Reprinted with permission from Michigan Radio.

Governor Rick Snyder

December 11, 2012

The Facts about Freedom to Work

WHAT IS FREEDOM TO WORK?

Freedom to Work, also known as right to work, is a simple measure that gives every worker the right to choose for themselves whether to join a union. It's based on the simple truth that Michigan workers should never be forced to join—or not join—a union.

WHY DOES GOVERNOR SNYDER SUPPORT FREEDOM TO WORK?

Governor Snyder is pro-union and pro-worker, and he supports Freedom to Work for two reasons. First, he believes that workers should be able to decide whether or not they want to join a union. Second, he believes that Freedom to Work is one more way that we can help Michigan's economy be more competitive, grow stronger, and produce more and better jobs for the people of our state.

WHO ELSE SUPPORTS FREEDOM TO WORK?

A majority of people in Michigan support a right to work law, according to a recent poll.

HOW WILL FREEDOM TO WORK HELP MICHIGAN'S ECONOMY?

Freedom to Work will help Michigan attract the new businesses and new industries we need to compete in the 21st century. That will help our economy recover faster and set us on the path to more and better jobs for years to come.

HOW DOES FREEDOM TO WORK IMPACT WAGES?

According to the Wall Street Journal, "of the 10 states with the highest rate of personal income growth, eight have right-to-work laws," and according to an economic study, there is a 23% higher rate of per capita income growth in right-to-work states. Another study finds that had Michigan adopted a right-to-work law in 1977, per capita income for a family of four would have been $13,556 higher by 2008.

Not only do right-to-work states provide more jobs, the workers in those states enjoy a higher standard of living. Yes, there are some right-to-work states where workers receive lower wages, but that's because the cost-of-living happens to be lower in those states. Moreover, workers in right-to-work states don't have to pay mandatory union dues or make forced political contributions, so they end up with even more take-home pay.

HOW DOES FREEDOM TO WORK IMPACT BENEFITS?

Right-to-work does not affect workers' ability to bargain for their benefits in any way. If workers feel that management is mistreating them, they're still free to unionize and fight for their benefits through collective bargaining. All right-to-work does is give workers the freedom to choose whether or not to join a union. If they believe unionizing is in their best interest, they're free to do that. If they're happy without unionizing, they're free to do that, too.

DOES FREEDOM TO WORK PREVENT PEOPLE FROM JOINING A UNION?

Absolutely not. Freedom to Work in Michigan will allow everyone the freedom to choose whether or not they want to join a union. Workers will not be forced to join a union, just as no one should ever be forbidden to join a union.

HOW DOES THIS LEGISLATION IMPACT POLICE AND FIRE UNIONS?

This legislation has no impact on police and fire unions. It respects and preserves the status afforded to police and firefighters under Public Act 312, which reflects the hazardous nature of their jobs. We must preserve the loyalty and intra-unit solidarity that are crucial elements in the ability of our police and firefighters to perform their dangerous public safety missions.

"The Facts about Freedom to Work," December 11, 2012, http://www.michigan.gov.

Stateside Staff, Michigan Radio

December 10, 2014

It's been two years since hordes of people descended on the state Capitol to protest the passage of "right-to-work" legislation in the lame-duck session.

Lawmakers and Gov. Rick Snyder argued it was only fair that union workers decide whether they actually wanted to pay dues to the union. They also said businesses would move to Michigan if it became a right-to-work state. Labor leaders and others called it a ploy to weaken unions and Democrats.

So what have we seen in the two years since right to work came to Michigan?

Patrick Anderson, CEO of Anderson Economic Group, and Charles Ballard, an economics professor at Michigan State University, both say not much has changed. They say the power of organized labor in the state has been in a steady decline now for the last five decades.

Ballard says 50 years ago, 45% of Michigan workers were unionized. Today, that number is at 16%—the same rate it was when the right-to-work law passed.

Ballard also notes the lack of evidence confirming that the passage of the right-to-work law has led to an increase in job creation within the state. He says this is due to the fact that right-to-work wasn't a sudden shift, but merely a ratification of what had been going on for a long time.

Ballard says the cases made by both sides when the law passed were overblown. Anderson agrees, noting this year's midterm elections and the complete lack of attention right to work garnered from politicians from both the Democratic and Republican parties.

Anderson says the message right to work ultimately sends is that Michigan has become a much friendlier state for employers. He says it will take some time before we start to see the effects of the law.

"Two Years Later, What Effect Has 'Right to Work' Had on Michigan?," Stateside Staff, Michigan Radio, December 10, 2014, http://michiganradio.org. Reprinted with permission from Michigan Radio.

CHAPTER 14

Arsenal of Democracy: World War II

Because of Michigan's industrial capacity, the state played an important role in war production through the first half of the twentieth century. During wartime, the demand for labor rose with the boost in production, and therefore women were welcomed into jobs that were previously reserved for men. Further, thousands of southerners migrated north to work in these industrial jobs. While this led to social tension that sometimes burst into violence, Michigan factories continued to churn out war materiel: tanks, transport vehicles and replacements parts, machine guns, airplanes and airplane engines, and several other items. Michigan was so important to war production during World War II that the state was dubbed the "Arsenal of Democracy." By February 1942, no commercial automobiles were in production; the auto industry in Michigan was devoted entirely to the war effort. Alongside the tremendous efforts in war production during World War II, hundreds of thousands of Michiganians served in various aspects of the war.

A Progress Report on Work for Defense

General Motors

February 20, 1941

To Our Stockholders:

In a message dated November 20, 1940, there were summarized for the information of stockholders the orders placed with General Motors under the National Defense Program up to that time. It was stated that, in addition to orders then definitely received, plans and studies for further defense material production were in progress in many of the Corporation's divisions.

The summary on the center spread of this message is for the purpose of bringing stockholders up to date on the status of the orders previously reported and to inform them of new developments in the defense activities of the Corporation.

The progress achieved in the past four months has been in three important directions. Quantity delivery has been accelerated where facilities for production already existed or could be rapidly adapted. Construction of new plants and of plant extensions is going forward rapidly preparatory to the production of items requiring such new facilities. And finally, as a result of studies carried on in cooperation with defense authorities and representatives of the outside industries involved, the Corporation has assumed important additional tasks in the aviation phase of the defense program, this extending the effective scope of its technical skill and management experience.

For the year 1940—and in reality this means chiefly the last few months of 1940—deliveries of special defense materials from United States and Canadian plants of General Motors amounted to approximately $60,000,000. Included were the deliveries to British, Canadian and United States governments. This amounts to 3 1/3% of the total sales volume of General Motors in 1940. The net income realized on such business in 1940, before federal taxes, was 1.5% of the Corporation's total net income for the year, before deducting federal taxes.

Defense materials for which basic production capacity existed previously, or could be adapted—for example, military trucks and transport vehicles, Diesel engines and other items—have been and are being produced in expanding volumes. Special army trucks for British and United States use are being turned out in quantities at Chevrolet plants in the United States. Additional orders for British and Canadian motorized equipment are being filled from Canadian factories. The Cleveland Diesel Engine Division, which has just completed an extension of its plant, is continuing deliveries of propulsion and auxiliary engines for naval use, with production scheduled in coordination with the ship-building program. General Motors accessory plants are producing quantities of electrical equipment, motors, instruments, gauges and small parts of many kinds, mostly under contract but in some cases under sub-contracts in cooperation with other companies engaged in defense work. . . .

As a second extension of General Motors activities in the airplane defense program, preparations are now in progress to manufacture parts and sub-assemblies for approximately 100 twin-engine bombers monthly. The Fisher Body Division will handle this program for General Motors. Most of the work will be done in Fisher Body plants, but some will be allotted to others of the Corporation's plants. The bombers will be assembled by North American Aviation, Inc., which has announced plans for erecting an additional plant at Kansas City, Kansas. Studies of airplane parts manufacturing techniques were begun by the Corporation some months ago. These are now being rounded out by the assignment of supervisory employees and technicians to the North American Aviation plant in California for first-hand experience. It is expected that parts and sub-assemblies will be in production in sufficient time for final assemblies to start by summer and that 12,000 men will be employed when this program is fully under way.

In addition to what might be termed the physical aspect of progress in production for defense, forward strides are also being made in gearing General Motors resources of technical skill and management experience to defense requirements. The tasks involved in planning and preparation, as well as in the production of defense materials, call for the best available talent in every technical field. The demands made upon the engineering and supervisory personnel are multiplied, not only by reason of the variety and complexity of the problems presented, but also because of the urgency under which all activities must be conducted. Careful integration of activities, therefore, is basic to progress production-wise. . . .

General Motors, as a continuing policy, seeks to implement on the broadest front its desire to cooperate with those responsible for the direction of the National Defense Program. As the program has developed, it has been possible to assume new responsibilities—and in an expanding way. . . .

Alfred P. Sloan, Chairman

From "A Progress Report on Work for Defense," a GM stockholders report, 1941.

One Million Machine Guns

General Motors

The Browning Machine Gun project was the first "all-out" major war contract that the Government assigned to us during this war. With the exception of aircraft and engines, more General Motors people are engaged in making machine guns than any other class of war product. Four of our accessory divisions were chosen to do the work—AC Spark Plug, Brown-Lipe Chapin, Frigidaire, and Saginaw Steering Gear. They were selected for the job because of their experience in the manufacture in volume of small, accurate, interchangeable parts. Although machine guns are radically different from other products previously made, these divisions, because of their skill in the technique of mass production, were able to organize for the efficient, progressive manufacture of them in minimum time.

While the accessory divisions and their subcontractors, within and without General Motors, did and are doing the good job all of us expected they would do, the attainment of the millionth gun in production, and the fine history of gun production leading up to that attainment, is definitely an accomplishment worthy of the highest recognition. For this outstanding accomplishment we wish to compliment those who had a part in it. Naturally, the task has been accomplished by no one person, but by many individuals who have worked long and loyally that the job be well done. Their great patriotic achievement was an important factor in making "too little and too late" a thing of the past.

The Ordinance Department, Small Arms Division, the Colt's Patent Fire Arms Manufacturing Company, the Machine Gun Integration Committee, the suppliers of equipment and materials, all have contributed importantly in the progress of our machine gun production, and have played a most important part in making possible the production mark just attained. We appreciate their cooperation and the teamwork that made this job possible.

This was a teamwork job all around, and appreciation, too, is extended to the accessory division heads and their coworkers here in Detroit, to the general managers of the different accessory divisions and to their immediate coworkers on the machine gun project, and to the thousands of fine men and women who have worked so well, cooperated so faithfully, and made a success of one of the biggest and most important jobs we have ever had to perform.

CE Wilson
President

A Note from the Front
Corporal George

Dear Sir.

I am now on the front lines here. No doubt you heard of our battle in which the machine guns played a major part from the very first shot to the last. Yes sir, they sure put out and I feel very proud to brag to the fellows that I used to work on them. Not a jam from the start to the finish. I can't start telling how glad we marines are to have them. I feel as safe behind one as I did working on them. Thanks to G.M. machine guns I am alive to write this.

So let all the jap army come as long as I'm behind the Browning machine gun.

Sincerely Yours
Corp. George

"One Million Browning Machine Guns" and the note from Corporal George are from
"One Million Browning Machine Guns: A Chapter in the History of General Motors War Production,"
General Motors company pamphlet, 1944, Perry Archives.

Glamour Girls Wear Overalls
Polaris Flight Academy

It's a far cry from Flint, Michigan, to War Eagle Field, Lancaster, California, and it's even a farther cry from society debutaunting to driving a truck. But the transition can be made—and has been. As witness the experience of the Misses Jeanette Buckingham and Betty Bishop, two of our tug-chauffeurs at Polaris.

Reared in the lap of luxury; sent off to college; and then taking their ordained places as attractive members of Flint's "Younger Set," these young women were enmeshed in the social routine of operas, parties, bridge, dances, tennis and an occasional fling at Red Cross activities or perhaps even lending their names and social prestige to further a Community Chest drive, when along came the WAR.

Like everybody else, Jeanette and Betty wanted to do something about it. For a year they fooled around, attending lectures and making bandages for the Red Cross; taking first-aid courses and the like, but at the end of that time they were definitely fed-up. Being normal, red-blooded American girls, they craved action. So, one bright and uppity morning, they simply packed their duds in the rear of a car, said good-bye to the folks and set out for the West Coast, where, they had heard, opportunity was knocking at the door.

For no particular reason they headed for San Diego. But at Bishop [California], the snow was just ripe for skiing and they couldn't resist the temptation to stay over for a few days. And right there was where FATE stepped in, in the person of our Johnny Buckley. (That was before our John joined up). Anyhow, Johnny happened to be doing a little skiing near Bishop, and met the two girls from Flint. "San Diego," Johnny said, scornfully, "that's no place to go. The thing for you girls to do is come to War Eagle Field. We've got just the right job for you." Well, the guy must have been persuasive, for a few days later Jeanette and Betty showed up at Polaris [Flight Academy], donned overalls and went to work. And there they have been now for upward of a year.

If Jeanette and Betty are fair samples of the kind of girls they rear back in Michigan, we're all for that state. Those two gals not only do their work well, they're so darned good-natured about it they have been an inspiration to their fellow workers. They fitted up a little cabin near Dude Ranch and every morning promptly at 7, you'll find them on the job, herding those cute little tugs about like nobody's business.

Trouble is, we may not be able to keep these jewels. Just at present they both cuddle a yen to get overseas duty. Don't care where they go or what they do, so it's in the thick of things. Whether they stay or go, we wish 'em the best of luck. They're swell people.

"Glamour Girls Wear Overalls," clipping from Polaris Flight Academy internal publication, Oversize Box 1,
Arthur Giles and R. Spencer Bishop Papers, Genesee Historical Collections Center.

A Young Woman Learns Electronics in the Navy

Mary Liskow

October 4, 1943

Dear Folks,

Letters seem to be getting a thing of the past. I haven't even gotten your next to last one answered yet. We're in the middle of leaving again as I told you on the phone. It seemed so good to hear your voices again that I didn't get much done that evening either. Just walked around in a trance. Your voices sounded so natural—more like I was calling from Jans than hundreds of miles away.

I meant to ask you to send my [Girl Scouts] jack knife if you can find it. I think it may be in my first aid kit. It comes in very useful in cutting wires and cord. Most of the girls bought them here at ships store, but I think mine is better & will be grand for this work.

So much happens when I don't write each day or so. I have carefully kept from telling anything much about school, but find that others are writing home about their work. What I tell you wouldn't help or hurt anyone but it might be a good idea not to mention too much of it outside.

Last Monday we started a new class on instruments. It started out with the fundamentals of electricity then branched into two wire parallel circuits, series, and single wire parallel. We had theory all morning, that is how electricity is created, where it flows and how to harness it. Then into shop which is a ground school type. We worked on boards with fuses, switches, and small flashlight bulbs in sockets. You had to wire the master switch and fuse then wire the instrument panel which had ten switches, some of which worked more than one light. The lights were placed to represent landing lights, identification lights, running, etc., on a regular plane. We had to run series, single and double wire parallels through the entire board. Then we were graded by the number of lights that were burning at the end of a four hour tussle with soldering iron and wire. That's where the phone call came in, so you can see that I was a little tired and wiser by that time. While we were doing elec the first part of the week we also were having ordnance. What a course that is! We do field stripping of a Browning 30 cal aircraft machine gun. We finish knowing all the parts and how and where to put them, how and where to install same in place. They're unhandy to drop on your feet as they weight about 36 lbs. Next week we would have had 50 cal. In between these classes we had swimming one day, drilling another, and hand-to-hand (how to take off a man's ear politely and make him eat it) another. Then swimming, etc.

Tuesday we had more elec and guns.

Wednesday we really started [instrument training,] there are about 200 in one plane. Of these we had to learn 20 in three days—how they were installed and how they ticked. Practical experience in that was gained by standing on my head in a "crashed plane."

From "Letter to Parents," October 4, 1943, Mary Liskow Papers, Bentley Historical Library.

A Strange Coincidence in France

Lieutenant Colonel Alexander Jefferson

I was tailing Charlie on my target, which meant I was on the last plane. We shot up radar stations. As I went across the target at about fifty feet, I heard this big BOOM! A hole came up through the floor, and when I looked up, there was a hole atop the canopy. I surmised afterward a gunshell came up and exploded, so I pulled up in a half-loop and fire came up, and I bailed out at about eight hundred feet. My buddies, all fifteen, went ahead of me. They saw the airplane go in, but they didn't see me get out of it.

(A KIA was sent home to my mother.) I remember seeing the tail go by. I pulled the ripcord. I pulled it out and looked at it; and just at that time she opened, and I hit the ground. Intelligence had told us to roll over, dig a hole, and hide your chute and get to the free French, because this was southern France. I hit the ground and rolled over, and I looked up, and a German said, "Ya." I landed in the middle of the guys who shot me down. They treated me with all the respect of an officer. . . .

They took me immediately to the officer who was in charge of the coast artillery. They took me about two or three miles down the beach to a little house sitting right on the water. Out on the porch was a glass table, and sitting at the table was a German officer. I saluted, and he said in perfect English, "Have a seat, lieutenant." I was scared. I sat down. The porch went right down about one hundred yards to the ocean. Beautiful white sand. He said, "Have a cigarette." My own cigarettes, by the way. The first thing they did was take your cigarettes, and take your watch and your Parker fountain pen, and your eyeglasses. We had Ray-Bans. It turns out the guy was a German who had gone to the United States to the University of Michigan for a doctorate in political science and had gone back to Germany, and they put him in the Army. He asked if I'd been to Washington. I went to Howard University, but quite naturally I said no. He described Washington, the black area, Howard University, the night clubs, the crystal caverns.

"You ever been to Detroit?" He described the Valley—the Three 666 nightclub on Adams Street, the little joint across the street where the girls were. He described how to get the Oakman streetcar downtown around the library, how it would turn and go north on Hastings. He described Sunnie Wilson's bar. He described the hotels on John R, the Gotham. He had been there. . . .

[Afterward, Lt. Col. Jefferson was taken into Germany to be interrogated.] They knew more about us than we knew about ourselves. They had a large book, about two feet long and a foot wide. Across the front it said "332nd Fighter Group, Negroes, Red Tails." When the guy opened it up, he thumbed through all the pages and finally stopped. He said, "Lieutenant, isn't that you?" It was my class picture. They knew your father's social security number, how much money he made, how much he paid in taxes on his house, where he went to high school. . . .

They were all listed—all the generals, the colonels, the lieutenant colonels, the majors, the captains, all the enlisted personnel.

I enjoyed sitting there because I hadn't had a cigarette in three, four, five, six days.

From *Untold Tales, Unsung Heroes: An Oral History of Detroit's African American Community, 1918–1967,*
edited by Elaine Latzman Moon (Detroit: Wayne State University Press, 1994), 228, 230–31,
with the permission of Wayne State University Press.

CHAPTER 15

Fight for Equality: Civil Rights

There is a common misconception that because of the Great Lakes state's role in the antislavery movement, Michigan whites were tolerant of blacks and other races. While many whites accepted blacks and others, there were still far more who were reluctant to do so. In other words, being antislavery did not necessarily translate to racial tolerance. This sometimes led to social tension, and several times this high racial tension broke out into violence, the well-known episodes occurred in 1863, 1943, and 1967. The term "civil rights movement" probably conjures images of the 1960s, but by that time the work for civil rights for blacks had been going on for more than a century.

A Resolution Requesting Justice

Colored Citizens of the State of Michigan

William Lambert, whose speech follows this note, was instrumental not only in civil rights, but in the Underground Railroad in Detroit. He worked closely with other abolitionists, including George DeBaptiste.

1843

Mr. Lambert, in taking the chair, remarked as follows:

"Friends and Fellow-Citizens: It is with great reluctance that I receive the honor [of being appointed chairperson of the convention] that you have been pleased to confer upon me. Not that I wish to shrink from the duty I owe to my oppressed fellow citizens. But, because—besides my limited education, youth and inexperience—I have been deprived of that encouragement, aid and culture which we should have received to enable us to fulfill those noble designs for which the Great Author of the universe, created man. This is the reason why I so reluctantly receive the responsible station to which you have been pleased to call me. As this is the first time that we, the oppressed portion of the citizens of this State, have assembled in convention to consider our political condition, the eyes of the public are gazing upon us with great interest, to behold the course that we are about to pursue; many are waiting for an opportunity to belittle us, by taking the advantage of our inexperience, to use as a handle in argument to sustain them in their position of depriving us of those inalienable rights, which we have assembled to consider and deliberate upon; others are standing cheering us on, aiding and assisting us in the great cause of Human Liberty and Equal Rights; a subject with which Ireland is now threatening to revolutionize the combined powers of Great Britain—a subject that is now agitating the world. Yes, fellow citizens, we have convened to deliberate upon a subject which is now fast revolutionizing public opinion, and promises to extend human liberty and equal political rights to all the oppressed of these United States. Therefore it behooves us, as the representatives of the oppressed of this State, to act with that calm, cool, and brotherly affection, and unanimity of feeling, sentiment and action, which would be becoming to an oppressed people wishing to be free; for we are placed in a very responsible station, the future destiny of our people in this State for years yet to come, depends greatly on our conduct here in convention assembled; if our acts be good, they will give life, vigor and energy to the efforts of our friends who have enlisted in our cause, and will command honor and respect for our people and ourselves. Many of our oppressors who are now halting between the two opinions of right and expediency will flock to our standard and eagerly aid and assist us in promoting our cause, for which we have now assembled. But if our acts be bad, they will only be so many disparagements to be used in the mouths of our oppressors, to impede the progress of our political advancement, and in a great measure would palsy the soul and cripple all the powers of our people and their friends . . ." [. . .]

The business committee reported by Wm. Lambert, their chairman, the following preamble and resolution which, after being ably supported were unanimously adopted:

Whereas, We, the oppressed portion of this State, have been called upon by the deprivations experienced daily by our oppressed brethren and ourselves, to assemble in convention to consider and deliberate upon the cause of our being deprived of our rights as citizens of the State; and whereas we find ourselves existing in this State, (many native born,) with no marks of criminality attached to our names as a class— no spots of immorality staining our character—no charges of disloyalty dishonoring our birthright; and whereas we yet find ourselves, the subjects and not the objects of legislation, because we are prevented from giving an assenting or opposing voice in the periodic appointments of those who rule us;

And *Whereas* we are thus made passive instruments of all laws, just or unjust, that may be enacted, to which we are bound to subscribe, even while we have no instrumentality, either in their formation or adoption;

And *Whereas* said laws in their operation, act upon us with destructive tendencies, by subjecting us to taxation without representation—by allowing us but a scanty and inadequate participation in the privileges of education—by shutting us out from the elective franchise, a right which invigorates the soul, and expands the mental power, and is the safe-guard of the liberty and prosperity of a free and independent people, and by being deprived of this right, we are virtually and manifestly shut out from the attainment of those resources of pecuniary and possessional emoluments, which an unshackled citizenship does always insure.

And *Whereas* for the same avowed prescriptions in the privileges of the government, did the fathers of the Revolution of 1776, declare these United States to be absolved from allegiance to the British crown, and established a republican form of government for their future protection, laying its foundation upon the broad platform of those noble principles set forth in the Declaration of Independence, which declares that all men are born free and equal, and endowed by their Creator with inalienable rights, among which, are life, liberty, and the pursuit of happiness; That to secure these rights, governments are instituted among men, deriving their just power from the consent of the governed; that the people have a right to institute, alter or abolish forms of government whenever they fail to secure the ends for which they were established; that to enable all men to exercise their right to institute governments, they should enjoy the right of suffrage, that this right, is a natural right belonging to man, because he is a person and not a thing, an accountable being, and not a brute; that government is a trust to be executed for the benefit of all, that its legitimate ends are the preservation of peace, the establishment of justice, the punishment of crime and the security of rights;

And *Whereas* the fathers of the revolution pledged to each other their lives, their fortunes, and their sacred homes, for the maintenance of those noble republican principles, and thereupon established the Constitution of the United States, which guarantees to every State in the Union, a republican form of government, and expressly declares that the citizens of each state shall be entitled to all the privileges and immunities of citizens in the several states; and whereas the first three clauses in the first article of the Constitution of this State, (Michigan) expressly declares, 1st. That all political power is inherent in the people. 2d. Government is instituted for the protection, and benefit of the people, and that they have the right at all times to alter or reform the same, and to abolish one form of government and to establish another, whenever the public good requires it. 3d. No man or set of men are entitled to excusive or separate privileges;

And *Whereas*, we, the oppressed, form a portion of the people of this State, and are deprived of all the rights and privileges guaranteed to the people;

Therefore, be it resolved by this Convention, That we enter our solemn protest against the word "white," embodied in the first clause of the second article of the State Constitution, which provides for all white male citizens, the exclusive and separate privilege of the exercise of the elective franchise, of which we are deprived, and which is also contrary, and gives the lie to the third clause of the first article of said Constitution, which expressly declares that no man or set of men are entitled to exclusive or separate privileges.

Resolved, That as the long lost rights and privileges of an oppressed people are only gained in proportion as they act in their own cause, therefore it is our duty, here in the convention assembled, to breathe out our sentiments without reserve against all political injustice.

Resolved, That this Convention declare it to be a violation of the Declaration of Independence, the Constitution of the United States, and not in accordance with a republican form of government—contrary to the first article of our State Constitution—injustice of the most aggravated character, either to deprive us of a just and legitimate participation in the rights and privileges of the State, or to make us bear the burdens, and submit to its enactment, when all its arrangements, plans, and purposes are framed and put into operation, utterly regardless of us, and which in their practical operation act upon us with destructive tendency.

Resolved, That we the representatives of the oppressed of this State, will continue to write, publish, cry aloud and spare not, in opposition to all political injustice, and all legislation, violating the spirit of equality until the first and second articles of our State Constitution shall cease to conflict with each other and the blessings of Equal Political Liberty, shall have been extended to all men of whatever clime, language or nation within this State, and also the United States, which professes to be the land of the free, and an asylum for the oppressed of all nations.

Resolved, That the Declaration of Independence, is the text-book of this nation, and without its doctrines be maintained, our government is insecure.

From "Minutes of the State Convention, of the Colored Citizens of the State of Michigan, Held in the City of Detroit on the 26th and 27th of October, 1843 for the Purpose of Considering their Moral & Political Condition, as Citizens of the State," through *Colored Conventions*, http://coloredconventions.org/items/show/245.

The Moon Is Green Cheese

Democratic Free Press *(Detroit, MI)*

April 30, 1846

"Suppose some negro shall raise and arm a black band, march into the legislating halls, and force the two Houses to concede negro suffrage to save their lives."

Supposing the moon to be made of green cheese it would not be more verdant than the man who put forth so silly a supposition as that contained in the above extract.

Untitled, *Democratic Free Press* (predecessor of the *Detroit Free Press*), April 30, 1846.

Rights and Qualifications of Voters

Judge Daniel Goodwin

November 7, 1848

Gentlemen:

I have just received your favor of this date making certain inquiries relative to the duties and responsibilities of inspectors of election under our laws and constitution, and I hasten to respond thereto.

The qualifications of a voter are established by Act. II, Sec. I, of the Constitution [of Michigan], and by Amendment No. 1, of 1839.

They are, that a person voting shall be

1. A white male.
2. A citizen of the United States, or have been a resident of this State at the adoption of our Constitution.
3. Twenty one years of age.
4. That he has resided within this State six months preceding the day of election, and is then a resident of the township or ward where he offers his vote.

Ordinarily it has been up to the province of inspectors of election to decide upon all of the qualifications of voters, but their duties are somewhat limited under our Statutes. Our laws still leave them the Judges, in some respects, but in others, it enables each individual, on his own responsibility, under the solemnities of an oath, to determine whether he has the legal qualifications. This as to the last three requisites enumerated above, the inspector can only administer to the voter a proscribed oath, and if he swears that he has those qualifications, his vote must be received even though the inspectors are satisfied that he has sworn falsely. The remedy is by punishing the illegal voter for his perjury.

But the oath prescribed by Statute for you to administer to a challenged voter does not touch the first qualification. A woman, a negro, or an Indian, might take the oath and yet commit no perjury. In this respect therefore the inspectors are the sole judges of the qualification, and it is their duty in all cases, first to determine whether the person offering to vote is a "white male." If they decide he is not, they should neither receive his vote nor administer to him the oath relative to his other qualifications. If they decide that he is a white male, they can then administer the oath and receive his vote under it.

White males only are entitled to vote under our constitution, and as each Inspector is sworn to support "the constitution of this State" "and faithfully discharge the duties of the office of Inspector" he commits perjury in his office, if he suffers a person of any other class to put a vote in the ballot box, . . .

But the question may be asked, who is meant by "white," in our Constitution? After an examination and careful consideration of all the judicial decisions which have been given on this question, I am of the opinion that the word is used in its common and usual acceptance among us, when applied to the distinction of races. It is used to designate those who are regarded as of pure Circassian blood; and this embraces all the European nations and those descended from them. It is not applied to those of mixed or amalgamated blood. Though the white blood greatly predominates in a quadroon, or in the offspring of a white person and an Indian, half-breed, yet no one would classify them as white. And had the framers of our Constitution used the word in an enlarged sense, as embracing not only those of pure white blood, but all those in whose veins white blood might preponderate I feel sure that they would not have left their meaning doubtful. But they used the word without qualification: and the practical inquiry under the constitution is not whether a person is nearer "a white," a negro or Indian, but whether he is absolutely "a white."

"Rights and Qualifications of Voters," November 7, 1848, printed in the *Detroit Free Press*.

Defense of Ossian Sweet

Clarence Darrow

In 1925, Dr. Ossian Sweet bought a house in an area of Detroit that was reserved for whites. Dr. Sweet was black, and immediately upon his arrival to his new home, a mob of whites formed outside his home, threatening Dr. Sweet by throwing stones at the house. Someone inside the house fired a gun into the crowd, killing a white man. Dr. Sweet and his family were arrested for murder. Clarence Darrow defended Dr. Sweet and his family and surprisingly secured an acquittal—from an all-white jury.

November 25, 1925

Eleven people are on trial charged with a crime which might involve imprisonment for life, which is something. In the next place, back of it all, hanging over all of it and overshadowing it is the everlasting problems of race and color and creed that have always worked their evil in human institutions. If I thought any of you [in the courtroom] had an opinion against my clients, I would not worry about it because I might convince you; it is not so hard to show men that their opinions are wrong, but it is the next thing to impossible to take away their prejudices. Prejudices do not rest upon facts; they rest upon the ideas that have been taught to us and that began coming to us almost with our mothers' milk, and they stick almost as the color of the skin sticks. It is not the opinion of anyone but these twelve men [on the jury] that I am worrying about; much else is it the evidence in this case, for I know just as well as I know that you twelve men are here at this minute that if this had been a white crowd defending their homes, who killed a member of a colored mob. . . . I don't need to say that no one would have been arrested, no one would have been on trial, and I would not have worried, and you know it, too. My clients are here charged with murder, but they are really here because they are black. . . . Now, I would guess that a good share of you twelve men are not only holding in your hands the future and the destiny of my eleven clients, but to a certain extent are determining the problems of two races—not fully for it will take ages to determine that fully—but you happen to be a jury on one of the most important matters that enter into the settlement of this question. If I felt sure that none of your minds had any prejudice against my clients, I would have no fear. I do want you to be as unprejudiced as you can be.

"Argument of the Defence," November 25, 1925, Box 1, Ossian Sweet Papers, Burton Historical Collection.

De Facto Segregation

Alice E. M. Cain Newman

My grandmother and father bought property out on Eight Mile Road when it was first developed, and that's where my memories really begin. We were right on Eight Mile Road, because my dad had a business. On north side of Eight Mile was a black-owned commercial strip. One side of Eight Mile was Ferndale; that's the side we lived on. The other side was Detroit. So we were in Ferndale, but it was right on Eight Mile. 164 Parkside.

The community, as far as I can remember, was all black, and all had built their own homes. They were frame houses. It was very nice. It was safe, it was clean, and the businesses were black-owned. Down farther, I remember there was a Kroger on the Detroit side, further down toward Woodward.

This is the part that I think you might find interesting. We black kids had to go to school over in Ferndale. I went to Jefferson High School first. They really didn't want us. They treated us horribly. They treated us very, very bad. I can't remember how many black kids were there. They just didn't want us there. They let the children abuse us. They would call us nigger. They'd call us black, and teachers wouldn't do anything about it, not a thing. If they were reprimanding the children, they didn't let us blacks know anything about it, which made us hostile too.

My grades were terrible. At home and in the community I was so well-loved and respected; and at school, where I was spending so many hours a day, I was treated like dirt. At that time they marked with one, two, three, four, and five. I got nothing but red fives. I would just be devastated.

The whites decided that they were going to put a school in the black community, and that was the Grant School [built in 1926]. My grandmother was Mrs. Robinson. She and another woman and I don't know how many others really fought the school because they knew it was just for segregation reasons. However, the more I think about it, the happier I am that it happened, because I was doing so poorly before then.

When that black school finally got up there, they brought in young black teachers who were college graduates. There was a lady out there named Mrs. Pearl Wright who was the assistant principal. They put in a white principal, Mr. Kern; but all of the teachers were young, black women. I'm going to tell you the difference in my grades was remarkable. I remember they had some citywide intelligence test, and my intelligence score was one of the highest in the city.

There was one white family who lived in the area, had a little boy. She was a widow or not married; there was no husband. The people got together and moved her out of that community so that her little boy wouldn't have to go to school with all the blacks.

The people in the white area moved her out. They got together, with her permission, and found her a house near to where her child would go to Jefferson School. . . .

We moved from there, forcibly, because of urban renewal. I think it was about 1930. The city wanted to widen Eight Mile Road. When the city came through to buy the property, the owners fought it for a long time. They had to hire an attorney. Eventually they had to sell. I'm using the word urban renewal; and, of course, that wasn't a word I knew at that time; but I know what they would call it now. They broke up the community. They broke up business. . . .

I was resentful because, when I had to leave, it broke up my life, my whole pattern—the friends I had made, the teachers that I loved. We moved up north, up into the Idlewild area. My grandmother had fine china, fine silver, linens and really the best of everything. My dad had a German Page car. Have you ever heard of that? It was a big car. He bought it used as well as a Model T Ford. I guess it was made by Graham Page Company. It was a big car, real big car. I remember my dad never drove. My uncle drove. We were on Woodward Avenue, in Highland Park, and the police officer stopped my uncle because he had that big car. Of course, he could show that the ownership was legal. He stopped him just because he was black with a big car.

From *Untold Tales, Unsung Heroes: An Oral History of Detroit's African American Community, 1918–1967*, edited by Elaine Latzman Moon (Detroit: Wayne State University Press, 1994), 72–73, 74–75, with permission from Wayne State University Press.

Response to Detroit's "Loyalty Amendment"

Michigan Committee on Civil Rights

August 18, 1949

As the Second Red Scare unfolded after World War II, "loyalty" became a theme throughout the country. President Truman in 1947 enforced his Loyalty Program, which required federal administrators to participate in a "loyalty oath." Rumors of communist subversion were commonplace. To combat this "threat," one Detroit official declared all the city's workers should take an oath of loyalty, and those who refused would be subject to an investigation. This led to amending the city charter to legally allow city officials to administer loyalty tests. This amendment had great support in the city, though most blacks opposed it for numerous reasons.

To: Members of Drafting Committee on Proposed Loyalty Amendment
From: Olive R. Beasley, Executive Secretary, Michigan Committee on Civil Rights
 The Honorable Common Council of the City of Detroit

Gentlemen:

We respectfully call the attention of the Honorable members of the Common Council of the City of Detroit, individually and collectively, to paragraph 3 of our memorandum addressed to the Honorable Common Council on July 14. This memorandum dealt with the proposed amendment to the City Charter commonly known as the "loyalty oath."

We stated in part,

"We believe that the Communist Party can turn the action now contemplated against them to their own advantage, that they will be able to exploit an ill-advised charter amendment attack upon them by legal action of their own which might be well be supported by court decision and thus seriously embarrass Common Council and the City of Detroit.

For these reasons, we feel that it is very important that Common Council avoid hysteria and haste in this important decision of city policy. Certain things, we think, need saying. This kind of hysteria . . . plays into the hands of our domestic fellow-travelers as neatly as any plot hatched within the walls of the Kremlin. The contemplated wholesale investigation, the stampede to tamper with an important provision of our City Charter, obviously without time for careful consideration of alternatives, are invitations to invasion of civil rights that must not be taken lightly. The anomaly of such a tactic is that it puts the Communists, and their supporters, in the position of being the alleged defenders of civil rights and "martyrs." . . . Thus, more harm is done to Democracy than the Soviet fifth column ever hoped to do. Cumulatively, we have had no little experience in purging from our midst Comrades who would ride the coat-tails of the liberal movements, and we are convinced that today's crusade would be beneath ridicule were it not for its inherent dangers."

We, therefore, urged the Common Council to pursue the sounder cause of appointing a special citizens commission to study the matter of loyalty among the employees of the government of the City of Detroit. We felt that many responsible community organizations would welcome the opportunity to join in such a study. . . .

Unwittingly, we are sure, the Common Council is making the Communists and fellow travelers "the defenders of civil liberties." . . .

We feel very apprehensive that the unbecoming haste to submit the proposed charter amendment, of questionable legality and effectiveness, to the referendum in September might cause findings of unconstitutionality in the courts of this state and land, and the Common Council, as much as it does not wish to do so, will aid and abet and extend comfort to the Communists.

Respectfully yours,

Detroit Chapter, Michigan Committee on Civil Rights

Memo, Beasley to Members of [Detroit] Drafting Committee, Michigan Committee on Civil Rights, August 18, 1949, Box 2, Olive Beasley Papers, Genesee Historical Collections Center.

Pro-Busing Flier

Support Peaceful Integration

The school buses are set to roll January 26th. Many of us have fears of the type of violence that erupted against students in Boston and Louisville. We must not allow this to happen! We must all support *peaceful* integration and oppose any violence directed at students, Negro, Anglo-American or Mexican. Anti-busing groups such as MAD (Mothers Alert Detroit), MAP (Metropolitan Area Parents), and CFAS (Committee to Fight the Attacks on our Schools) are advocating various tactics ranging from boycotting schools, to tampering with buses so they can't run, having older children throw things at the buses and children, "spying" on neighbors whose children do attend schools, and preventing students from entering schools through physical "persuasion." The members and followers of these groups are concerned working parents who are worried about the safety of their children, and getting a quality education. The leadership of these groups, however, Carmen Roberts, Donald Lobsinger, etc., have made their violent intentions known publically. In spite of their open claim of "peaceful opposition," they intend the boycott as a cover for more violent activities to keep the buses from rolling.

It is obvious that the Detroit Only Plan is limited. In some regions, like 1 and 8, it changes nothing. That is because the best plan, Metro area busing, was vetoed by the Nixon Supreme Court. Those people calling for a defeat of the Detroit Only Plan have nothing to put in its place that will insure both *integration* and quality education. Quality education does not automatically happen just because your children attend the school across the street, the "neighborhood school." No! Quality education is a question of money. Without money, the Detroit school system can't afford smaller teacher-pupil ratios, better science and gym facilities, new school buildings, bi-lingual education—things that will provide true quality education. MAD, MAP, and other "anti" groups never seem to mention how we can get these things. That's right, the only thing Donald Lobsinger and Carmen Roberts are about is "keeping the Negroes out." They are merely using the issue of "neighborhood schools" as a smokescreen for their white chauvinist attacks on minorities that will only lead to further divisions in our community.

Parents don't be used! Don't play into the hands of MAD-MAP and the KKK by boycotting the schools or stopping the buses or students. Support the *peaceful integration* of the schools. Help to build the unity of working class parents, Anglo-American, Negro, and Mexican that we need to force the state of Michigan to provide full state funding for all school districts. Join the real struggle for quality education—full state funding for all students and Metro Area Busing to insure integration. Accompany your children to school on Jan. 26th and make sure that no MAD-MAP or any other "anti" group stops or harasses them!

Anti-Busing Flier

Resist Forced Busing: Boycott the Public Schools

The U.S. Code, Title 42, section 2000 C-B reads: ". . . provided that nothing herein shall empower any official or court of the United States to issue any order seeking to achieve a racial balance in any school by requiring the transportation of pupils or students from one school to another or the school district to another in order to achieve racial balance or otherwise enlarge the existing power of the court to insure compliance with Constitutional standards."

Definition (b) of the above section states: "Desegregation means the assignment of students to public schools and within such schools without regard to their race . . . but desegregation shall not mean the assignment of students to public schools in order to overcome racial imbalance."

Speaking of the April 1971 decision of the U.S. Supreme Court authorizing the busing of children to achieve racial balance in the public schools, U.S. Congressman John R. Rarick, addressing the House of Representatives, said recently:

"Freedom of choice is not an empty slogan. Freedom of choice is the heart and soul of American liberty. The American people still understand this and we must understand that there is a point beyond which the great law-abiding majority cannot be pushed. We are perilously near that point.

"I state plainly and simply that this action of the Supreme Court of the United States is founded neither in any possible construction of the Constitution nor in any possible understanding of the law.

"It is a classic example of the arbitrary and unfettered exercise of naked power.

"Long years ago, Thomas Jefferson warned free men of this very possibility, when he dramatically pointed out that of all tyranny, judicial tyranny is the most fearful.

"If the Constitution of the United States forbids a State to assign pupils to a school solely because of their race, it makes no difference whether the object of such assignment is segregation or forced integration under the newly invested 'Doctrine of Racial Proportion.' If government has no power to forcefully segregate, it has no power to forcefully integrate.

"It does not take a genius to understand that the State either has that power or does not. Until 1954, it had such power. The Constitution did not change, but in 1954 the Warren Court decided the power had vanished. The Warren Burger Court has now decided that although the State has no such power, the court has.

"What the preposterous decision amounts to is that racial school assignments are unconstitutional if they are made by the States, but constitutional if made by the courts.

"These decisions are a gross distortion of any possible interpretation of the Constitution."

To state it another way, IF RACIAL DISCRIMINATION IN THE ASSIGNMENT OF PUPILS TO THE PUBLIC SCHOOLS IS PROHIBITED BY THE U.S. CONSTITUTION, IT IS PROHIBITED NO MATTER THE END TO BE ACHIEVED.

That is to say, if racial discrimination in order to achieve segregation is unconstitutional, it is EQUALLY UNCONSTITUTIONAL if its purpose is to achieve integration.

Both materials regarding busing are taken from Box 1 of Carmen A. Roberts Papers (Pro-Busing and Anti-Busing folders), Bentley Historical Library.

On Busing and the Riot

William Lowell Hurt

In the early 60s we were bused out to totally white areas in the city of Detroit, beyond Seven Mile and Livernois or Seven Mile and Southfield. They were taking a lot of the students who excelled, who had good grades. They bused kids to predominantly white schools on the outskirts of the city of Detroit, integrated those schools. They didn't do it with Board of Education buses. We were assigned to those schools, and would take city buses.

There were some negative responses, because all the black students that went to the school got off of city buses, and at that point in time, the city buses would pull up right alongside the school. They had city bus stops right in front of the school. Every morning these busloads of black students would get off the bus, and there would be all these white and Jewish students standing in line and milling around the outside. Bus after bus would pull up and there would be nothing but black students getting off of these buses.

We grew up in an area at a period in time where it was racially mixed. I mean, we didn't look at the white kids as being any different than the white kids that we played with in the neighborhood. We got in trouble, got chased by the police, hid on top of garages, hid inside of people's garages and basements, and there were white kids with us. So a lot of us didn't really think anything was strange about going to a school that was mostly white.

I was about fourteen at the time of the riots. I remember the Sunday morning that the riots started. My uncle called over to our house about six o'clock that morning and told my dad and mom that they should get up and look at what's happening on 12th street. He said people have started rioting down around Clairmount, or just below Clairmount. He really didn't know what had caused that riot. We sat on our front porch that whole day and that following Monday and literally witnessed the riot move north up 12th street from Clairmount.

They were in the process of putting in a Clark gas station on the corner. They had dug the foundation and had actually put the gas drums in and had filled the drums. The Clark station was getting ready to open that following week, the week of the riots. But it hadn't officially opened. These gas tanks were filled, and this was kitty-corner to our house. My mom, being the nervous sort of person that she was, once the riot started to get into full gear, the only thing that she could think of when the people started burning the buildings was that this gas station was going to explode and take our house with it.

But we sat there and watched people in the middle of July, walking up 12th street with fur coats on. Obviously they had stolen these things. We watched them pull, drag, the old guy who ran that shoe repair shop out in the middle of 12th street and literally beat him mercilessly, simply because he was white.

We saw people looting, just breaking windows at the supermarket up the street on the corner above Calvert and 12th. A crowd gathered outside, and this one guy who was obviously leading them broke the window and was the first person in the supermarket. I recall how my friends and I always laughed about this because he was the first person into the supermarket and all he came out with was about two oranges. We saw people walking up and down the street with arms full of clothes, or jewelry or walking with television sets and radios they had looted.

Our parents, the kids' parents who lived on our side of 12th street, none of them took part in the looting. Our parents were very, very strict. I'd have friends come down to my porch and watch what's happening because we were right on the corner of 12th. But even that got dangerous, because the police would drive by and see five, six, or seven black male youths sitting on the porch, and they'd tell us to break it up.

They had something in that point in time called the "Big Four," and they drove around in these black Chryslers or Fords and were usually three white police officers with one black officer that was driving. Nobody messed with the "Big Four." They would whip your head on the spot. There was a certain amount of fear and through that fear a certain amount of respect for the "Big Four." No one liked them, but no one messed with them either.

We had outside of our home, on the corner, three National Guards. On the side of the house we had two. And between our house and the house that was next to us, we had another National Guard stationed. National Guards were stationed up and down the block and along 12th and Boston to protect our neighborhood from brick-throwing, rioting, and destruction. All of the moms in our block club would get together and make these guys huge dinners and would feed the soldiers every day. They would give them breakfast, lunch and dinner. That stopped abruptly.

Our living room was in the back of the house; and we had this big, huge, glass window that was a sliding glass door. You could come from the backyard into the living room of our house. A number of homes received threats, via bricks thrown through their windows with messages attached to them, saying that if you continue to feed the National Guard troops, your house will burn. So food stopped. Soldier stopped getting fed.

We started writing a phrase on the side of the house, on the windows; and all store owners who wised up to what was happening would put the signs in their windows that said, "Soul Brother," or "I'm a Soul Brother," or something like that. That was almost like painting the blood over the top of the house to let death pass over, because they didn't mess with the houses that had those signs or the stores that had the signs.

There was a little party store right across the street on the other side of 12th, and my mom sent me out to the store to get some milk or something, and I came running out the side of our house. I ran out of the house and got into the middle of the street when the National Guard hollered, "Stop!" I literally froze in the middle of the street. They called me over and asked me where was I going, what was I doing; and I told them that, hey, I live right here and my mom was just sending me to the store. They made me go back in the house, made my mom or my dad come out and explain to them where I was going, what I was going for, and then stood there and watched as I went across the street to the store and came back.

Then one night, my younger sister was just an infant at that time, and they had pinned a sniper down on the roof of the building across the street on 12th. My mom got up about eleven-thirty or twelve o'clock. The police had turned off all of the street lights up and down 12th Street, so it was pitch black. My mom got up to go downstairs to get my sister a bottle. When she turned on the light in the living room, which was in the back with that big glass door, the light hit like a floodlight; and she got about two steps when the National Guard and the police said over a megaphone she had about five seconds to turn that light out or it would be blown out because it was giving their position away and illuminating them to the sniper. She turned the light out, and I remember how she crawled back up the steps. She was so scared. She made us sleep under our beds that night because of the gunfire. The next morning I got up, went out in the backyard, and saw spent shells. And our garage on the alley side was just riddled with bullets.

At first the riots were a matter of just looting stores and people roaming. Then it got real ugly. I mean, it turned more violent, where there were snipers and gunfire, and we were literally under martial law. If there was a group of four or five blacks walking down the street together, they were broken up. The police would stop them, break them up, and make some of them go a different way. It was really scary. I remember how firemen stopped coming into the neighborhood because they were being shot at. That is why you had so many buildings that were just gutted.

From *Untold Tales, Unsung Heroes: An Oral History of Detroit's African American Community, 1918–1967,* edited by Elaine Latzman Moon (Detroit: Wayne State University Press, 1994), 371–74, with permission from Wayne State University Press.

The Idlewild Resort Company

E. W. B. Curry

Because of segregation practices, official and de facto, blacks had limited recreational opportunities, including hunting, fishing, and camping. In response, a resort town was created in the early twentieth century near and around Idlewild Lake to give blacks the opportunity to freely engage in those activities. The town that emerged eventually became an important center for African American culture, and in continuing that tradition, Idlewild recently began hosting an annual homecoming music festival.

January 21, 1919

To all Lovers of Our Race:

I am glad to speak a good word for the Idlewild Resort Company. It is my duty to inform my friends of any good project that I believe will help this race to higher things. I have made a long study of the Idlewild movement and have been convinced that it is worthy of our support. It is a good, safe investment. Idlewild, in Michigan, will, in a few years, be the center of attraction for our educational, fraternal, business and religious meetings in the summer. I have purchased lots in Idlewild and will secure more this Spring. The Curry Institute is planning a Summer Normal for Teachers to be conducted there. The place is ideal in every way and I shall do all I can for the advisement of the Work.

Yours for humanity,
E.W.B. Curry
President
Curry Normal and Industrial Institute

> From appendix 3 of *Black Eden: The Idlewild Community* by Lewis Walker and Ben C. Wilson
> (East Lansing: Michigan State University Press, 2002), 242.

Understanding Is Goal of the Idlewild Community

Norma Lee Browning

Idlewild, Mich., September 28, 1950

—Adventure lies around every bend in the road for anyone willing to take potluck wherever he finds it. Throw away your time tables and plane schedules. Say "hello" to a man in a bean patch and see where it leads you.

It led me from a pickle farm to a cabbage rattle at a Townsend meeting, from an unplanned trip to a golf course to a midnight lunch in this little known lake resort spot near a whistle stop called Baldwin.

I had hitched a ride south with Mrs. Virginia Grant in her light car heading toward Michigan's detour merely to say "hello" to her brother and sister-in-law, Bill and Alice Wuthenow, who turned their farm into a golf course. Instead of continuing south I accepted their invitation to ride with them north, to a friend's summer cottage at Idlewild.

We arrived about 8 p.m. Our hosts, Mr. and Mrs. Milton Winfield of . . . Chicago, greeted us at the door and graciously ushered us into their large, beautifully furnished home overlooking Lake Idlewild. The living room had fiber carpeting, colorful rattan furniture, many books, and a television set.

Mrs. Winfield, a charming, pretty little woman in a long aqua colored hostess gown, led us to the enclosed veranda-sunporch and introduced us to the other guests.

There were Dr. Cortez A. English and his girlish-looking wife, Amelia. Dr. English is a dentist in Grand Rapids. He was graduated from the University of Michigan 25 years ago, second highest in his class. There also were Mrs. Welbourn A. Mollison, and her son, Welbourn Jr., a graduate of the Illinois Institute of Technology, now a law student at John Marshall; and James H. Cowan, once a University of Chicago student, a graduate of Oberlin, and a chemistry professor in Washington, D.C.

At a glance you could tell it was rather a distinguished gathering. They were not much different from other people of similar backgrounds. Their manners, dress, conversation, and food were the same. Only their color was different. They were Negroes.

"I can remember the first time I ever realized I was different from anyone else," said Winfield, a soft voiced, tall, skinny man whose nickname is Beans. "I used to be in show business. I was one of Jeanette Adler's child actors. We were on the road and we stopped at a hotel one night. They wouldn't give us a room. We spent the night on a bench in an empty, unheated building. Miss Adler never told me but that's the night I found out."

Beans was a song and dance performer at the old Princess theater . . . until he was 17. He worked for a railroad 10 years, became manager of a Chicago cafe, and then went into real estate business. He has been married "to the same woman" 32 years, he boasts, and has a son, Milton Jr. in business with him.

Dr. English said the Negroes don't want social equality, only equal opportunities. "If I could make $200,000 a year in Mississippi, I'd stay right here in Grand Rapids," he said. "You can go in the same door [in Grand Rapids] with a white man without being arrested."

About 85 percent of Dr. English's dental patients are white, he said. Some, like Bill and Alice Wuthenow and other around Fremont and White Cloud, go to Grand Rapids regularly to have Dr. English take care of their teeth. He also has patients from New York, Miami, and Chicago. A girl in the cosmetics department of a . . . [Chicago] department store goes to Grand Rapids every six months for dental care from Dr. English.

The doctor used to be a cotton picker, then worked his way thru college as a summer porter at Mackinac Island. He believes that Negroes, like other Americans, can succeed at about anything they choose if they only work hard enough.

"The trouble is," he said, "too many people judge a whole race by its poorest examples. There are illiterates and criminals in all societies. And there are the refined and educated in all of them."

"They talk about improving conditions for the Negroes," said young Welbourn Mollison. "What is needed first is to improve people's minds."

Welbourn's grandfather, Willis Mollison, won reputation as a criminal lawyer in Mississippi. His uncle, Irving Mollison, was the first Negro federal judge to serve in the continental United States. His father is an industrial chemist in Chicago.

Idlewild was started as a summer resort for Negroes 35 years ago by a Negro woman, Lela Wilson, now in her 60s. She sold 50-foot lots for $19.50 each to Negroes only with the hope that they would improve the grounds and build up the place into one of the finest summer resorts in the Midwest. Her dream has been fulfilled.

Idlewild's winter population of 300 swells to nearly 2,000 during the summer months and fall. The cottages are owned by doctors, dentists, lawyers, and teachers, many of whom drive down to Bill and Alice's golf course, 30 miles away, where they are as welcome as anyone else.

"We don't ask to be treated any better or any worse than anyone else," one of them said. "All we want is to be treated like people."

"'Hello' to Stranger Leads City Girl to Rural Friendliness," by Norma Lee Browning, September 29, 1950, *Chicago Daily Tribune*. Reprinted with permission from PARS International, on behalf of the *Chicago Tribune*.

CHAPTER 16

The Buckle of the Rust Belt: Economic Decline

Not long after World War II, Michigan's economy began to decline. Because of its dependence on the automobile, changes in that industry deeply affected the state. In the 1950s, other states began competing for auto-manufacturing jobs and military production contracts, automation was on the rise, which replaced human laborers with machinery, and demand for skilled labor increased—a resource in which Michigan was losing ground. As a result, industrial jobs were moving out of Michigan. A generation later, foreign automobiles began competing in the American market, exacerbating this problem. With the serious declination of the automobile industry in the state, its citizens who remained felt the brunt. Areas in which the auto industry once flourished experienced poverty, crime, and crumbling infrastructure. The 1980s were especially difficult for Michigan, and leaders have been touting the "comeback" for many years.

Life in the Projects

Gloria Manlove Hunter

We lived on the third floor [in Brewster Housing Projects, Detroit], and right up over our apartment was the roof, which we made our private domain. We [children] had our club up there. The roof was a world on its own. You traveled by roof. In the three-story apartment buildings the kids knew we could travel all through the court by roof, because if you went into somebody else's court, you could get beat up; that was enemy territory. You jumped from one roof to another. Mom didn't know. Kids had a world of their own. We would climb around the walls. Sometimes if she wasn't home, we would monkey-climb from the first floor all the way up to the third floor and get the window open and come in the apartment.

Sometimes we had to almost do it for survival. If we stayed out on the weekends until it was dark, the prostitutes and the pimps would be pulling the "Murphy" on the white man. These men would tell white men that would come into the area that there were prostitutes in these apartments, and they would take the money. The guy would say, "Okay, you give me twenty-five dollars, and you go up to apartment 675; and in that apartment there's a woman there for sex." When these white men would get there, sometimes they would be drunk or they would be angry. And the doors were steel, so the men would be hollering and beating on the door. They would try to set a fire; they tried to burn the place.

Whoever thought that using cement and steel wasn't a bad idea was correct, because when Mom and her neighbors would finish with the paper, they'd put it outside the door. We kids would collect it for sale or the papers went to the incinerator. These guys got together one night, and they decided they were going to burn the door down to get to this woman. And had it been wood, it would have burned. But since the whole building was brick and steel, it wouldn't have burned. They would try to kick the door down or take the handles off the door. . . .

Sometimes when we got home, the lights would be off in the hall. If a light was out, you didn't know if one of the junkies had screwed the lightbulb out because he was out there shooting up. You didn't know if it was a prostitute turning tricks in the hall. You didn't know if it was a setup.

So you would stand there and holler, "Hey, Ma." She would come to the window and tell us to come in the building or not to come in the building. If she told us to come in the building, it was just that the light had gone out. If she said don't come in the building, you couldn't go in because you were afraid someone would harm you. So you learned to walk the walls. We'd start at the first-floor window ledge. Somebody would boost you up, or you would stand on something like a rock; or you could jump and grab the ledge. And you could go from the first floor to the second floor. Then we'd get to the third floor, and we'd crawl in the window, and we'd be in the house.

From *Untold Tales, Unsung Heroes: An Oral History of Detroit's African American Community, 1918–1967*, edited by Elaine Latzman Moon (Detroit: Wayne State University Press, 1994), 324–25, with permission from Wayne State University Press.

The Quality of General Motors' Automobiles

David E. Davis

At the time he delivered this speech, Davis was the editor of Car and Driver *magazine.*

April 5, 1983

I've been invited here this morning to tell you what my readers, my staff, and I think about the quality of General Motors products as compared to their domestic and imported competition.

I want you to bear that fact in mind as you listen to my comments. You *asked* me to come here, I didn't volunteer. I've been led to believe that you want the unvarnished truth, so that's what I'm going to give you. If you don't like it, you at least have the consolation of knowing that I'm not charging you anything . . .

I've been doing my best to be a thorn in the side of the domestic automobile industry since 1953, when I was 22 years old and first became a professional drum beater for imported cars.

You see, I was involved in a Volkswagen dealership in Ypsilanti, Michigan, in 1953. Unfortunately, that was about 200 years before the Midwest was ready for imported cars, but I was out there, pointing the way toward financial ruin for the rest of you.

Professors from the University of Michigan who, in those distant days, used to believe that a 1952 Ford station wagon was the epitome of automotive practicality and good sense, would visit us on Saturday afternoons to be patronizing about our little economy cars, and to knock the dottle out of their pipes on our fenders. At night we'd be visited by activist UAW members, free-lance xenophobes, who would paint rude patriotic messages upon the windshields of new cars on our back lot. Southeastern Michigan was ill-prepared to deal with imported car visionaries like us in the early fifties. . . . By the autumn of 1954 we had become one of America's first bankrupt Volkswagen dealers. . . .

In 1969 I went back to Campbell-Ewald [advertising agency] to launch the [Chevrolet] Vega. You remember the Vega? The little car that does everything well, right?

Well, I stumped the country in that little sucker's behalf for six months and I'm surprised that no former Vega owner has ever seen fit to set fire to my house, or shoot me from ambush.

You know, some of the best engineers at General Motors worked on that project, and it still turned out to be the worst car GM ever built. Every time I go on a trip, I tremble in anticipation of the dead Vegas I'm going to see at the roadside, or the ones I'll pass as they coast to a stop in a great cloud of smoke and steam.

Frank Witchell, your former vice president, engineering staff, was one of the guys responsible. Back when the Vega was still news, he and I got drunk and talked about what went wrong. He said, "You know, literally hundreds of good guys worked on that car, and not *one* of them arrived at a meeting and said, "I got it, you guys, what we'll do is we'll build this really shitty little car!"

Lest you get the idea that I'm completely sold out to the importers, I should tell you that I was also a Packard salesman, and that I ran presses and worked as an assembler in several Ford plants, one Briggs manufacturing plant, and a Fisher Body plant in Pontiac.

Building cars at night made it possible for me to go to school during the day. Working on the assembly during those years also gave me a point of view about the industry that I've always believed was somewhat different from that of my peers, whether I was putting out a car magazine or working at one of your advertising agencies.

Finally, having spent a fair bit of time as a retail car salesman gave me some special insight. I know that many of you have spent time in the plants, getting your hands dirty, but how many of you have actually sold cars, one at a time, and had to face the angry customer when he or she storms back into the dealership to complain that the new car isn't all you promised it to be.

I don't envy those poor guys who have to go one-on-one with the public today. Unless they're working in Toyota or Honda dealerships.

We just completed a 30,000 mile test on a Toyota Celica Supra. The car averaged 21 miles per gallon for the duration of the test, and didn't cost us one thin dime in maintenance. That was an especially good car, even by Japanese standards, but it's still representative of our overall experience with Japanese cars.

We have three long-term cars from GM in our fleet right now. One, a J-Car, has held up pretty well. It has very few squeaks and rattles and it does the job. It's not a great car, but it's a sound car.

We have a V-6, four-speed S-Truck that's had a funky feeling clutch from the very start. When this was first pointed out to the dealer, we got the usual, "They all do that," routine. Eventually, however, the thing was in for speedometer cable repair—another persistent annoyance—and the dealer service people took it upon themselves to make a repair. When the truck was taken apart, a failed throwout bearing was discovered and that had also wounded the pressure plate, so a number of parts had to be replaced on warranty. Right now, we're at the mercy of the parts department. They say they have everything needed for reassembly except one "retainer gasket . . ."

You might also be interested in the fact that this unit was handed over to us with a sizeable clump of some mystery substance painted right into its hood at [the] assembly plant, even though the thing was at the GMPG [proving ground] for rebuild by the engineers for at least a month before we got it.

That last point is an important one. Generally speaking, the cars we get have had very special preparation. This is true of every PR fleet in the business. We've occasionally found somebody's checklist in the glove box that attests to the extraordinary lengths good PR people will go to to make sure that cars delivered to car magazines are the best they can be.

Please bear that in mind when I tell you that our 1983 F-Car is the *worst* long-term car we've ever had.

Our test F-Car arrived in Ann Arbor last July with 38 miles on the odometer. The paint was blotchy. The deck lid was a different color from the rest of the body. Particles of dirt were imbedded in the paint on the roof. The shifter came apart in our hands. The engine overheated at redline. The cigarette lighter would pop into the rear seat when hot.

We weren't concerned until the transmission began acting up two months later. For some reason, it was reluctant to upshift . . . , and when it finally did so, the shift was so rough that it snapped your head back. We had the bands readjusted, and that fix held for 1000 miles.

The driver's electric window failed at 10,000 miles, and squeaks developed in the instrument panel and the hatch. The transmission began to leak fluid, and after a routine 80 mile per hour run on the freeway the catalyst would turn red hot and automatic transmission fluid would pour from the sealed pan.

New clutch plates were installed at 11,000 miles. 800 miles later the transmission failed completely in Cleveland. Our technical editor left the car at a dealership and flew home, waiting for the transmission to be rebuilt. The oil pump had broken, causing a 12-inch crack in the case.

When we flew to Cleveland to retrieve the F-Car, we'd driven just 30 miles on the return trip when the shifting became erratic again. We nursed it home, and our local dealer installed a new hand-built transmission that we got from Hydramatic.

Two months later, transmission and rear axle seals began to leak, and the electronic control module had to be replaced. It took another month for our dealer to get the parts.

The car now runs reasonably well, although our gas mileage has averaged only 13 miles per gallon and we've used twelve quarts of oil in the last 21,000 miles. There are rattles in the suspension and the interior, and the hatch still squeaks. We still have 9000 miles to go on the test.

If this sort of thing can happen to us, with cars that have received special attention from your engineers, what must the poor customer experience?

What all of this proves, I guess, is that quality can't be "prepped" into a product. If it isn't there when the product is conceived, it won't be there after the product has been driven for three or four thousand miles.

David Smith, of Wards [automobile magazine], gave me a line that I've been using ever since I heard him say it. . . . We'd just been told that the quality of the then-new GM-X cars wasn't good enough for a typical for the Japanese consumer. The man talking to us was the president of Nissan, Mr. Ishihara. The Japanese couldn't understand how General Motors could start with a clean sheet of paper, commit so many millions of dollars, and then come up with an X-Car. Smith said, "Quality is a management decision." And for me, he put the whole business of automotive quality into perspective.

My feeling, and that of my staff, and, unfortunately, that of a huge number of consumers, is that General Motors has been in the business of *simulating* quality. We get the feeling that quality control has meant exactly that at General Motors—controlling the amount of quality that gets into cars. And I'll tell you something else, if ever there was a time to decontrol quality, this is it.

General Motors Conference Speech, Box 9, David E. Davis Papers, Bentley Historical Library.

The State Financial Crisis

Committee to Save Michigan

More than 150 leading citizens of Michigan have formed the Committee to Save Michigan, a coalition which will urge the Legislature to quickly adopt a balanced program for a long-term solution to Michigan's grave financial crisis.

The Committee's main activities will be directed toward providing public education on the magnitude of the state's financial problems and on solutions to the crisis.

[Ed Harden, president of Story Oldsmobile] said that "the budget crisis in this state is unprecedented and requires immediate action by the Legislature. Michigan deserves no less than a principled, bi-partisan effort to achieve a long-term solution."

[Lawrence Owen, mayor of East Lansing] said that "Without a long-term solution to our state's massive budget deficit, we cannot begin the overdue work on creating jobs, which we all need desperately."

The Committee has focused on four main principles:

- Spending cuts within a reasonable range of those proposed by Governor Blanchard ($225 million).

- A revenue increase to ensure that Michigan's budget is balanced.
- An additional tax increase to eliminate deviations from generally accepted accounting principles.
- Continued efforts toward efficient management of state government and elimination of unnecessary programs.

The Committee, which is still in formation has offices at 116 E. Ottawa in Lansing.

Committee to Save Michigan Press Release, 1984, Box 6, James Blanchard Papers, Bentley Historical Library.

Speech on Economic Recovery

J. Phillip Jourdan

Jourdan was chief of staff to Governor Blanchard.

December 13, 1983

On January 1, 1983, Governor James J. Blanchard took office confronted by a fiscal and economic crisis of unprecedented dimensions in Michigan. No previous administration had ever inherited the dual scourges of chronically high unemployment and huge budget deficits.

Unemployment rates had been in double digits for more than three years and still hover today around 12 percent. Governor Blanchard found the current year's budget $900 million in the red, coupled with long-term debts of $823 million accumulated from several years of accounting maneuvers.

These phenomena are not unrelated, of course. A one percent increase in Michigan's unemployment has a doubly disastrous effect on the state's budget: reducing revenues by $45 million and raising expenditures by $40 million.

In the past, when faced with cyclical downturns in the state's economy, we have looked longingly to Washington for help. Now, we would probably be satisfied for a period of "benign neglect" because the current federal policies are only exacerbating our problems. The federal deficit and resulting high interest rates continue to threaten our long-term revitalization. In short, the governor knew from the outset, we could only look to ourselves for help.

The state had reached the point where it could not even borrow on a short-term basis to raise the cash flow necessary to make quarterly payments to school districts and to local governments. With Michigan's credit rating in shambles, and the state teetering on the brink of bankruptcy, Governor Blanchard knew he could not responsibly put off the day of fiscal reckoning that had been postponed for so many years.

The response would have to be bold, decisive and creative. Further, it would call for courage and vision on the part of the legislature. This has been borne out by the tragically misguided recall movement. Finally, action would require a spirit of determination, commitment, cooperation, and even short-term sacrifice on the part of Michigan's people.

From the outset, the Governor's economic development strategy has been guided by three themes or principles: Investment, cooperation, and quality. In every effort this administration has advanced, you will find a commitment to investment, cooperation, and quality.

Speech on Economic Recovery, J. Phillip Jourdan, Chief of Staff, Box 6, James Blanchard Papers, Bentley Historical Library.

State of the State, 1987

Governor James Blanchard

February 4, 1987

We celebrate this year the 150th anniversary of Michigan's statehood. It is a celebration that all of us can share. For the state of our State is strong—and it's getting stronger. Today in Michigan, there is a renewed sense of opportunity, pride, energy and vision—a renewed sense of hope and determination. That's the spirit which connects us with Michigan's first pioneers. That's the spirit which propelled Michigan to the forefront of American ideas and prosperity. And that's the same spirit we must unleash to master our next challenge—the challenge of rapid economic change—of global change. And we can meet that challenge! For like those first Michiganians, our generation has already proven itself to be more than a match for the tough challenges of turbulent times. Four short years ago, our state was mired in a depression—stuck in economic quicksand that we did not create. Some people thought the situation looked hopeless. Some thought that bankruptcy was the only solution. Some thought there was nothing that could make a difference—that the more we struggled the faster we would sink. But others—those with the real Michigan spirit—knew otherwise. And so from the grit and pride and resourcefulness of our people was born the Michigan Comeback.

At first we set two major goals:

- We would rescue Michigan from the brink of bankruptcy and return fiscal stability to our state; and
- We would create jobs for our people and put Michigan back to work.

Two specific goals to guide this state government. Two concrete goals to summon the cooperative efforts of all the men and women of Michigan. Together, the men and women of this legislature, the men and women of my administration, and the men and women of the entire state went to work to accomplish these two goals—to begin the resurgence of our great State. And four years later, the results are in. Four years later, we can look at the work we did together with a sense of pride in ourselves and each other. In just four short years, Michigan has come back! Here are just some of the things we have accomplished together: Four years ago, our state budget showed a $1.7 billion deficit. Our credit rating was the worst in the nation. Today, our budget is balanced. Our tax rate is below where it was four years ago. Our credit rating is the best in the nation. Four years ago, our unemployment rate was 17.3%; we had 700,000 people out of work; more people out of work than some states have people. People were leaving Michigan to search for opportunity elsewhere. Today we have cut the unemployment rate in half—it is below 8%, still too high, but so much better. We have created nearly 400,000 new jobs in just four years; today there are more people working in Michigan than ever before in our state's history.

Let me repeat that. We now have more people working in Michigan than at any time in our State's history. So Michigan has more than come back, we're moving ahead.

And for the first time in nearly two decades, we are gaining in population, as more people come to Michigan to find opportunity and to create more opportunity. Across the board and across the state, the people of Michigan have joined hands to go to work for Michigan. Together we have created the Michigan Comeback.

Now it is time to create the future!

James Blanchard State of the State Address, Box 179, James Blanchard Papers, Bentley Historical Library.

Response to Governor Blanchard's State of the State

Michigan Legislative Black Caucus

February 4, 1987

The 1987 "State of the State" message given by Governor Blanchard does not reflect the "State of Blacks" in Michigan. Although we can cite isolated improvements for the black community during the Blanchard years, for the most part high unemployment and levels of poverty existence have continued and accelerated.

The improvements in quality of life Jim Blanchard speaks of in 1987 have not yet reached the majority of black Michiganians.

The best single indicator of quality of life is income. This determines how much people can spend, save, and invest.

The median income of black households in Michigan is little more than half of white households. Nearly four times as many whites receive income from capital such as interest, dividends, and rent. And the average amounts are nearly twice as much for Whites as for Blacks.

Although Blacks are approximately 15% of the households in the state, we receive only 10% of all money income. As the income scale descends below $10,000, we find increasing proportions of black households in each income category. Shockingly, over twice as large a proportion of Blacks as Whites are in the lowest income category—$5000 or less.

Although the income categories between $10,000 and $20,000 show approximately equal ratios of both races, as you move above these income categories, black representation falls off severely.

In the highest income category of $50,000 or more, the proportion of whites is two and a half times that of Blacks.

So, in 1987, we find that blacks in Michigan remain disproportionately concentrated in the lowest paying jobs, and in those jobs with the least future. The major question is why? Surely we deserve better.

In 1982, black votes were crucial to the Governor's victory over Republican candidate Richard Headlee. Voting as a bloc, Blacks successfully offset strong Headlee support outside of Detroit.

We voted for Jim Blanchard because he was a Democrat; we voted for him because union leadership promoted him as a dynamic progressive; and we voted for him in his role in saving Chrysler Corporation.

But most of all, a vote for Jim Blanchard was a vote against Dick Headlee and the Reagan philosophy.

While structural unemployment affects all classes of workers, Blacks have been particularly hard hit because of a financial inability to retrain for new careers. This is no secret, and it's not an easy problem to resolve, but at minimum it deserves attention.

The silence on this issue is frightening. It's almost as if Michigan is saying to the black worker "we don't need your labor anymore." Indeed, some of the problem can be attributed to new technology and foreign competition. But the shifting of factories old and new from inner-city locations to suburbs has also been a major factor in the equation.

Virtually all blacks live in urban areas of the state. In contrast, only two-thirds of Whites live in these areas. Furthermore, through the darkest years of Michigan's economy, the black concentration in urban areas has continued to increase, while the absolute number of Whites in these areas continue to decline as they migrate to suburban and rural areas.

These shifts have all but destroyed urban Michigan. Black communities in Lansing, Flint, Detroit, Saginaw, and Pontiac are among a few that derived a significant amount of economic support from industrial occupations. Most of these workers and the communities they supported cannot survive without a replacement for jobs lost.

The failure to develop an urban strategy, when combined with structural unemployment and racism, spells disaster for Michigan's black communities.

Press Release of Michigan Legislative Black Caucus, February 4, 1987, Box 18, James Blanchard Papers, Bentley Historical Library.

Short Biography of John Engler

Michigan's Former Governors

First elected in 1990 as Michigan's 46th governor, Governor John Engler is now America's most senior governor. Engler was elected chairman of the National Governors Association in August 2001.

A common sense Midwestern conservative who believes strongly that every child should have the chance to succeed, Engler has made improving education Michigan's number one priority. With boldness and vision for the future, Governor Engler also cut taxes, reformed welfare, right-sized government and implemented the biggest road repair and rebuilding plan in state history. Under his watch, the quality of Michigan's water, land, and air resources has steadily improved.

In 1994, Engler led the fight to enact proposal A—a ballot proposal overwhelmingly approved by voters to fund schools fairly and cut property taxes. Now, all children have a foundation grant that follows them to the public schools of their choice, including more than 180 charter public schools. With funding issues resolved, high standards and rigorous assessments have helped improve student performance. To encourage academic achievement, Governor Engler created the Michigan Merit Award—a $2,500 scholarship for college or training—that is awarded to high school students who pass their proficiency tests in reading, writing, science, and math.

Governor Engler has signed 32 tax cuts into law, saving taxpayers nearly $32 billion. The state inheritance tax and capital gains taxes have been eliminated. Personal exemptions for children, seniors, and the disabled have been increased. The personal income tax rate is being reduced to 3.9 percent—the lowest level in a quarter century—and Michigan's main tax on business is being phased out completely.

Engler's economic policies have helped to create more than 800,000 jobs in Michigan, cutting the state's unemployment rate from over 9 percent the year he took office to 3.4 percent in 2000—the lowest annual level ever recorded. For an unprecedented five years in a row, Michigan has led the nation with the most new factories and expansion projects. As part of the nation's most forward-looking economic development strategy, $1 billion is being invested in a "Life Sciences Corridor" from Ann Arbor to Grand Rapids, and a high-tech cybercourt to hear business disputes is also in the works. In addition, Governor Engler's NextEnergy initiative is positioning Michigan to be an international cluster of innovation in the development and commercialization of alternative energy technologies, including hydrogen fuel cells.

Governor Engler has strengthened Michigan's role as guardian of the Great Lakes, fought water diversions, and invested more in clean water than any governor. Thanks to reforms of environment laws, Michigan leads the nation in reclaiming contaminated brownfield sites while preserving green space and farmland.

"Governor John Engler Biography," Michigan's Former Governors, http://www.michigan.gov.

State of the State, 2003

Governor Jennifer Granholm

February 5, 2003

Together, we have inherited one of the most severe budget crises this state has ever known. This year the total state budget is $285 million short. I have already asked my department directors to cut their budgets by at least 4 percent and I am asking the Legislature to pass an Executive Order that will carve $158 million from the General Fund budget right now to bring us into balance.

Unfortunately, the current school budget crafted last year and based on last year's assumptions has now also come up short. Michigan law requires that our school budget be balanced . . . and with good reason. Two weeks ago, the law forced a $127 million cut in school aid. A cut to education is a cut to the heart—to this heart. It was painful, even if mandated by law.

The General Fund budget problem we inherit for the budget year ahead is $1.7 billion. Just how much is $1.7 billion? Let me give it to you straight. We could close every prison in the state and still not have enough to close the gap. Or, we could close every Secretary of State's office, shut down the Michigan State Police, lock up every State Park, cut out the entire Legislature, shut down the Attorney General's Office, and shut down the Departments of Agriculture, Military and Veterans Affairs, Environmental Quality, and Natural Resources . . . and still not close the gap. In other words, some twenty percent of the services we now provide through the General Fund budget we cannot afford.

It will not be easy, but in March I will present a balanced budget. The fiscal year 2004 budget will ensure that our government lives within its means, but it will have to cut deep to do so. We will work to protect what matters most, but every department, every agency, every local government and every citizen will feel the scale of this problem. You are all invited to be part of the solution.

How did we get here? Quite simply, we cut taxes but not spending, and we continue to spend more than we take in. That must stop. You can use your MasterCard to pay your Visa bill, and even transfer that balance to your Discover card, but eventually the bill will come due. Today is Michigan's due date and we, the Michigan family, must make tough choices to pay the bill and balance the budget. Though I did not create this problem, I will see that we fix it.

How will we do it? By doing what every Michigan family does when times are tough. We will work harder, cut waste and tighten our belts. We will save every dollar, and we will invest in the things that really matter. We have already started. In my first month on the job, I directed the Department of Management and Budget to review every state contract for cost overruns and potential cost savings. I will direct the Administrative Board—which signs-off on state purchases—to hold up contracts that represent a major expense. And I have asked my Department Directors to cut every contract with an outside vendor by at least 7 percent.

I am cutting the fleet of state vehicles by 1,000 cars, calling in cell phones and credit cards, stopping subscriptions, color copying and pay stub mailings. I have directed each state agency to use up every pad of paper, and sheet of stationery in existence, even if my predecessor's name is on them. I don't need them to say "Granholm." I need them to say that we're giving the taxpayers a frugal government.

In these first five weeks on the job, I have focused my attention on the budget, but I have not been consumed by it. Already we have done great work for the people of Michigan.

Jennifer Granholm, "Michigan: Greatness through Challenge," State of the State Address, February 5, 2003, http://www.michigan.gov.

CHAPTER 17

Preserving the State: Environment and Health

nvironmental concerns came to the forefront in the 1960s and 1970s, and it took little time before great efforts were undertaken to preserve and protect our world. Clean water, clear air, and litter-free land are important to the residents of Michigan, who cherish the Great Lakes and wish for stable agriculture and industry.

Bottle Battle

Return to Returnables Committee of ENACT

Michigan passed a law in 1976 requiring consumers to pay a deposit of ten cents per container on bottles of carbonated beverages. This program is successful; from 1990 to 2012, nearly 97% of the deposits paid were redeemed. The following flyer was distributed by the group Environmental Action for Survival in Ann Arbor in 1970.

THIS IS AN OPEN LETTER WHICH WAS DELIVERED TO:

President Robben Fleming [University of Michigan]

John Feldkamp, Director of University Housing

Mr. Edward Salowitz, Associate Director of University Housing

Mr. Robert West, Business Manager, North Campus Commons
and people concerned about their environment

Empty cans, bottles, and other non-returnable containers are seriously depleting our non-renewable natural resources and are cluttering our surroundings. These containers are being used up at an astronomical rate: 26 billion bottles and 48 billion cans last year. We are running out of materials to make these cans. We are running out of places to hide them. The mountain of cans is rising.

As concerned individuals, we fell that the University should initiate action to end this problem. As immediate action we demand that the University change its contract with the Coca-Cola Company and Servomation, Inc. to ban the use of non-returnable containers in their vending machines.

Furthermore we demand that the Coca-Cola Company and all other beverage manufacturers completely abolish the manufacture and use of non-returnable containers and return to returnables.

The Return to Returnables Committee of ENACT

TO UNDERSCORE OUR DEMANDS WE WILL RETURN EN MASSE THE MOUNTAIN OF CANS WE HAVE COLLECTED. SHOW YOUR SUPPORT

Wednesday, March 11 [1970], at 1:00

Open letter to President Robben Fleming, Box 1, David Chudwin Papers, Bentley Historical Library.

An Agreement on Great Lakes Water Quality

International Joint Commission of the United States and Canada

Agreement, with annexes and texts and terms of reference, signed at Ottawa April 15, 1972; Entered into force April 15, 1972.

International Joint Commission
United States and Canada
1974
Agreement between the United States of America and Canada
on Great Lakes Water Quality

The government of the United States of America and the Government of Canada,
Determined to restore and enhance water quality in the Great Lakes System;
Seriously concerned about the grave deterioration of water quality on each side of

the boundary to an extent that is causing injury to health and property on the other side, as described in the 1970 report of the International Joint Commission on Pollution of Lake Erie, Lake Ontario, and the International Section of the St. Lawrence River;

Intent on preventing further pollution of the Great Lakes System owing to continuing population growth, resource development and increasing use of water;

Reaffirming in a spirit of friendship and cooperation the rights and obligations of both countries under the Boundary Waters Treaty signed on January 11, 1909 and in particular their obligation not to pollute boundary waters;

Recognizing the rights of each country in the use of its Great Lakes waters;

Satisfied that the 1970 report of the International Joint Commission provides a sound basis for new and more effective cooperative actions to restore and enhance water quality in the Great Lakes System;

Convinced that the best means to achieve improved water quality in the Great Lakes System is through the adoption of common objectives, the development and implementation of cooperative programs and other measures, and the assignment of special responsibilities and functions to the International Joint Commission;

Have agreed as follows: . . .

General Water Quality Objectives

The following general water quality objectives for the boundary waters of the Great Lakes System are adopted. These waters should be:

a. Free from substances that enter the waters as a result of human activity and that will settle to form putrescent or otherwise objectionable sludge deposits, or that will adversely affect aquatic life or waterfowl;

b. Free from floating debris, oil, scum and other floating materials entering the waters as a result of human activity in amounts sufficient to be unsightly or deleterious;

c. Free from materials entering the waters as a result of human activity producing color, odor or other conditions in such a degree as to create a nuisance;

d. Free from substances entering the waters as a result of human activity in concentrations that are toxic or harmful to human, animal or aquatic life;

e. Free from nutrients entering the waters as a result of human activity in concentrations that create nuisance growths of aquatic weeds and algae.

From *Evolution of the Great Lakes Water Quality Agreement* by Lee Botts and Paul Muldoon (East Lansing: Michigan State University Press, 2005), 245–47.

Cattlegate

In 1973, the Michigan Chemical Corporation accidentally shipped bags of fire retardant to the Michigan Farm Bureau Services, each believing the bags were filled with a cattle-feed additive. Unfortunately, the flame retardant was mixed with cattle feed and distributed to farmers across the state. Thousands of animals were poisoned, from which some died. More than a million others had to be destroyed. Moreover, families across the state consumed meat and other products from these poisoned animals.

Testimony of Dr. H. Dwight Mercer

May 29, 1975

My name is H. Dwight Mercer. I am a veterinarian representing the Bureau of Veterinary Medicine, Division of Veterinary Research.... Mr. Chairman, I am pleased to have the opportunity to appear before you today to present the results of a survey conducted by the Food and Drug Administration, assisted by others, during the period March 16–21, 1975, to determine the health status of dairy herds exposed to polybrominated biphenyls. During the early summer or fall of 1973, a shipment of Firemaster BP-6 (a polybrominated biphenyl) was inadvertently sent to several Farm Bureau Feedmills in the State of Michigan. The Firemaster BP-6 was mixed into animal feeds instead of the normal feed additive magnesium oxide, and as a result, widespread and high level contamination of livestock rations occurred. During the ensuing months since this event, an estimated 172 dairy and beef herds representing approximately 18,000 animals, 32 swine herds representing approximately 3,500 animals, 16 sheep flocks representing approximately 1,200 animals, and 92 chicken flocks representing 1,500,000 birds have been destroyed and buried at Kalkaska, Michigan. The chemical contaminant was first identified as [PBB] in April, 1974. The first 34 herds were quarantined in June, 1974, and were found to contain 2.6-134.8 [parts per million PBB] in milk fat. The feedmills involved were cleaned in July, 1974, and constant monitoring of feeds produced in these mills since that time, has revealed only sporadic trace levels of PBB in feeds. In February, 1975, the Michigan Department of Agriculture reported that they had identified 286 herds of cattle, an estimated 37,000 animals, with PBB levels from trace, that is in amounts less than 0.02 ppm to 0.3 ppm in body fat or milk fat. Based upon MDA contacts with many of these herd owners, it was estimated that approximately 50% of the animals in these low level contaminant herds were experiencing adverse clinical signs. Clinical signs reported included lower milk production, some death losses of cows especially shortly after freshening, some animals drying up half way through their lactation period, death loss in calves, weak or still-born calves, and some calves born with deformities. Associations were being made between these alleged indicators of illness due to PBB exposure and the food from animals on Michigan farms.

Testimony of Dr. Walter Meester

May 29, 1975

I'm Dr. Meester from Grand Rapids, Michigan, Clinical Pharmacologist, Toxicologist, and I see patients which are poisoned either intentionally or accidentally. Many drug overdoses, obviously. Many children which are accidently poisoned, but during the last six months, I've seen a number of patients who live on farms that are either quarantined or they are not quarantined. Patients who come to me to express a concern about the fact that they have been eating products from their animals, living on their farm, which may have consumed PBB contaminated feed. Many of these farmers are living on quarantined farms, and some of these farmers have a variety of symptoms. These symptoms vary from arthritic type conditions to peripheral neuropathies, gastro-intestinal problems, nervous problems, headaches, malaise, weakness, general weight loss, a loss of appetite. These are mostly non-specified, a wide variety of problems. Many of the farmers, however, that have come, have no symptoms at all. They simply have a genuine concern about whether or not—if they have PBB in their blood, or PBB in their body, whether or not this may not in the future cause a problem, so I have taken time out of my practice to examine these people and to evaluate their symptomatology for what it may be. Very often I'm asked the question, "Could it be that PBB levels in the blood or in my fat might be related to such and such a symptom?" I always answer their question by saying, "There is no way that I can prove that such and such a symptom is related to PBB in your blood." I don't think there is anybody in this country that can prove that, simply because there is no scientific data whatsoever to prove that. It would be totally unacceptable, totally unethical, to take a group of humans and give them a given level, a given dose of PBB and then determine whether or not they start having symptoms. However, if you say that PBB present in their blood and present in their fat may not be related to symptomatology, is equally fallacious.

Testimony of Larry Crandall

May 29, 1975

I, Larry K. Crandall, on this 29th day of May, 1975 would like to make this following statement pertaining to PBB and my family's health. My family consists of my wife, Gloria, age 30, my daughter, Lori, age 7, my son Brad, age 4 and I am 33 years old. We have consumed products, milk and meat, raised on our own farm for many years. In addition to my immediate family others directly consuming home grown products from our farm, are my parents, Mr. and Mrs. Frank Crandall from Battle Creek, also. They consumed meat and milk, my grandparents, my wife's parents, my sister and her family, consuming meat only. Contaminated products were consumed for approximately one year. None of the fore-mentioned individuals have shown any problems that we feel could be attributed to PBB. With the reports emulating from the various individuals concerning possible PBB problems, I made the decision in March to have my doctor, Dr. Paul J. Diamante, M.D. of Battle Creek, perform a biopsy on myself to determine the degree of contamination. I felt the information could be useful for the Public Health Service and they sent a kit to Dr. Diamante with complete instructions and a questionnaire to be filled out concerning our health . . . My fat sample showed 3.0 ppm in the body fat and blood level of 0.012 ppm of PBB. I was told by Dr. Humphrey of the Michigan Department of Public Health that this should be considered low level and that many control people had about the same blood level. Again, I have felt as well as possible under the circumstances this past year. By this I am referring to the great emotional drain and psychological blow resulting from the disruption of our farm business and the destruction of a life time of dairy progress. This has affected us and I'm sure every other farmer in the state involved in PBB. The animals that contaminated our families are buried in Kalkaska.

PBB Public Hearing Transcript, May 29, 1975, I. A. Bernstein Papers, Bentley Historical Library.

Testimony of Tom Butler

June 10, 1976

I'm Tom Butler, Gregory, Michigan, Livingston County, I guess a former dairy farmer. We still got 30 scrub, bred heifers left but I don't know what we're going to do with them; I guess if things stay as they are somebody's going to eat them because I sure wouldn't sell them to a farmer for dairy stock. But, it's kind of a funny deal in our family, we got so sick, it just come so gradual, apparently as we look back now. Just kind of snuck in on is insidiously and we just didn't know. . . .

My brother-in-law got some corn from us about the last month, and he put the rest of his cattle most of them in a stanchion and took real good care of them—says we'll really fix these up good, grained them heavy, got the grain from us, for the hay from us. Why I know, I figure it's pretty good stuff. And gee whiz, the bull died. The vet come out, checked the boys, said gee I don't think he's going to die. The bull was dead the next morning. [Not] too long ago . . . our cows got worse, too, the more we give them that corn the worse they got. . . . [The] lab found traces [of PBB] in our vegetables.

It doesn't seem to me that our family could be this sick if there is no human significance and I've been refused life insurance for bromide ingestion.

PBB Public Hearing Transcript, June 10, 1976, I. A. Bernstein Papers, Bentley Historical Library.

Ruling on Native Americans' Fishing Rights

Judge Noel Fox

A large number of Native Americans remained in Michigan, having avoided the harsh removal policies of the nineteenth century. Members of Indian tribes, as independent and sovereign communities, are governed under different sets of laws, oftentimes their own constitutions. Native American communities and the U.S. government are bound by treaties, even those created and agreed upon more than a century ago. One issue that arose as a result of such a treaty was Indian fishing rights on the Great Lakes. By the terms of the Treaty of Washington (1836), Michigan's Native Americans who were signatories of the treaty maintained fishing rights in Lakes Huron, Michigan, and Superior. In the twentieth century, Michigan's Indians returned to their traditional practice of using nets to catch fish in these lakes, counter to state regulations. The following is U.S. district court judge Noel Fox's ruling on the matter in United States v. Michigan (1979).

Declaratory Judgment and Decree

Judge Noel Fox

This judgment and decree are based upon the Findings of Fact, Conclusions of Law and Opinion of the Court entered in this case, all of which by this reference are hereby made a part hereof as though set forth herein. No language herein shall be interpreted as superseding the Opinion of the Court, which shall control if in any respect it appears to be in conflict with any Finding herein. It is hereby ORDERED, ADJUDGED AND DE-CREED that the right of the Plaintiff tribes to fish in the waters of the Great Lakes and connecting waters ceded by the Treaty of 1836, 7 Stat. 491, is as follows:

(1) Each of the Plaintiff tribes, the Bay Mills Indian Community and the Sault Ste. Marie Tribe of Chippewa Indians, is a present-day tribal entity which . . . is a political successor in interest to the Indians who were party to the Treaty of Ghent and the Treaty of 1836. Their members can trace their ancestry to the Indians who were ben-eficiaries of the Treaty of Ghent of 1814 . . . and the Treaty of 1836. Members of these tribes and their predecessor bands and the individual ancestors of their members have fished the ceded waters of the Great Lakes under claim of aboriginal right, Treaty of Ghent and Treaty of 1836 right from ancient times until the present.

(2) The Indians who comprised the Ottawa and Chippewa bands which were signatories to the 1836 treaty occupied the ceded territory of Michigan for centuries. They lived off the fruits of the land, continuing the dependence of Upper Great Lakes Indians upon the Great Lakes fishery dating back several thousand years. The culture, subsistence and livelihood of these Indians centered around and depended upon the Great Lakes fishery. In the spring the Indians would gather in large fishing villages of around 200 persons, where they would remain until the onset of winter. These villages were on the shores of the Upper Great Lakes in locations with convenient access to productive fishing grounds. Fish comprised up to sixty-five percent of the usable meat in the Indians' diets at these times. In winter the villages would break up into small family groups which would disperse inland to hunt. Various species of fish were taken depending upon the season and the method of fishing. Fishing took place throughout the ceded area, wherever the fish were to be found.

(3) The Indians' participation in the fishery of the ceded area evolved over time. The fishery was transformed when nets and gill nets became available at about the time of the birth of Christ. When the European market economy arrived, the Indians quickly adapted their fishing skills to serve it. Especially after the decline of the fur trade, fishing was the principal means of making a living and participating in trade with the non-Indi-ans. Long before the Treaty of 1836 commercial fishing took place throughout the treaty area, including the Whitefish Bay area, the Sault Rapids, the Michilimackinac area, and various other places in the Northern lower peninsula and lower Lake Superior. Indian participation in and dependence upon commercial and subsistence fishing continued throughout the 19th century, and remains important today.

(4) By virtue of their joint and amicable occupation of the land and water area ceded by the Treaty of 1836, the Ottawa and Chippewa Indians of Michigan possessed

aboriginal rights to occupy and use this area. By virtue of their use of the fishery of the Great Lakes and their connecting waters, the Ottawa and Chippewa bands, signatory to the Treaty of 1836, possessed an aboriginal right to fish in those waters for subsistence and commercial purposes. The United States and Britain recognized their sovereignty over these lands was limited by the Indians' aboriginal right to use and occupy these lands. The United States expressed this in the Northwest Ordinance and acknowledged an obligation not to take Indian lands or properly without the Indians' consent. The consent was to be accepted by the United States with the utmost good faith, justice and humility. The right of the Ottawa and Chippewa Indians to fish in the Great Lakes and connecting waters, along with their right to occupy and use the area generally, was expressly guaranteed to them by the United States in the 1814 Treaty of Ghent. At the time of the Treaty of 1836, they possessed both aboriginal and treaty guaranteed rights to fish for subsistence and commercial purposes in the waters of the Great Lakes and connecting waters.

(5) The United States was aware, when it negotiated the Treaty of 1836, that the Indians of the treaty area depended upon subsistence and commercial fishing for their existence and livelihood. The United States intended that the Michigan Indians be able to fish in order to maintain their livelihood and way of life then and in the future. By the treaty the Indians ceded certain rights to the United States, and reserved all rights not ceded. The Indians ceded to the United States a tract of country including areas of the Great Lakes belonging to them, described in the treaty. They excepted from this cession and reserved for themselves certain land reservations. The United States did not negotiate for, nor did it obtain, the Indians' right to fish off reservation in the ceded area. The Indians implicitly reserved and retained their right to fish. This right is confirmed by the Treaty. The right is further protected by Article Thirteenth of the Treaty, which stipulates for the "usual privileges of occupancy."

(6) The Indians understood that they would have to accommodate the exercise of their right to hunt on the ceded lands to the rights of settlers on the ceded land. They understood that they could continue to use the land to the extent necessary to continue to live their lives as before. By the terms of the treaty, specifically the retention of exclusive rights to fish in each of the areas where white men had previously sought fishing rights, they were led to believe consistent with the intention of the United States that they would not have to accommodate with settlers in the exercise of their fishing rights.

(7) The Indians understood the limiting language of Article Thirteenth "Until the land is requited for settlement" to mean that Indians could continue to exercise their fishing right for as long as Indians lived in Michigan. The phrase is ambiguous as to the term of possible occupancy and can only be enforced as it was understood by the

Indians. The United States inserted the clause into the Treaty only because it wanted to insure settlers access to particular plots of land. The limitation was not intended to affect Indian fishing. It is not possible to "settle" the Great Lakes and their connecting waters.

(8) The Indians assented to the Senate Amendment to Articles Second and Third because of the assurance that they could use their ceded territory indefinitely or so long as Indians lived in Michigan. . . .

(15) Nothing in the Treaties of July 31 and August 2, 1855 . . . abrogated, alienated, surrendered, granted away, extinguished or otherwise diminished the fishing right affirmed by the Treaty of Ghent and reserved by the Treaty of 1836.

(16) The fishing right reserved by the Indians in 1836 and at issue in this case is the communal property of the bands which signed the treaty. Their modem political successors, plaintiffs in this action, presently hold the right. It does not belong to individual tribal members who exercise it, although the rights were reserved for every individual Indian, as though named in the treaty. . . .

(17) The mere passage of time has not eroded, and cannot erode the rights guaranteed by solemn treaties that both sides pledged on their honor to uphold. The Indians have a right to fish today wherever fish are to be found within the area of cession as they had at the time of cession a right established by aboriginal right and confirmed by the Treaty of Ghent, and the Treaty of 1836. The right is not a static right today any more than it was during treaty times. The right is not limited as to the species of fish, origin of fish, the purpose of use or the time or manner of taking. It may be exercised utilizing improvements in fishing techniques, methods and gear.

Declaratory Judgment and Decree, *United States of America, v. State of Michigan,* 1979.
The decision can be found at http://www.saulttribe.com/history-a-culture/treaties.

Renewable Energy

Governor Jennifer Granholm

January 29, 2008

Lean government. Pro-job tax cuts, as never before. More capital as never before. Marketing Michigan as never before. A billion dollars in economic stimulus from new construction. Those powerful tools will help us bring and keep all kinds of businesses here. But let me talk for a moment about one sector that has blockbuster potential for Michigan: alternative energy.

Why alternative energy? Because—to borrow a line from Wayne Gretzky—if you want to win, "don't skate to where the puck is—skate to where the puck is going." The puck is going to alternative energy.

Any time you pick up a newspaper from here on out and see the terms "climate change" or "global warming," just think: "jobs for Michigan." Because of the need to reduce global warming and end our dependence on expensive foreign oil, the renewable energy and energy efficiency industries will create millions of good paying jobs. There's no question that these jobs are coming to our nation. The only question is, where? I say we will win these jobs for Michigan and replace the lost manufacturing jobs with a whole new, growing sector.

Why us? Because, no other state—indeed few places in the world—have what we have to offer: our wind, our water, our woods—and thanks to the working men and women of Michigan—our skilled workforce.

Look at each of these resources. The unique geography of our peninsulas makes us windy. Experts have said that we have the second best potential for wind generation and production in the country. In fact, the wind turbines we'd use to capture that power can be built right here in Michigan, because we have what's needed: manufacturing infrastructure; available factory space; a skilled workforce. And water—the Great Lakes—are one of the best ways to ship these huge turbines.

That Pure Michigan water will do even more for us. The natural movement, the waves of our Great Lakes waters, creates enormous energy. We are talking with businesses right now about coming to Michigan to convert water currents into electric currents.

And wood! The wood waste from the pulp and paper industry is being used to produce the next generation of biofuels. Cutting-edge companies like Mascoma, Chemrec, NewPage, and others are turning wood waste into fuel for your vehicles, and they want to come here because of our vast sustainable forests.

Our automotive base is also a huge asset: we are the automotive research capital of the world, and we are building the engines of the future—hybrids, clean diesel, electric, fuel cells, flexfuel—all of that is being, and will continue to be, researched, designed, and produced right here in Michigan.

There may be one or two other states that are sunnier than we are, but we are already a huge player in the solar energy industry. We have in Michigan the world's largest producer of the stuff that makes solar panels work. Polycrystalline silicon. Made by Hemlock Semiconductor right here in Michigan. They are in the middle of a billion dollar expansion, hiring 500 people in the Saginaw area. They have even bigger plans. And just last week, Dow Solar Solutions announced it was locating a new $52 million manufacturing facility in Midland, focusing on solar energy generating building materials. Saginaw Valley can be the Silicon Valley for the alternative energy business!

Even waste is being used: companies are taking household trash in landfills and converting it to green energy—the Lansing Board of Water and Light is doing it right now. Farms are turning animal waste into methane gas. Opportunities are everywhere in Michigan to create green energy.

Michigan must do as any successful business does. To compete, we need to capitalize on our natural advantages. For us, it's our geography and our history. Auto ingenuity. And our solar edge. Wind. Woods. Water. Workforce. Even waste. If we do this right, Michigan can be the alternative energy capital of North America, and create thousands and thousands of jobs.

But, for Michigan to win the race for those high-paying jobs, we have to out-hustle the competition. How? First, we must commit as a state to use alternative energy to meet our own energy needs. To understand the connection between renewable energy and jobs, just look at Sweden—a country with striking resemblances to our state: the same size population, similar geography with two-thirds of their land covered by forests, a strong automotive sector. Sweden set high goals for their use of renewable energy. The result? They created over 2,000 businesses and 400,000 jobs in their renewable energy sector. 400,000 jobs!

Alternative energy companies have watched closely as 25 other states have set aggressive goals for their alternative energy use. We have to meet and beat other states' goals here in Michigan if we are going to attract those companies here. That's why I am asking the Legislature to set ambitious alternative energy goals for Michigan—produce 10 percent of our electrical energy from renewable sources by the year 2015 and a full 25 percent by the year 2025. . . .

As soon as this Legislature acts on a comprehensive energy package, Consumers Energy and DTE will begin to jointly invest up to $6 billion in Michigan—much of it to build wind turbines and wind farms to produce electricity and to help businesses and homeowners install energy saving technologies. . . .

A renewable energy goal is a powerful tool to attract alternative energy jobs, but there are other tools, too. We are going to create Centers of Excellence across the state to bring alternative energy companies and Michigan universities together to create new products and new jobs. I'm also asking you to pass tax incentives for anchor companies in the alternative energy sector that get their suppliers to also locate in Michigan. And to make sure that ethanol is made here and sold here and is competitive with gasoline, I'm asking you once again to eliminate the gas tax for fuel purchases of ethanol and biodiesel at gas stations.

And we won't stop there. Michigan will do whatever it takes to compete and win those alternative energy jobs and replace those lost manufacturing jobs.

From Jennifer Granholm, "Creating Opportunity in a Changing World: Diversifying Our Economy, Educating Our People," State of the State Address, January 29, 2008, http://www.michigan.gov.

The Flint Water Crisis

The crisis in Flint was national news in 2015. A year before the widespread media attention, Flint's emergency financial manager chose to stop purchasing water from the Detroit Water and Sewer Department, which treated water from Lake Huron, and instead use the Flint River as the primary source of water for the city. This was to be a temporary move as the Karegnondi Water Authority constructed a pipeline that would bring water from Lake Huron directly to Flint. The switch caused a series of devastating problems.

Source Switch Press Release, City of Flint

April 25, 2014

City of Flint Officially Begins Using Flint River as Temporary Primary Water Source

Flint, Michigan—April 25, 2014—For the first time in fifty years, the City of Flint is using the Flint River—part of the Saginaw River watershed—as a primary water source for city residents. Today the valve to the pipeline from Detroit was closed and the Flint River officially became Flint's water supply. The temporary switchover is scheduled to support the city's primary water needs for the next two years while construction of the forthcoming pipeline from Lake Huron is completed by Karegnondi Water Authority. Officials from the City of Flint, the Genesee County Drain Commission and the Michigan Department of Environmental Quality were all on hand to witness the historic event.

The Flint River was once the primary source of water for city residents up to the 1960s. Over the past 40 years, it has provided water to city residents as a back-up to water provided to us by Detroit. During our partnership with Detroit, Flint has had to transition to the use of the Flint River for residential water on a few different occasions, with the most recent temporary switchover happening in 2009. Each temporary stint on local water proved three things to city employees and residents alike: That a transition to local river water could be done seamlessly, and that it was both sensible and safe for us to use our own water as a primary water source in Flint.

Even with a proven track record of providing perfectly good water for Flint, there still remains lingering uncertainty about the quality of the water. In an effort to dispel myths and promote the truth about the Flint River and its viability as a residential water resource, there have been numerous studies and tests conducted on its water by several different independent organizations. In addition to what has been found in independent studies, it is also the responsibility of the City of Flint Water Service Center to continually test the water provided to city residents. Michael Prysby of the Michigan DEQ Office of Drinking Water verified that "the quality of the water being put out meets all of our drinking water standards and Flint water is safe to drink."

For nearly 10 years Mike Glasgow has worked in the laboratory at the City of Flint Water Service Center. He has run countless tests on our drinking water to ensure its safety for public use. Mike has not only conducted tests on water provided to us by Detroit, but also on local water from nearby rivers, lakes and streams including the Flint River. When asked if over the last decade . . . he has seen any abnormalities of major concern in the water, his response was an emphatic, "No." In his words, "there has been nothing seen that was of major concern," during his ongoing tenure working in the lab. "The tests results have shown that our water is not only safe, but of the high quality that Flint customers have come to expect," announced DPW Director Howard Croft, "we are proud of the end result."

Apart from the water plant's devotion to ensuring that our water is good, Flint is doubly blessed in having the Flint River Watershed Coalition as a separate organization dedicated to monitoring the overall welfare of local bodies of water, overseeing more than 30 different nearby locations. Rebecca Fedewa has been director of the water-shed coalition since 2008. By virtue of her passion for her work and her position on the board, she is very conversant with the condition of the Flint River. In her words, "The Flint River is increasingly healthy, and completely suitable as a drinking water source." Fedewa and FRWC are working closely with the city "to monitor flows and habitats between the intake and the waste water treatment plant to ensure there are minimal to no impacts to the overall health of the river."

FRWC also invites city residents to be a part of their monitoring exercises during this spring in order "to gain firsthand knowledge in the health and vitality of our Flint River." Mayor Dayne Walling invited everyone at today's event to toast to Flint's water. "It's regular, good, pure drinking water, and it's right in our backyard," said Mayor Walling, "this is the first step in the right direction for Flint, as we take this monumental step forward in controlling the future of our community's most precious resource."

City of Flint Press Release, April 25, 2014,
http://somcsprod2govm001.usgovcloudapp.net/files/snyder%20emails.pdf.

Trihalomethane Contaminant Notice

March 2015

Important Information about Your Drinking Water:
City of Flint Did Not Meet Treatment Requirements

Our water system recently violated a drinking water standard. Although this incident was not an emergency, as our customers, you have a right to know what happened and what we are doing to correct this situation.

We routinely monitor for the presence of drinking water contaminants. Samples were collected for total trihalomethanes (TTHM) analysis from eight locations on a quarterly basis (May 21, August 21, November 20 of 2014, and February 17, 2015). The average of the results at ANY of the eight locations must not exceed the maximum contaminant level (MCL) for TTHMs, otherwise our water system exceeds the MCL. The standard for TTHMs is 80 micro grams per liter (µg/L). The location reporting the highest TTHM level was 105 ug/L; thus, our water system exceeds the TTHM MCL.

WHAT SHOULD I DO?

- There is nothing you need to do unless you have a severely compromised immune system, have an infant, or are elderly. These people may be at increased risk and should seek advice about drinking water from their health care providers.
- You do not need to boil your water or take other corrective actions. If a situation arises where the water is no longer safe to drink, you will be notified within 24 hours.

WHAT DOES THIS MEAN?

This is not an emergency. If it had been an emergency, you would have been notified within 24 hours. People who drink water containing trihalomethanes in excess of the MCL over many years may experience problems with their liver, kidneys, or central nervous system, and may have an increased risk of getting cancer.

WHAT IS BEING DONE?

We are currently working on solutions to correct the problem. We anticipate resolving the problem in 2015. Our most recent individual sample results were all less than half the 80 µg/L standard, however since compliance is calculated using a locational running annual average (LRAA) of the most recent four quarters, we are still out of compliance with the MCL at two of eight locations. . . .

Please share this information with all the other people who drink this water, especially those who may not have received this notice directly (for example, people in apartments, nursing homes, schools, and businesses). You can do this by posting this notice in a public place or distributing copies by hand or mail.

This notice is being sent to you by the City of Flint.

Notice sent to Flint residents, March 2015, from http://somcsprod2govm001.usgovcloudapp.net/files/deq1.pdf.

Geralyn Lasher [Michigan Department of Health and Human Services]
to Dennis Muchmore [Governor Snyder's chief of staff]

September 25, 2015

Today the City of Flint issued [a] "Lead Advisory" for residents to be aware of lead levels in drinking water and issued suggestions from the Genesee County Health Department as to what residents could do to reduce risk. These include:

- flushing cold-water pipes by running water for approximately 5 minutes,
- using only water from the cold-water tap for drinking, cooking and making baby formula
- installing a water filter that is NSF [National Sanitation Foundation]-certified for lead removal.

We worked with the Genesee County Health Department throughout the week to get them in a more pro-active mode to provide this guidance publicly and to encourage citizens to have the City test their water if they were concerned about the quality at their home. The health department also issued [a] fact sheet on Thursday providing additional information on the issue.

MDHHS epidemiologists continue to review the "data" provided by a Hurley hospital physician that showed an increase in lead activity following the change in water supply. While we continue to review this data, we have stated publicly that Hurley conducted their analysis in a much different way than we do at the department. Hurley used two partial years of data, MDHHS looked at five comprehensive years and saw no increase outside the normal seasonal increases. The Hurley review was also a much smaller sample than MDHHS data as ours includes all hospital systems in Flint as well as outside laboratories.

http://somcsprod2govm001.usgovcloudapp.net/files/snyder%20emails.pdf.

Dennis Muchmore to Governor Snyder

September 26, 2015

The memo and attachments below [referring to Lasher's correspondence of the previous day] have captured the latest information from the departmental side on Flint succinctly. [U.S. Representative Dan] Kildee is engaged in his normal press hound routine, which is unfortunate because he's really a smart, talented guy who needs to roll up his sleeves while [State Senator Jim] Ananich is looking for relief but doesn't know where it would come from and as usual is a positive force.

Frankly, I think both know that Walling went out on [absolution] effort due to the election, but of course can't say no. . . .

[Flint] can't reconnect to DWSD even if they wanted to as they sold the connector line. And, especially with the new rate increases in Detroit, their citizens would be less able to pay than they already are. The water certainly has occasional less than savory aspects like color because of the apparently more corrosive aspects of the hard water coming from the river, but that has died down with the additional main filters. Taste and smell have been problems also and substantial money has been extended to work on those issues.

Now we have the anti everything group turning to the lead content which is a concern for everyone, but DEQ and DHHS and EPA can't find evidence of a major change per Geralyn's memo. . . . Of course, some of the Flint people respond by looking for someone to blame instead of working to reduce anxiety. We can't tolerate increased lead levels in any event, but it's really the city's water system that needs to deal with it. We're throwing as much assistance as possible at the lead problem as regardless of what the levels, explanations or proposed solutions, the residents and particularly the poor need help to deal with it.

It seems that continuing to find funds to buy local residents home filters is really a viable option and Harvey and all are pursuing more assistance in that work. Almost all the "experts" I've talked to are convinced the problem is in the old lines leading to homes and short of a massive replacement CSO type bond that wouldn't resolve the issue for a couple years, nature (temp reductions), filters and a final connect seems to be the best course of action.

Muchmore to Snyder, September 26, 2015,
http://somcsprod2govm001.usgovcloudapp.net/files/snyder%20emails.pdf.

Meegan Holland [Director of Communications for Governor Snyder] to Governor Snyder

December 24, 2015

While the [Flint] City Council voted in March 2013 to move to the KWA pipeline, it didn't designate the Flint River as an interim water source. But the DEQ had approved the river as a backup source for emergency purposes in 2006. The treated water met safety standards in quarterly tests by the Flint WTP, but Flint never tested its effect on the distribution system.

In an email review of key DEQ managers to determine if there was an effort to conceal information, only one email exchange raised red flags. The EPA had asked DEQ in February 2015 if Flint had a corrosion control program; the DEQ responded the city had an optimized program in place. But in April the EPA asked again, and the DEQ said that the Flint Water Treatment Plant (WTP) was not doing corrosion control. DEQ later explained that its first response referred to its program to monitor a new water source (in this case, the Flint river) for lead/copper for two consecutive six-month periods to determine optimal corrosion treatment. The report says there's no reason to believe that DEQ willfully misrepresented information to the EPA. It also concludes that ODWMA [Office of Drinking Water and Municipal Assistance] employees appeared to have notified management properly about the unfolding Flint water situation.

DEQ did not consult with the EPA on how best to apply the Lead and Copper Rule (LCR) monitoring practices after the switch to Flint [River] water, but from past experience, DEQ believed it was doing so correctly by doing two rounds of six-month monitoring on the new water source before determining optimal corrosion control. The EPA disagreed with DEQ's interpretation of the LCR, but later stated that the LCR was open to interpretation. It then clarified the rule; the upshot: corrosion controls already in place when Flint was on Detroit water should have been maintained after the switch.

DEQ should have notified the Flint WTP to start corrosion controls once the first round of six-month sampling results arrived in late March 2015 and showed the water exceeded acceptable lead levels.

DEQ doesn't oversee the Flint WTP so it doesn't have any accountability measures to ensure the WTP is collecting water samples from tier 1 homes, i.e., residences with lead service lines, soldering, or plumbing. Instead, DEQ relies on Flint's certification of sample sites.

Meegan Holland to Rick Snyder, December 24, 2015,
http://somcsprod2govm001.usgovcloudapp.net/files/snyder%20emails.pdf.

Snyder's Statement

December 29, 2015

The following statement was prepared by Meegan Holland for Governor Snyder.

When I became aware that the city of Flint's water showed elevated lead levels and that the state's handling of the situation was being questioned, I requested funding to switch the source back to the Great Lakes Water Authority and appointed an independent task force to identify possible missteps and areas for improvement.

The task force has done an exceptional job, reviewing stacks of documents and interviewing scores of Flint, Genesee County, state and federal officials.

Although the task force's final report is not yet completed, it has made me aware of some interim findings and corrective steps that I have decided to take immediately in order to restore trust in how the state keeps its citizens safe and informed.

We'll continue to work with the community members to make sure we hear and respond to their concerns.

In addition, MDEQ Director Dan Wyant has offered his resignation, and I've determined that it's appropriate to accept it. I'm also making other personnel changes at MDEQ to address problems cited by this task force.

But changes in leadership and staff are not enough. I understand there can be disagreements within the scientific community. That is why I have directed both the departments of Environmental Quality and Health and human Services to invite every external scientist who has worked on this issue to be our partners in helping us improve Flint water. Let's share research on water and blood lead level testing so we can arrive at accurate and mutually supported conclusions. Together, we should work to affirm that we're using the very best testing protocols to ensure Flint residents have safe drinking water and that we're taking steps to protect their health over the short and long term.

I want the Flint community to know how very sorry I am that this has happened. And I want all Michigan citizens to know that we will learn from this experience, because Flint is not the only city that has an aging infrastructure.

I know many Flint citizens are angry and want more than an apology. That's why I'm taking the actions today to ensure a culture of openness and trust. We've already allocated $10 million to test the water, distribute water filters, and help in other ways.

Last week, I called Flint Mayor Karen Weaver, and we're going to meet soon to discuss other ways the state can offer assistance.

These are only initial steps—we fully expect to take more actions following the recommendations of our task force. When it comes to matters of health and quality of life, we're committed to doing everything we can to protect the well-being of our citizens.

Meegan Holland to Rick Snyder, December 29, 2015,
http://somcsprod2govm001.usgovcloudapp.net/files/snyder%20emails.pdf.

Summary Statement of the Flint Water Advisory Task Force

March 2016

The Flint water crisis is a story of government failure, intransigence, unpreparedness, delay, inaction, and environmental injustice. The Michigan Department of Environmental Quality (MDEQ) failed in its fundamental responsibility to effectively enforce drinking water regulations. The Michigan Department of Health and Human Services (MDHHS) failed to adequately and promptly act to protect public health. Both agencies, but principally the MDEQ, stubbornly worked to discredit and dismiss others' attempts to bring the issues of unsafe water, lead contamination, and increased cases of Legionellosis (Legionnaires' Disease) to light. With the City of Flint under emergency management, the Flint Water Department rushed unprepared into full-time operation of the Flint Water Treatment Plant, drawing water from a highly corrosive source without the use of corrosion control. Though MDEQ was delegated primacy (authority to enforce federal law), the United States Environmental Protection Agency (EPA) delayed enforcement of the Safe Drinking Water Act (SDWA) and Lead and Copper Rule (LCR), thereby prolonging the calamity. Neither the Governor nor the Governor's office took steps to reverse poor decisions by MDEQ and state-appointed emergency managers until October 2015, in spite of mounting problems and suggestions to do so by senior staff members in the Governor's office, in part because of continued reassurances from MDEQ that the water was safe. The significant consequences of these failures for Flint will be long-lasting. They have deeply affected Flint's public health, its economic future, and residents' trust in government.

The Flint water crisis occurred when state-appointed emergency managers replaced local representative decision-making in Flint, removing the checks and balances and public accountability that come with public decision-making. Emergency managers made key decisions that contributed to the crisis, from the use of the Flint

River to delays in reconnecting to DWSD once water quality problems were encountered. Given the demographics of Flint, the implications for environmental injustice cannot be ignored or dismissed.

The Flint water crisis is also a story, however, of something that *did* work: the critical role played by engaged Flint citizens, by individuals both inside and outside of government who had the expertise and willingness to question and challenge government leadership, and by members of a free press who used the tools that enable investigative journalism. Without their courage and persistence, this crisis likely never would have been brought to light and mitigation efforts never begun.

Flint Water Advisory Task Force Final Report, March 2016,
https://www.michigan.gov/documents/snyder/FWATF_FINAL_REPORT_21March2016_517805_7.pdf.

CHAPTER 18

Challenges Old and New: Michigan's Infrastructure

According to a popular joke, there are two seasons in Michigan: winter and road construction. While it seems true to some people, it is an odd joke since, for the past few decades, Michigan has been notorious for its terrible roads. In Michigan, building and improving infrastructure is an old but ongoing issue.

Build a Canal at the Sault

John R. Williams

October 24, 1831

To the Honorable the Senate and Representatives of the United States in Congress assembled—

The memorial of the Undersigned, Citizens of the United States, inhabitants of the Territory of Michigan; Respectfully showeth . . .

The Commerce of the Great Lakes has attained such a degree of magnitude and increasing importance as to claim the fostering care and attention of the National Legislature.

The Territory of Michigan is yet principally National domain. The appropriations made by Congress for Memorial to Congress for roads and other improvements enure very materially to the interest of the United States; by accelerating the Sale of Public Lands and by facilitating the transportation of public and private property, through the Territory; and a great desideratum has also been attained by inducing a rapid settlement by the influx of an overflowing population . . .

The People who have selected Michigan as their destined abode have principally emigrated from the States of the Union. They have borne with them to their new home that love of liberty and veneration for the Constitution & Laws of the land of their sires which constitutes the patriotism & pride of every American Citizen. Important objects have been secured to the Nation by the Spirit of emigration; which has changed the frontier wilderness, into a well cultivated region of Country. These considerations are too well known and understood to be overlooked or depreciated. The time is fast approaching when our frontier borders will form a barrier at once populous, formidable, and secure, against the future inroads of aggression of foreign enemies. The United States have only to aid and encourage those desirable objects. And fortunately the flourishing state of the National Treasury added to the unparalleled prosperity which happily prevails throughout our country furnish ample means for the improvement of every portion of the Union. . . .

But little has yet, comparatively speaking, been done to develop the great Natural Advantages of these Regions.

The Commerce of these [Great Lakes] which has greatly increased since the year 1815 is yet in its infancy, although the Tonnage of Vessels already actively employed on these waters is multiplying in an increased ratio. Yet when the fertility of the Land—the Salubrity of the Climate and the various other natural advantages of our region are taken into view, it is not at all extravagant to predict, that a period of five years will at least double the Tonnage now afloat on the Great Lakes.

These are among the reasons which lead us to ask Congress the proper and accurate survey of the Coasts of Lake Huron, Michigan and Superior at as early a period as practicable. And that measures may also be taken to provide a Ship Canal to connect Navigation of the Lakes Erie, Huron, & Michigan with Lake Superior. Your memorialists are well informed that the expense of such a work would be very trifling, especially when compared to the advantages which would certainly flow from such improvement in navigation—among the benefits to be derived from such a Canal would be the facility of extending our Commerce to Lake Superior and its numerous tributaries, extending to our most northwesterly boundary and to the waters of the Mississippi and Missouri. The animating influence of the vast fisheries of Lake Superior would also contribute very essentially to the increase of Trade. Connected with these desirable results ought to be the opening & working of the extensive Copper Mines on or near the River Ontenagon. The United States expend annually a large sum of money for the purchase of foreign copper for the use of the Navy and for the Merchant Service. The Am't thus paid for imported Copper might not only be saved, but a sufficient quantity of that valuable article procured for exportation—which with the fisheries would furnish extensive employment not only for shipping but for sailors. Thus a good nursery for Seamen within our Continent would also thereby created.

John R. Williams to United States Congress, folder "1831 Oct-Dec," Box 15,
John R. Williams Papers, Burton Historical Collection.

Reminiscence of 1837

Supply Chase

At the first session of the Legislature after the State was admitted to the Union, a magnificent system of internal improvements was determined upon, and an act passed to borrow $5,000,000 to carry out the project.

Through the southern tier of counties was to be built a railroad, having its eastern terminus at the city of Monroe, and its western at New Buffalo. Commencing at Detroit and running through the second tier, was the Central, with its western terminus at the mouth of the St. Joseph. From Port Huron a railroad was to be built through the wilderness to the navigable waters of Grand River, or Lake Michigan. From Mt. Clemens was to be built a canal through the third tier of counties to the mouth of the Kalamazoo river. On the route of this last a corps of surveyors and engineers was employed, with headquarters at Mt. Clemens, and in the fall of 1837 the ceremony of breaking ground took place near the village. On this occasion an immense concourse of people was present from nearly all parts of the State where there were settlers. Gov. Mason and staff, many members of the State government, and a large delegation from the city of Detroit were in attendance. The first spadeful of earth was raised and deposited in the barrow by Gov. Mason, amidst the huzzas of the multitude, and every one thought the era of internal improvements was fully inaugurated. Whisky flowed profusely. Tables were spread in the adjacent grove, and a sumptuous dinner was provided, to which—after the oration was over—the government of Michigan, with all the invited guests, repaired, and did ample justice to the feast. Then came the toasts, with speeches and responses. It was a day of democratic glory. All were hilarious with joy and whisky. Distinctions were abolished. All were on a level. After a time an honored senator from Macomb county was placed upon the dinner table, amidst the crockery and glassware, and called on for a speech. This he attempted, but he never got beyond "Fellow citizens!" for his voice was drowned by the vociferations of the crazy multitude by which he was surrounded.

This was the day of great expectations. Mt. Clemens was to be the great port of transshipment for the immense productions of interior Michigan when the wilderness had disappeared and the banks of the Clinton and Kalamazoo canal had become studded with busy and thriving cities.

But alas for the great canal! It dragged its slow length along until it reached Rochester, Oakland county, where it made a permanent halt, and I do not remember of but a single craft that ever navigated its waters. A portion of it is still used as a mill-race, but the wooden locks have long since gone to decay.

"A Pioneer Minister" by Supply Chase, *MPHC*, vol. 5, 59–60.

Address to the Legislature

Governor Stevens T. Mason

1839

It affords me the highest gratification to renew my congratulations on the successful progress of our internal improvements. Each division of the system has been prosecuted with an energy and activity highly credible to those to whom they are instrusted. The Central road is under contract as far as Jackson, being a distance of 73 miles from Detroit, and location are now on progress as far as Kalamazoo, 140 miles from Detroit. By the agreement with the contractor, that portion of this road between Ypsilanti and Ann Arbor should have been ready for the iron rails as early as the month of October, but for some cause is not yet completed. On the Southern road a commendable energy has been evinced; 30 miles of this road—as far as Adrian—will be ready for laying the iron early in the ensuing spring. It is under contract as far as Hillsdale, and the engineers are completing the final locations on the third division as far as the village of Branch. The Saginaw and Clinton canals are in active progress; the same may be said of the Northern railroad, which has been placed under contract for clearing and grubbing from Port Huron to Lyons. The contract for the construction of the canal around the falls of the Sault Ste. Marie has been let, and the work itself will be commenced at an early day.

Stevens T. Mason, address to the Michigan Legislature, January 1839. Quoted in
"Internal Improvements" by O. C. Comstock, *MPHC*, vol. 1, 46.

Bad Benzie County Roads

Traverse City Record Eagle

August 2, 1922

In all of the State of Michigan, but two counties have failed to see the wisdom of coming into the county road system—Benzie and Oceana. And just now, the former is paying the penalty for its near-sightedness.

Tourists who have traveled M-11 state trunk highway between Traverse City and Manistee, will tell you why. They will not tell you of a long detour south of Benzonia, nor will they tell you of the detour around Silver Lake in Grand Traverse county, for these are indications of road work where improvements are being made. They will tell you, however, of one terrible stretch of road, perhaps a mile and a half long, between Honor and Beulah, that is a disgrace to Benzie county, and the greatest reason in the world why Benzie should come under the county road system.

Here is a small stretch of highway that has been utterly neglected, and that links the splendid gravel road from Honor with the splendid road leading into Beulah—a stretch of road that is hazardous, dangerous and an imposition on the tourist.

So bad is it, and so disgraceful to M-11 that members of the State highway Commission and the Grand Traverse Roads commission are laying out another route into Beulah to avoid this bad stretch, also avoiding Honor, which town must suffer because of the road it tolerates.

Tourists leaving Traverse City for Manistee are advised to leave M-11 near Bendon, and take the old route to Beulah, skirting Honor and the bad road. Tourists leaving Manistee for Traverse City are advised to take the Copemish route.

Accordingly, one of the finest pieces of roads in Northern Michigan, M-11, is suffering because Benzie county has ignored the county system and has failed to improve one small span of highway.

From *Traverse City Record Eagle* as quoted in *Michigan Roads and Forests*, vol. 19, no. 26, p. 6.

A Quick Guide to Roads and Road Funding in Michigan

Country Road Administration of Michigan

2009

In order to understand where Michigan is today in terms of road funding, it is necessary to understand where we have been in the past.

When we look at Michigan's record for the last 45 years, we find that Michigan has done a pretty decent job of funding such important areas as health and education. Roads, unfortunately, are a different story.

As the chart on the right indicates, since at least 1964, roads have been Michigan's "forgotten priority"—Michigan has continuously ranked in the bottom nine states in per capita state and local expenditures on roads. Today, Michigan still ranks in the bottom four states.

PER CAPITA STATE AND LOCAL EXPENDITURES
(MICHIGAN'S RANK IN THE NATION)

Expenditures	1964	1974	1984	1988	1992	2006
Health	5	8	9	3	12	11
Education	11	7	10	7	11	8
Roads	43	44	42	44	49	47

Source: U.S. Census Bureau.

Given this track record, it should be no surprise that Michigan's roads are in worse shape than those in many other states. Many of the states that, for years, have ranked higher than Michigan in per capita road spending, do not have the freeze/thaw cycles that Michigan experiences each spring and fall, which take a tremendous toll on paved road surfaces. Nor do road agencies in many of these states spend millions of dollars on snowplowing and salting. . . .

THE BOTTOM LINE

It is clear that the condition of Michigan's roads won't catch up with that of roads in other states as Michigan ranks in the bottom seven states in per capita road funding . . .

When there's not enough money to adequately maintain roads, the road surfaces deteriorate, winter road maintenance services are reduced and, in urban areas, roads become increasingly congested. This ultimately has a negative impact on both business and quality of life. And because the road agencies can't afford to spend enough in any community, the communities get frustrated and accuse the road agencies of spending all their money in other communities. And road agencies must compete with each other for the scarce road dollars. This undermines the cooperative spirit necessary to most efficiently maintain the road system on which Michigan relies.

"A Quick Guide to Roads and Road Funding in Michigan," Country Road Administration of Michigan, 2009.

Changes to the Sales and Gas Taxes Made by Proposal 1

Stateside Staff, Michigan Radio

April 22, 2015

Three weeks from now, we will know the fate of Proposal 1, the plan that would raise around $1.2 billion for road funding by increasing the state's sales tax. It would also raise money for schools and restore the earned income tax credit for low- to moderate-income families to the 2011 level.

Many people wonder why Proposal 1 isn't more straightforward. Why doesn't it clearly state: "You pay a higher sales tax and it goes to roads?"

According to Gov. Rick Snyder, it's the current tax structure that makes this proposal sound complicated.

"We have a really complicated system today and what this will do is actually simplify it," Snyder said. "The starting point is the mess and this would be a much better solution."

Currently at the pump, 19 cents per every gallon goes to fund transportation. This is the largest source of revenue for state transportation today, Snyder said. The balance of state taxes paid at the pump—the retail sales tax—then goes to local government and schools.

"And a lot of people don't know that," he said. "A lot of people believe everything at the pump goes to transportation."

In order to increase transportation funding, this proposal would increase the 19 cents a gallon contribution to the transportation fund to a little under 42 cents a gallon.

"Now the issue is going from 19 to 42, if you leave the retail sales tax, our prices at the pump get awful high, much higher than other states," Snyder said. "So, the easy way to solve that is to say, 'let's eliminate the retail sales tax off of fuel so everything paid at the pump will go to transportation.'"

To eliminate the retail sales tax on fuel, however, would generate a funding gap for local government and schools. To solve this issue, Snyder said that Proposal 1 would then increase the retail sales tax on other goods and services.

A bipartisan two-thirds vote in both the House and the Senate placed the proposal on the ballot. Should it pass, it would ensure that state transportation raises the $1.2 billion it needs.

"Everything at the pump will go to transportation," Snyder said. "Our pump prices won't get too high. We'll not create a problem for schools and local government, in fact we'll have some additional resources to invest. In addition, public transportation does well and there'll be some tax relief for lower income people through the earned income credit as you said, to help offset the tax increase."

"Foggy about Proposal 1? Gov. Snyder Explains How a Sales Tax Increase Would Help Fix Roads," by Stateside Staff for Michigan Radio, April 22, 2015, http://michiganradio.org/post/foggy-about-proposal-1-gov-snyder-explains-how-sales-tax-increase-would-help-fix-roads. Reprinted with permission from Michigan Radio.

Michigan Voters Reject Road Funding Ballot Measure, Proposal 1

Mark Brush

May 5, 2015

We in Michigan have been talking about fixing our roads for years.

"Just fix the damn roads," was the mantra Michigan lawmakers heard over and over from their constituents.

Now the refrain sounds more like "just don't fix the damn roads this way."

Voters overwhelmingly voted "no" on Proposal 1—the statewide road funding ballot initiative that would have raised the state's sales tax from 6% to 7% in order to change the way fuel is taxed in Michigan. The changes in fuel tax would have generated new road funding. . . .

Now it's back to the drawing board for Michigan lawmakers.

And political analysts have their doubts as to whether this Legislature—a Legislature that is decidedly more anti-tax than the last one—will find a way to come up with the necessary funds to fix the state's ailing road system—a need experts have pegged at anywhere from $1.8 to $2 billion, and rising.

The state's biggest supporter of the measure, Gov. Rick Snyder, issued the following statement after news of the defeat:

"It's essential that making Michigan's infrastructure safer remains a top priority. While voters didn't support this particular proposal, we know they want action taken to maintain and improve our roads and bridges. The 'relentless' part of relentless positive action means that we start anew to find a comprehensive, long-term solution to this problem. Doing nothing isn't an option as the costs are too great. Michiganders need to be able to get behind the wheel and not worry about dodging potholes or seeing plywood to catch crumbling concrete under overpasses. We appreciate that this bipartisan plan was supported by so many groups—business leaders and unions, public safety officials and local governments, teachers, and the list goes on. I plan to work with my partners in the Legislature on a solution that gives Michigan residents the safe roads they need and deserve and bolsters our growing economy."

Shortly after the proposal was voted down, politicians and pundits took to their pulpits to tell you exactly what this election result means:

- a simple message of "no new taxes";
- a rejection of the state legislature;
- a call for more progressive taxation:
- a failure by Gov. Snyder.

"Michigan Voters Reject Road Funding Ballot Measure, Proposal 1," by Mark Brush for Michigan Radio, May 5, 2015, http://michiganradio.org/post/michigan-voters-reject-road-funding-ballot-measure-proposal-1. Reprinted with permission from Michigan Radio.

The Cost and Funding of a Bridge across the Straits of Mackinac

Charles E. Fowler

The author is writing to Chase S. Osborn, former governor of Michigan.

May 18, 1921

Dear Mr. Osborn:

The writer has read your letter to Mr. Shipman and can assure you there is nothing visionary about the scheme for crossing the Straits from an engineering point of view, although the problems would be in many respects unprecedented. The need for this is certainly very great and I quite agree with Mr. Earle that it should be taken in hand at least put on the map.

The traffic at the present time, of course, would not more than pay the cost of operation and any interest on bonds or dividends would only come about from an increase of traffic or else from a real estate operation in connection with the scheme. The bridge in its initial shape would cost at the present time $20,000,000.00 and should be eventually expanded to a cost of about $30,000,000.00, but by the time anything could be really started, there is no question in my mind but what a reduction of one-third of these amounts could be realized.

The writer is very loath to make this public until it has been determined whether there is any way by which Bois Blanc Island can be acquired as I understand most of it could be bought up for about $10.00 an acre and with the bridge complete from the main land to the island, the property could be sold out at a great enough profit to pay for the cost of the bridge, at least so I am informed. However, in my opinion there would be no difficulty in getting through the Chamber of Commerce in the various cities, subscriptions to this project for $1,000.00 each or an average of that amount from some 30,000 people so that the method of financing is not visionary as it might appear from a hasty consideration. There are certainly this number of people in Michigan who are patriotic enough to carry such a small amount of stock until traffic develops and dividends would be paid even if the Bois Blanc Island idea was not adopted. . . .

Very respectfully yours,
Chas. E. Fowler
Consulting Engineer

Charles E. Fowler to Chase Salmon Osborn, May 18, 1921, folder "May 16–20, 1921," Box 48,
Chase Osborn Papers, Bentley Historical Library.

Manistee and the Economic Benefits of the Straits Bridge
Manistee Board of Commerce

December 29, 1952

To All Manistee County Industrialists:

We have been asked to survey the industrialists of this area to learn, if possible, what effect a bridge across the Straits of Mackinac would have on your business.

We would appreciate learning to what extent you would use the bridge in your business and whether or not it will increase truck shipments to the north, once the bridge is constructed.

Your comments written on the bottom of this page and returned to this office over your signature will be deeply appreciated.

Yours truly,
Eugene Emunson
Secretary-Manager [Manistee Board of Commerce]

.   .   .

[RESPONSES]

Gentlemen:

1. Bridge would open up areas for truck shipment of wood to Filer City if necessary.
2. Bridge would give truck shipment for boxes and board to N. Mich for SK Plant, our plant closest to Soo, etc. & would replace present around lake route via Chicago. Also Wisconsin due to shorter mileage. —WL Schmarcht

.   .   .

A bridge would probably make it practical for the haulers of uncrated furniture to deliver into the UP. Lumber would also move by truck from the UP. —EJ Burns

.   .   .

We believe that a bridge across the Straits of Mackinac will have no effect on our business. —Fallen Drop Forge Co., BV Dixon

.   .   .

This bridge would help us to some extent as we do ship quite a bit of material across the straits and prefer truck shipments to any other. Makinen Tackle Company —William Makinen

.   .   .

This bridge would be of no use to us. —Manistee Mfg. Co.

.   .   .

Gentlemen: It is our feeling that all of our northern boat dealers would use this bridge in coming to our plant for picking up their boats. At the present time they all come across by car ferry.

Very few of our boats are shipped by truck, therefore our business would not increase truck shipments to the north to any degree. —LA Holmes, Century Boat Co.

.   .   .

We do not see, at the moment at least, where a bridge across the straits would have any effect whatever upon our business. There is some possibility of slightly increased truck shipments north, but we would not expect anything very substantial along that line. —CH Morton, Morton Salt Co.

·   ■   ■

Would have no effect on our business. Would not use the bridge. —Manistee Iron Works.

·   ■   ■

Dear Gene: In answer to your question, I don't believe from our angle of manufacturing this bridge would do us any good in Manistee except when completed it will bring a few more people through our city. I do believe this project would be very beneficial to the country as a whole if it were built at a time when labor needs something to do. All projects of this manner are good to think about from this angle. This is my personal opinion only. —KR Hansen.

·   ■   ■

Such a bridge would have no effect what-so-ever on our shipping. —The Standard Lime and Stone Co., AT Houser

·   ■   ■

Gene: A bridge across the Straits would have no effect whatsoever on our truck ship-ments. —Will Hudson, Great Lakes Chemical

·   ■   ■

We believe it will help our business but cannot say how many trucks a day would use it trucking salt from our plant. —unsigned

Open letter of Manistee Board of Commerce, December 29, 1952, Manistee Historical Museum, "Mackinac Bridge" folder.

Response to the *Wall Street Journal*

Emerson Smith

October 30, 1957

On October 23, 1957, the Wall Street Journal published a piece about the Upper Peninsula and the opportunity and/or economic trouble the Mackinac Bridge might bring to the region. The author expressed the belief that the bridge would be a modern improvement for the "vast and primitive" peninsula.

Dear Sirs:

Before me is a story on the Mackinac Bridge and the Upper Peninsula which recently appeared in the Wall Street Journal, written by Dan Cordtz. It paints an unwarranted picture about the economic picture of St. Ignace, which is situated at the northern terminal of the bridge. The facts are generally inaccurate in this story, and reference is made to the Upper Peninsula as primitive and isolated, all of which is *now to be corrected* with the opening of the bridge. The inference throughout the story is that residents of the Upper Peninsula have been underprivileged. One friend in New York wrote me to the effect that living in the Upper Peninsula should be more tolerable from now on.

This writer is not alone in stretching the truth. The Chicago Tribune, Cincinnati Enquirer and other papers have pictured the bridge as bringing civilization to a wilderness. Heretofore the leading question by tourists has been "Where are the Indians?" Now, I presume they will want to see the primitive people, and get a look at the "wilderness" before it is magically transformed by the Mackinac Bridge—that is, unless they are wise to the "bunk" in their reading material.

It is true there is room for development in the Upper Peninsula, and there is need for economic improvement. The bridge will help to bring that improvement about, for it is like a needed highway in a land where transportation is somewhat handicapped.

Also, we have vast tracts of National Forests, which give the idea that there is a lot of wilderness in this country. The thinking people of the Upper Peninsula, however, are hoping to preserve these wooded lands, although busy real estate men and others are now trying to get these lands in private hands. Obviously, if the forces of "civilization" and the desire for profit at any cost predominate, the Upper Peninsula may become as unattractive and as unfit for human life as the overrun congested city areas have become.

There are fewer underprivileged people percentagewise in the Upper Peninsula than in New York and other crowded areas. Perhaps, the per capita income is smaller here but the benefits of the country and the income are undoubtedly spread to the satisfaction of the residents. Our brand of Americanism, like upper New York State, is of the best, and we do not have breeding places for communism.

Emerson Smith to *Wall Street Journal*, October 30, 1957, folder "Correspondence, 1957,"
Box 1, Emerson Smith Papers, Bentley Historical Library.

RECOMMENDED READING

ANISHINAABEG AND OTHER MICHIGAN INDIAN GROUPS

Edward Benton-Banai, *The Mishomis Book: The Voice of the Ojibway* (Hayward, WI: Indian Country Communications, 1988).

Charles Cleland, *Rites of Conquest: The History and Culture of Michigan's Native Americans* (Ann Arbor: University of Michigan Press, 1992).

Michael McDonnell, *Masters of Empire: Great Lakes Indians and the Making of America* (New York: Hill and Wang, 2015).

Helen Hornbeck Tanner, ed., *Atlas of Great Lakes Indian History* (Norman: University of Oklahoma Press, 1987).

Michael Witgen, *An Infinity of Nations: How the Native New World Shaped Early North America* (Philadelphia: University of Philadelphia Press, 2012).

ANTISLAVERY AND THE CIVIL WAR

Jack Dempsey, *Michigan and the Civil War: A Great and Bloody Sacrifice* (Charleston, SC: The History Press, 2011).

Carol Mull, *The Underground Railroad in Michigan* (Jefferson, NC: McFarland Co., 2015).

Frederick Williams, *Michigan Soldiers in the Civil War* (Lansing: Michigan Historical Center, 2002).

THE AUTOMOBILE INDUSTRY

Richard Crabb, *Birth of a Giant: The Men and Incidents That Gave America the Motorcar* (Philadelphia: Chilton, 1976).

George S. May, *A Most Unique Machine: The Michigan Origins of the American Automobile Industry* (Grand Rapids: Eerdman's, 1975).

BRITISH MICHIGAN

Denver Brunsman and Joel Stone, *Revolutionary Detroit: Portraits in Political and Cultural Change, 1760–1805* (Detroit: Detroit Historical Society, 2010).

Michael McDonnell, *Masters of Empire: Great Lakes Indians and the Making of America* (New York: Hill and Wang, 2015).

Nelson V. Russell, *The British Regime in Michigan* (Northfield, MN: Carleton College, 1939).

Keith R. Widder, *Beyond Pontiac's Shadow: Michilimackinac and the Anglo-Indian War of 1763* (East Lansing: Michigan State University Press, 2013).

CIVIL RIGHTS

Elaine Latzman Moon, ed., *Untold Tales, Unsung Heroes: An Oral History of Detroit's African-American Community, 1918–1967* (Detroit: Wayne State University Press, 1994).

Lewis Walker and Benjamin C. Wilson, *Black Eden: The Idlewild Community* (East Lansing: Michigan State University Press, 2007).

ECONOMIC DECLINE IN MICHIGAN

Phyllis T. H. Grummon and Brendan Mullan, *Policy Choices: Framing the Debate for Michigan's Future* (East Lansing: Michigan State University Press, 1995).

IMMIGRATION TO MICHIGAN

George P. Graff, *The People of Michigan: A History and Selected Bibliography of the Races and Nationalities Who Settled Our State* (Lansing: Michigan Department of Education, 1970).

C. Warren Vander Hill, *Settling the Great Lakes Frontier: Immigration in Michigan, 1837–1924* (Lansing: Michigan Historical Commission, 1970).

THE ENVIRONMENT

Thomas Dietz and David Bidwell, eds., *Climate Change in the Great Lakes Region: Navigating an Uncertain Future* (East Lansing: Michigan State University Press, 2012).

Joyce Egginton, *The Poisoning of Michigan* (East Lansing: Michigan State University Press, 2009).

THE FRENCH AND MICHIGAN

Robert Englebert and Guillaume Teasdale, eds., *French and Indians in the Heart of North America, 1630–1815* (East Lansing: Michigan State University Press, 2013).

Michael McDonnell, *Masters of Empire: Great Lakes Indians and the Making of America* (New York: Hill and Wang, 2015).

Marcel Trudel, *The Beginnings of New France, 1524–1663* (Toronto: McClelland and Stewart, 2016).

LUMBER, RAILROADS, AND MINING

Willis Dunbar, *All Aboard: A History of Railroads in Michigan* (Grand Rapids: Eerdman's, 1969).

Jeremy W. Kilar, *Michigan's Lumber Towns: Lumbermen and Laborers in Saginaw, Bay City, and Muskegon, 1870–1905* (Detroit: Wayne State University Press, 1990).

Larry Lankton, *Cradle to Grave: Life, Work, and Death at the Lake Superior Copper Mines* (New York: Oxford University Press, 1991).

Rolland H. Maybee, *Michigan's White Pine Era, 1840–1900* (Lansing: Michigan Historical Commission, 1970).

MICHIGAN HISTORY

Willis F. Dunbar and George S. May, *Michigan: A History of the Wolverine State,* 3rd ed. (Grand Rapids: Eerdman's, 1995).

Roger L. Rosentreter, *Michigan: A History of Explorers, Entrepreneurs, and Everyday People* (Ann Arbor: University of Michigan Press, 2014).

Bruce Rubenstein and Lawrence Ziewacz, *Michigan: A History of the Great Lakes State,* 5th ed. (Malden, MA: John Wiley & Sons, 2014).

MICHIGAN TERRITORY AND EARLY STATEHOOD

Denver Brunsman, Joel Stone, and Douglas D. Fisher, *Border Crossings: The Detroit River Region in the War of 1812* (Detroit: Detroit Historical Society, 2012).

Kim Crawford, *The Daring Trader: Jacob Smith in the Michigan Territory, 1802–1825* (East Lansing: Michigan State University Press, 2012).

Don Faber, *The Boy Governor: Stevens T. Mason and the Birth of Michigan Politics* (Ann Arbor: University of Michigan Press, 2012).

Mary Karl George, *The Rise and Fall of Toledo, Michigan* (Lansing: Michigan Historical Commission, 1971).

Frank Woodford, *Mr. Jefferson's Disciple: A Life of Justice Woodward* (East Lansing: Michigan State University Press, 1953).

Anthony J. Yanik, *The Fall and Recapture of Detroit in the War of 1812* (Detroit: Wayne State University Press, 2011).

ORGANIZING LABOR

Sidney Fine, *Sit Down: The General Motors Strike of 1936-1937* (Ann Arbor: University of Michigan Press, 1991).

Doris McLaughlin, *Michigan Labor: A Brief History from 1818 to the Present* (Ann Arbor: Institute of Labor and Industrial Relations, 1970).

WORLD WAR II

Alan Clive, *State of War: Michigan in World War II* (Ann Arbor: University of Michigan Press, 1979).